OXFORD STUDIES IN D

OXFORD STUDIES IN DEMOCRATIZATION

Series Editor: Laurence Whitehead

. . . .

Oxford Studies in Democratization is a series for scholars and students of comparative politics and related disciplines. Volumes will concentrate on the comparative study of the democratization processes that accompanies the decline and termination of the cold war. The geographical focus of the series will primarily be Latin America, the Caribbean, Southern and Eastern Europe, and relevant experiences in Africa and Asia.

OTHER BOOKS IN THE SERIES

Institutions and Democratic Citizenship

. . . .

AXEL HADENIUS

OXFORD

UNIVERSITY PRESS

OXFORD

UNIVERSITY PRESS

Great Clarendon Street, Oxford OX2 6DP

Oxford University Press is a department of the University of Oxford.
It furthers the University's objective of excellence in research, scholarship,
and education by publishing worldwide in

Oxford New York

Athens Auckland Bangkok Bogotá Buenos Aires Cape Town
Chennai Dar es Salaam Delhi Florence Hong Kong Istanbul Karachi
Kolkata Kuala Lumpur Madrid Melbourne Mexico City Mumbai
Nairobi Paris São Paulo Shanghai Singapore Taipei Tokyo Toronto Warsaw

and associated companies in Berlin Ibadan

Oxford is a registered trade mark of Oxford University Press
in the UK and in certain other countries

Published in the United States
by Oxford University Press Inc., New York

© Axel Hadenius 2001

British Library Cataloguing in Publication Data

Data available

Library of Congress Cataloging in Publication Data
Hadenius, Axel, 1945—Institutions and democratic citizenship/Axel Hadenius.
p. cm.—(Oxford studies in democratization)
Includes bibliographical references and index.
1. Democracy. I. Title. II. Series.
JC423. H258 2001   321.8—dc21   2001021642
ISBN 0–19–924429–4
ISBN 0–924666–1 (Pbk.)

1 3 5 7 9 10 8 6 4 2

Printed in Great Britain
on acid-free paper by
T.J. International Ltd,
Padstow, Cornwall

For Karin, Hildur, Ingegerd, and Carl

Preface

This book contains two parts with a broad theme in common. Each addresses, from a different angle, the relationship between institutions and democratic citizenship. The aim in Part I is to contribute to the debate on democracy's preconditions. The focus is mainly on contemporary matters. Drawing on studies inspired by group theory, organization theory, conflict-resolution theory, and so forth, I try to specify societal traits which serve to further democracy. My general argument is that the development of these traits is determined to a significant extent by institutional factors, that is, the nature of the state.

This critical factor—the state—is the object of analysis in Part II. In an historical review that takes us far back in time, we trace the roots of state structures. The prospects for democracy in modern times have been greatly affected, I maintain, by the varying paths of institutional development we shall discover in the course of this review. What is more, the differing modes of state have displayed a variable capacity for governance; and some have provided more favourable conditions for economic development, others less. The evolution of state structures thus tends to have consequences across broad areas of political and social life.

One scholar in particular has inspired this work: Alexis de Tocqueville. It is the analytical approach that he pioneered which serves as a common intellectual underpinning for the two parts of this book.

Several colleagues have read earlier versions of the manuscript and furnished valuable comments. I would like to express my gratitude to the following persons in particular: Karl-Göran Algotsson, Michael Bratton, Nils Elvander, Lauri Karvonen, Leif Lewin, Arent Lijphart, Charles Parker, Dietrich Rueschemayer, Jan Teorell, and Sten Widmalm. This book is dedicated to my loved ones: Karin, Hildur, Ingegerd, and Carl.

Contents

List of Figures

List of Tables

Introduction

It has been well-known since the days of Hobbes that people require a state for coordinating their actions and protecting their well-being. Through its coercive power and administrative capacity, the state can provide a series of goods in general demand. In order to guarantee social order, justice, and efficiency, society needs a functioning state.

The problem is that the state can become, owing to its monopoly of force and its superior administrative capacity, a mere tool in the hands of the powerful: a means for accumulating power and enjoying its fruits. The state may thus become a burden for the society and citizens it is supposed to serve. The standard method for protecting ourselves from these dangers—the abuse of power in its various guises—is to establish institutionalized forms for citizen control over the state, that is, democracy. Society tries by this means to govern the state by which it is governed (Sartori 1987). But how is such popular governance possible?

On this point there is, as we know, more than one opinion. I shall focus here, however, on the idea—or cluster of ideas—according to which democracy's fortunes depend on the existence of democratic norms and power resources among citizens. Democratic government, I will argue, is contingent on a certain type of civic culture. This civic culture is linked, in turn, to a particular pattern of societal organization. Furthermore, the generation of these preconditions depends in a high degree on the institutional setting, that is, the structure of the state.

Since we are interested in the institutional setting, there is reason to begin with Montesquieu. This Frenchman devised a programme for institutional pluralism, that is, the separation of powers. In order to prevent despotism and the concentration of power, he argued, power must be met and balanced by counter-power, through the method later known as checks and balances. Montesquieu's primary interest lay in how various organs within the state apparatus could be matched against each other, creating mutual balance and control thereby. He proposed that the legislative, executive, and judicial powers be held, as far as possible, apart from one another.

It is well-known that these ideas greatly influenced the American Founding Fathers, who expressly set up an institutional system in the spirit of the French *marquis*. Such a system provided the means, as they saw it, for preserving popular government. Yet we encounter, when reading *The Federalist Papers*, a certain hesitancy towards this idea, especially in the case of James Madison. For despite the fact that fairly rigorous constitutional arrangements had been applied in several American States, extensive improprieties and abuses had occurred. Madison concluded that formal regulations would not in themselves be sufficient for maintaining sound popular government: a conclusion which would prove, over the course of time, to apply to many other parts of the world besides. An additional important basis for constitutionalism and popular rule was to be found, in Madison's view, in the character of the surrounding society: in whether or not it embodied a social and organizational pluralism. A society containing 'a great variety of interests, parties, and sects' was the surest guarantee against the emergence of tyrannical rule (Hamilton, Madison, and Jay 1961: 335). If popular government is to be upheld, Madison warned, there must also be an active, pluralist society.

The Tocquevillian Argument

While the importance of societal conditions was a subsidiary idea in Madison's writings, it became a major theme in Tocqueville's study of American democracy. According to Tocqueville, what sustained American democracy, and what endowed it with such vitality, was the highly developed network of popular associations. These voluntary organizations were linked, in turn, to an active system of local self-government. Through their involvement in popular organizations, and their participation in democratic organs of local self-rule, citizens were socialized into a democratic civic spirit: what Tocqueville called the virtue or mores of the people. Tocqueville believed it was on account of this political culture, which combined engagement in matters of public concern with tolerance and respect for the views of others, that public organs in the US were able to function democratically. Through civic participation and practice in their daily lives, American citizens had cultivated a tradition of democratic cooperation. The French visitor saw in this a distinct contrast to conditions in his homeland, where for hundreds of years a high degree of political centralism had been paired with the absence of an active civil society.

Like Montesquieu, Tocqueville was a champion of institutional pluralism. He regarded the division of powers between different state organs as a necessary feature of democratic government. He particularly emphasized the value of a vertical—central/local—division of duties within the state, and he warmly advocated federalism and local autonomy. Most importantly, however, he added a new dimension to the institutionalist perspective. The relationship between the public bodies themselves was not his prime object of analysis. Institutions, in Tocqueville's view, do not function in isolation. The important thing, as he saw it, was the impact of institutions on societal life. What mattered for democracy was the fostering—or not—of certain attitudes and political skills among ordinary citizens.

As Tocqueville understood the matter, it was essential that popular rule be entrenched in the civic culture, in the mores of the people. Herein lay the foundations of democratic government: it had to be rooted in the habits and hearts of the citizens. The institutional framework, for its part, could serve to support this purpose— or to thwart it.

From this perspective, Tocqueville laid the basis for a theory of how a civic spirit favorable to popular government could grow forth and gain strength. Democratic culture developed, according to Tocqueville, in a process of learning by doing. The key to understanding the American phenomenon lay in the highly developed system of local self-government:

. . . the strength of free peoples resides in the local community. Local institutions are to liberty what primary schools are to science; they put it within people's reach; they teach people to appreciate its peaceful enjoyment and accustom them to make use of it. (Tocqueville 1969: 62–3)

By taking part in the running of local affairs—by meeting, discussing issues, reaching decisions, and implementing them—citizens learned the habits of cooperation. By combining their strength they could increase their resources, thus acquiring the power to defend their interests. This collective process, with its active civic interaction, had a mental effect besides: it called forth a spirit of affinity and community. By doing things together, both in public organs of decision-making and in the civic organizations they had established in so uncommon a degree, American citizens learned a sense of public spirit and mutual concern. In this way, Tocqueville thought, popular self-government could foster the civic virtue underlying democracy. By its very practice, then, and the spirit cultivated thereby, popular government could reinforce its own preconditions.

Tocqueville took the view, in other words, that it was the quality of the people as citizens which ultimately determined the quality of public and political life. In this he continued an intellectual current with deep historical roots. Aristotle described the good citizen as the ideal practitioner of the political duties. What he had in mind here was the prevalence among citizens of social virtue: a willingness to work for the public good, and not just on their own narrow interests' behalf. We find similar notions in Machiavelli, who held the patriot in the highest regard: the citizen and soldier who is prepared to endure great sacrifice, even to give his life, for his country and his people.

In its British and American variant, this tradition, known usually as republicanism, came to be manifested in a defence of the independent, competent, and broad-minded citizen. This was a person possessed of enough time and interest to engage in public business, and able to prefer the common interest to his own. For a long time—up to the 1700s—this was mainly considered an ideal for the gentry: it was the well-to-do landowning gentleman who was best able to embody the noble civic virtues. Later, in the United States especially, it was the independent, self-sufficient farmer who was seen as the natural bearer of the republican ethos (Shklar 1991: 6ff, 63ff; Morone 1990: 5ff, 39ff; Wood 1991: 95ff; Lakoff 1996: 65ff).

In the French setting, the republican tradition was associated above all with the writings of Rousseau. Taking his inspiration from Montesquieu, who averred that virtue—*la vertu*—was the distinguishing feature of the republic, Rousseau argued that democratic government required citizens of a special sort. Democracy rested on a high level of popular involvement and broad participation in its practice, and it presumed close community ties and a developed sense of solidarity. Only thus was government in the common interest possible. This implied that popular government could be applied only in small units. It presupposed, furthermore, a high degree of equality between citizens, both in regard to wealth and status and in regard to—preferably simple—habits of life (Rousseau 1919: 83–4).

These traditions were fused, one might say, in Tocqueville's studies of American democracy.[1] He emphasized civic spirit—the mores

---

[1] 'His passion for civic virtue always had a strong ring of Rousseau', Larry Siedentop points out (1994: 67). One difference between Rousseau and Tocqueville, however, bears emphasizing here. While the former warned strongly against

of the people—as that system's unique and distinguishing feature. At the same time, he stressed the importance of the organizational framework: how self-government was practised through vital local institutions and an extensive network of voluntary associations. He also attached importance to two critical features of the American farmer society: on the one hand, its striking equality and simplicity in forms of life; and, on the other, its widespread ethos and practice of independence, patriotism, and self-reliance. In addition to his penetrating description of these and related conditions, however, Tocqueville did something more. He laid the foundation, on the basis of these observations, for an institutional theory of political learning. It is herein above all that his contribution to social science lies.

The one side of this theory concerns political education and socialization: how civic spirit—the republican ethos presupposed by popular rule—can be developed through the practice of democratic government. This idea played a central role in the writings of John Stuart Mill as well. Like Tocqueville, by whom he was clearly influenced,[2] Mill emphasized the educative role of political participation. Through taking part in elections, debates, and meetings, and especially through performing their public duties, serving as office-holders, jurymen, and so forth, citizens became habituated, in thought, word, and deed, to working for the common good. They were taught to look beyond their narrow self-interest and to regard their own actions as a part of a larger effort to promote the public good (Mill 1991: 78ff). Herein lay the basis, moreover, for Mill's normative advocacy of democracy. The goodness of a government could be ascertained, as he saw it, by 'the degree in which it tends to increase the sum of the qualities in the governed, collectively and individually' (Mill 1991: 40). The primary strength of a popular state lay in the fact that, more than any other type of state, it was capable of fostering the intelligence and virtue of its citizens. In gloomy tones, Mill described the circumstances arising when 'this school of public spirit' is lacking. Under such conditions, the citizen is merely a subject. He follows laws and ordinances but feels no obligation towards society:

There is no unselfish sentiment of identification with the public. Every thought and feeling, either of interest or of duty, is absorbed in the

autonomous civic organizations, seeing in them a threat to the general interest, the formation of free associations was something which the latter warmly welcomed, both as a way for citizens to exert external influence and as a way for them to practise self-administration.

[2] Mill (1991: 171); Siedentop (1994: 111–12).

individual and in the family. The man never thinks of any collective interest, of any objects to be pursued jointly with others, but only in competition
with them, and in some measure at their expense. (1991: 78)

Under such conditions, in which all are cast into rivalry with their
fellows, everybody suffers. The reason for this state of affairs,
according to Mill, lies in the lack of public arenas: organs for common decision-making, in which people can meet together and join in
shared endeavours for the common good.

The matter just mentioned illustrates the other side of the theory
as well, that having to do with the institutional framework.
Suitably designed, institutional structures can contribute to good
civic virtues and to an active and cohesive civil society. When badly
designed, however, this framework can lead to society's ruin. For
Tocqueville, this gloomy latter scenario was represented by his
homeland, about which he wrote another book—which is much less
well-known but as surely worth reading—upon finishing his studies
of the young American republic. In Tocqueville's view, the far-reaching centralization of state power that had taken place in France
under royal rule, and which had been retained under subsequent
regimes, had had devastating effects on social life. Organs for local
self-government which once had existed had been systematically
dismantled, and civic self-organization had ceased along with them.
The result was a virtually complete draining of public engagement
and activity. Cut off from participation and influence, citizens lost
interest in public life. But this was not all. They had also become
strangers to one another, and they had lost the ability to manage
their own affairs. Many matters of common concern which once had
been handled by the citizens themselves later had to be assigned—
to ensure that they would get done at all—to the state.

This centralized state structure had been established in order to
break down the feudal and parochial patterns previously characterizing French society, and in this it had been largely successful.
The localism, regional splintering, and aristocratic dominance
which had marked the previous system had been abolished. It was
replaced with a highly cohesive and centralist form of government.
The country was governed, from the smallest village up, by a large
and hierarchical bureaucratic corps responsible to the king. This
administrative apparatus was then taken over in all essentials by
the revolutionaries, who simply removed the king. With the military rule of Napoleon, moreover, the centralist character of this system became yet more pronounced. In this way, a fundamental
institutional structure came into being, and it left its mark on
French society for a very long time. Through all political upheavals,

the relation of the state to the citizens remained unchanged: it was still a relation between authority and subject. To this extent, 'the old régime' had survived. Thus no foundation existed, in Tocqueville's view, for the emergence of the active citizenship he had found in such abundance in America (Tocqueville 1969: 53ff; see also Siedentop 1994: 113ff).[3]

What Tocqueville set forth, we have seen, was an institutional theory of learning. The civic norms and capacity required for democracy are best developed within a certain institutional framework. He described how the generality of persons in the young American democracy took part actively in various kinds of associations. This endowed them with the habits of democratic cooperation and self-government, habits which could be profitably applied in public life also. Through their socialization into the democracy of daily life, citizens in the young republic developed attitudes and resources that promoted active political citizenship. This positive scenario was the product in turn of the special state structure which had been established in North America. It was precisely the lack of a comparable institutional context in Tocqueville's own country that made conditions there different. In France, a kind of guardian state had been established over the course of many centuries, and it had powerfully retarded the emergence of democratic citizenship. Royal rule had led to the creation of a state power capable of subduing the regionalized aristocratic order. This had been done at the price of undermining institutions which had provided channels for influence and arenas for popular intercourse and participation, and which could have furnished the basis for democratic development. This royal autocracy was in time overturned, certainly, but it was subsequently re-established—a number of times, in fact—only to collapse again in the face of popular protest. A despotic system had thus been broken time after time, and had been replaced by a system of popular rule. What had not changed, however, was the administrative structure of the French state apparatus. The centralized guardian state had been maintained and even strengthened. These institutional conditions restrained and reduced the democratic potential of citizens. It was herein that Tocqueville

---

[3] It may be worth noting here that Tocqueville was surprised, upon arriving in America, to discover that a hundred thousand citizens had joined together in order to counteract, through temperance and good example, the widespread abuse of alcohol in society. He concludes: 'One may fancy that if they had lived in France each of these hundred thousand would have made individual representation to the government asking it to supervise all the public houses throughout the realm' (Tocqueville 1969: 516).

detected the major difference between the two countries he studied, and more or less explicitly compared: in the presence, in the one case, of a state structure that supported and stimulated democratic activity, and, in the other, its absence.

Later Contributors

We find a similar approach when considering the work of another French student of society, a man who wrote a good half-century after Tocqueville. I have in mind Emile Durkheim. This scholar has attracted particular attention for his studies of how the forms of social solidarity and cohesion have changed over the course of social development. In Durkheim's view, the character of prevailing relations of solidarity, among which he distinguished between primitive mechanical types and developed organic types, primarily reflected the division of labour in society. On the one hand, it was important for society's welfare that such stable bonds between people existed; on the other, it was important that such bonds not become inhibiting and rigid. Here the state could play a two-sided role. The essential function of the state, in Durkheim's view, was of an emancipatory character. The emergence of the state had made possible the liberation of the individual from an intrusive and repressive social control. The state's secularizing struggle against the church in Catholic countries, for instance, had had such an import. At the same time, however, Durkheim saw in this a danger. He warned forcefully against the growth of an atomized mass society, in which individuals are held together solely by a superior authority. Like Tocqueville, he argued that such a form of social coordination 'from above' tends to become self-reinforcing:

when the state constitutes the sole environment in which men can fit themselves for the business of living in common, they invariably 'contract out,' detaching themselves from one another, and thus society disintegrates to a corresponding extent. A nation cannot be maintained unless, between the state and individuals, a whole range of secondary groups are imposed. (Durkheim 1984: liv.; cf. Tocqueville 1969: 515)

The state can therefore liberate, but, like other organizations, it can also stifle and choke. In order to obstruct the latter tendency, the power of the state must be limited and balanced by that of other collective forces in society. This pluralist function is best performed, according to Durkheim, by a network of professional organizations (Durkheim 1958: 62–3; see also Badie and Birnbaum 1983: 13ff).

This line of argument, with its emphasis on the role of organizations, has been followed up in more recent years by William Kornhauser especially. In Kornhauser's view, the strength of democratic institutions depends in large part on the character of interpersonal relations in society. The most favourable condition is the one he calls 'social pluralism'. This is characterized by the prevalence of strong 'intermediate relations' serving as links between the primary social units—the individual and the family—and the state. What he has in mind most especially is the existence of a multiplicity of voluntary organizations: religious congregations, trade unions, producer associations, and so on. Participation in such associations grants the individuals in question a collective strength with which they can defend their interests against the state and other social groups. A rich associational life is therefore a safeguard against oppressive and despotic tendencies in society. Such participation has an dynamic inner effect besides: it enhances feelings of affinity between people, and fosters interest in civic affairs.

As against such favorable conditions, which he describes in terms similar to Tocqueville's, Kornhauser poses a stark contrast: mass society. This is a society in which organizational bonds between persons are lacking. Individuals in such a society are atomized and unconnected with one another. Neither, accordingly, do they have any protection against the outside: 'Mass society is a *naked society*, where the direct exposure of social units to outside forces makes freedom precarious', says Kornhauser (1960: 23). Otherwise put, it is a weak society. Since it lacks the autonomy made possible by social cohesion, it can easily be dominated and led from above. An authoritarian political system is the typical companion of mass society. The deficient social power of coordination, and the powerlessness arising therefrom, have unfortunate consequences. Political behaviour oscillates between, on the one hand, alienation and passivity—the typical condition—and, on the other, rapidly flaring actions of an eruptive sort. The popular movements emerging from such circumstances frequently bear a populist stamp; they can even sometimes develop downright totalitarian tendencies. On account of their young and fragile structure, moreover, such movements are seldom lasting. Yet in certain cases they can, through the dammed-up forces they release, have a powerful impact on political life.

Enormous political swings and periodic convulsions are thus the distinguishing token of mass society. While pluralist society makes room, through its greater coordination capacity, for gradual and continuous changes in prevailing conditions, mass society can only, on account of its weakness, proceed to action through temporary and sometimes wholly spontaneous outbursts. Mass society contains, in other words, at least a latent revolutionary potential, while pluralist society provides the basis for the political scenario of reformism.

The characteristics of mass society have been particularly salient, Kornhauser claims, in France. Intermediary associations—meaning both political parties and interest organizations—have traditionally been weak in that country. Other forms for civic participation, on the local level especially, have been underdeveloped there as well. The contrast with conditions in Great Britain and the United States has been striking in this regard. The political history of the latter countries has consequently been very different. The traumatic experiences of Germany, moreover, with fascism and the destruction of democracy, can be explained in large part, in Kornhauser's view, by the weak development of social pluralism (Kornhauser 1960: 84ff).

Like Tocqueville, Kornhauser finds a large part of the explanation in the centralized structure of the state; this is the key, he argues, to understanding the political history of both Germany and France. In addition, however, he points to factors of a social and economic nature. Mass tendencies find their most fertile soil, in his view, among rootless and marginalized social groups. A society in the throes of rapid economic development, with extensive population removals and great changes in living conditions, can lay the basis for social atomization and its attendant political consequences. Economic depression and high unemployment can also issue in social and political outcomes of a similar sort (Kornhauser 1960: 159ff).

Among scholars in the Tocquevillian tradition, Robert Putnam merits mention here too. Like his illustrious predecessor, Putnam crossed the Atlantic to study how democracy works. He journeyed, however, in the opposite direction: from America to Italy. His aim was to investigate the organs for regional self-government which had been established in Italy during the early 1970s. He noticed, in the course of this research, that these institutions functioned very differently in different parts of the country. The dividing line went, roughly speaking, between north and south: in many significant respects, the results were better in the north than in the south. To explain this difference, Putnam adduces a strong correlation with the degree of 'civic engagement' in the various parts of the country. For measuring civic engagement, he uses an index based on variables indicating political activity—in the form of electoral participation and newspaper reading—and participation in voluntary local organizations. He concludes, on the basis of this correlation, that he has discovered a way to test the strength of the republican and Tocquevillian thesis: that it is the quality of the civic community which makes the big difference in political life. And, indeed, he finds the evidence confirms the Tocquevillian thesis, for it is in regions where citizens are active, cooperative, and cohesive that democracy functions best (Putnam 1992: 63ff).

Putnam furthermore shows that the degree of civic spirit—or 'civic-ness', as he calls it—in the various regions can be traced to the conditions prevailing in Italy as far back as medieval times. His main explanation fastens on the institutional legacies found in the different parts of the country. Regions with a long tradition of authoritarian government and political and administrative central-ism are those which are marked by the lowest degree of civic engagement in the 1970s; whereas the regions marked by high degree of popular engagement share a long history of political plu-ralism and decentralization. Putnam sees this relative permanence in the question of regional differences as illustrative of the phe-nomenon termed 'path dependence' by Douglass North: the fact that the conditions structuring our social and political behaviour tend to be of lengthy duration. Once established, institutional structures create patterns of social interaction, and, in a symbiotic adaptation, said structures and patterns of social interaction reinforce one another. These durable conditions assumed divergent forms in northern and southern Italy.

These differences are revealed in the fact that the public sector works much better in some parts of Italy than in others. The same can be said of the economy. Putnam is able to show that economic growth has been highest in those parts of the country marked by a high degree of civic engagement. He sums up his results with the following laconic formulation: 'Strong society, strong economy; strong society, strong state' (1993: 176).

Putnam then places these results in a broader theoretical con-text. He interprets the decisive factor—the degree of civic engage-ment—as an empirical indicator of 'social capital', a concept associated with James Coleman in particular. Where social capital is found, in the form of mutual trust and social networks, people wield civic power. It is this capacity which forms the foundation for social and economic progress, and it is this which endows citizens with the ability to check the power of the state and to exercise con-trol over its doings: 'Effective and responsive institutions depend, in the language of civic humanism, on republican virtue and practices.

Tocqueville was right: Democratic government is strengthened, not weakened, when it faces a vigorous civil society' (Putnam 1993: 182).

Themes and Arguments Developed in This Book

In the Tocquevillian view, it is active citizenship which gives society strength and infuses democracy with vitality. In adopting this general approach, Tocqueville linked up with an older republican tradition. He laid the basis for a theory of political learning, showing how, through practice, norm-systems and collective capabilities supportive of democracy can emerge. He emphasized, moreover, that such a dynamic can take place only under certain institutional conditions. Prevailing state structures may largely bar the development of democratic citizenship. This, in his judgement, had been the case in his homeland. But it could also be the other way round. The vigorous rule by the people he had encountered in the United States was due basically to a supportive institutional context. In Tocqueville, in other words, a republican and an institutionalist view are combined. Herein lies the novelty of his mode of analysis.

My ambition is to impart a higher degree of precision to this general approach. In Part I, the notion of democratic citizenship forms our point of departure. In Chapter 2, I try to illuminate how this idea can be explicated and understood. Emphasis is laid on the organizational side of the matter. Democratic citizenship denotes the aptitude of ordinary people to take part in political life and to exert influence upon it. This capacity has two sides: it is a matter of developing within society both a mobilizing—expressive—potential and a conciliatory—conflict-alleviating—capacity. Yet these qualities may come into conflict with one another. Upholding them simultaneously can therefore be difficult.

In Chapter 3, I examine three common organizational patterns, all of which represent weak forms of citizenship: clientelism, populism, and so-called social movements. In all three cases, certain qualities favorable to democracy are present, albeit in differing ways; others are absent.

The fourth chapter addresses the question of democratic development. I begin with a survey of the waves of democratization observed during the twentieth century. The matter of explanation is then addressed more explicitly. I deal first with socioeconomic theories, which I conclude are helpful in certain respects, even as they leave certain important questions unanswered. I attempt thereafter to clarify more precisely the connection between institutions and democratic citizenship. In clarifying the impact of institutions, I find three circumstances to be most important: (1) a long experience of political pluralism; (2) a separation of powers, particularly through substantial elements of decentralization; and (3) a rule-governed state apparatus.

Having stated these relationships, I continue in Chapter 5 by analysing the impact of institutions and of socioeconomic conditions in Africa, Latin America, and India. As so often in such comparisons, India stands out as a special and theoretically challenging case. Despite a low level of economic advancement, and notwithstanding an unfavorable social composition due to rigid cultural cleavages within the population, the democratic project has been more successful in India than in Africa and Latin America. The key, I conclude, is to be found in the nature of the institutions there. In India, more than in many other countries, favorable institutional circumstances have counteracted and mitigated troublesome conditions in the economic and social realms.

In the second part of the book, the focus shifts to the evolution of state structures. I begin in Chapter 6 by spelling out, from a Weberian perspective, the basic characteristics of the state. Various methods of governance at the disposal of the state are analysed. An historical review of the emergence of states follows thereupon. I devote particular attention to the autocratic state. In accordance with the precepts of Hobbes, states of this type seek to enforce social order through coordination from above. This was the dominant model for long periods.

In the Middle Ages in Europe, however, a new mode of government emerged: the interactive state, signified by a regulated intercourse between the state and society. Preconditions for the evolution of this kind of state are analyzed in Chapter 7. I argue that, due to a special societal composition prevalent in Europe, together with a particular institutional tradition, the 'miracle', as some have called it, was possible. I continue in Chapter 8 by illustrating how the medieval tendency, with its pluralism and constitutional rights, could be continued in certain countries, while eventually being broken elsewhere. England, Sweden, the Netherlands, and North America represent the former trend. Russia, Prussia, Spain, and France exemplify the latter. My argument is that these differing 'paths' in the development of state institutions have heavily affected the prospects for popular rule in modern times.

In Chapter 9, the development of states is examined further; particular attention is paid to their effects in the social realm. I draw here on the history of Europe. The basic question is how to explain the dynamic development which took place on this continent. Taking issue with two well-known explanatory themes—the economic approach launched by Barrington Moore, and the state-system theory championed by Otto Hinze and others—I argue that it was the development, at an early stage, of a special mode of state which explains the unique dynamism in Europe. I specify the basic traits of this mode of state—the interactive state—and contrast it with other models. The reason why this mode of state has proved the most successful is that it is able to develop, over the long run, a greater capacity than its competitors. This capacity is gained, I maintain, through the upholding of institutions which tend to stimulate, at one and the same time, effective governance and economic development.

I

Conditions of Democracy

2

Democratic Citizenship

As an introductory formulation of the notion of democratic citizenship, the following quotation from Judith Shklar's book, *American Citizenship*, may be fitting:

The good democratic citizen is a political agent who takes part regularly in politics locally and nationally, not just on primary and election day. Active citizens keep informed and speak out against public measures that they regard as unjust, unwise, or just too expensive. They also openly support politics that they regard as just and prudent. Although they do not refrain from pursuing their own and their reference group's interests, they try to weigh the claims of other people impartially and listen to their arguments. They are public meeting-goers and joiners of voluntary organizations who discuss and deliberate with others about the politics that will affect them all, and who serve their country not only as taxpayers and occasional soldiers, but by having a considered notion of the public good that they genuinely take to heart. The good citizen is a patriot. (1991: 5)

We see here a fairly comprehensive list of the qualities associated with active democratic citizenship. In order to bring some structure into the multiplicity, however, we may find it fruitful to distinguish between traits that we bear *as individuals* and those which join us to the various *collectivities* of which we are a part. This categorization resembles that introduced by Sidney Verba, Norman Nie, and Jae-on Kim in a study of political participation in different countries. They distinguish between 'individual-based' and 'group-based' forces driving political activity, and find that the effects of these factors on political behaviour are distinct but mutually reinforcing (Verba, Nie, and Kim 1978: 10ff). Our distinction recalls as well that between human and social capital suggested by James Coleman (1990), and followed up empirically by Robert Putnam, first in his study of Italy (1993), and later of his homeland, the United States (1995; 1997; 2000).

When we speak, on the individual level, of human capital in relation to politics, we refer to certain *attitudes*—of both a normative and a cognitive character—associated with active citizenship.

These include a developed political interest, a desire to become involved, and a wish to exert influence. The persons in question should also have a firm faith in their ability to make their voices heard. In their basic political attitudes, moreover, they should be open, tolerant, and broad-minded, and they should apply a rationalist and deliberative method: that is, they should be interested in seeking out facts and respectful of rational analysis (Inkeles 1974; Verba, Nie, and Kim 1978: 11; Eriksen 1995).

Alongside such attitudes favourable to democracy, certain *resources* are important as well. These embrace civic skills of various kinds. On the individual level, they include political competence and capacity: keeping well-informed on political and other questions, being able to take initiatives—for example, contacting a politician or other public person—and so on. Political resources are usually thought, furthermore, to include access to 'time and money': that is, on the one hand, the opportunity in terms of actually available hours to participate in political and similar activities; and, on the other, the ability to exert influence by means of pecuniary contributions to the activities and candidates one supports. Partly associated with these factors—competence and economic capacity especially—is another characteristic of crucial importance: independence. The active, democratic citizen stakes out his/her positions on an autonomous basis; nor is he/she found in relationships of dependence and submission[1] (Brady, Verba, and Schlozman 1995: 273–4; Shklar 1991: 64ff; Petersson, Westholm, and Blomberg 1989).

When it comes to social capital and to the collective dimension of citizenship, interest centres not on private individuals but rather, as Coleman (1990: 304) points out, on *relations between* individuals. Here too there is cause to distinguish between attitudes and resources. The former have to do with feelings of trust and affinity between people: an experience of identification with a larger whole, and a recognition of obligations towards it. This is a question of the emotive bonds of trust and solidarity with a unit of people to which we belong. This means our motives for action derive from more than just our narrow self-interest. We nurture as well the ambition to

---

[1] An example of dependence and subordination which would seem to inhibit independent action may be discerned in the following words of a Soviet steelworker. Describing the enterprise-controlled system for the distribution of goods, he explained: 'We're completely dependent on them. Food, clothes, apartments, furniture, day care, summer camps, vacations—everything is allocated by them according to their lists, with which they rule over our lives. Everybody has something to lose' (Crowley 1994: 604).

serve a common interest of some kind: a common interest tied to the collective with which we identify. The norms embodied in social capital are connected, in other words, with the ethos of republicanism: with the will to promote the public good.

As far as resources are concerned, the question turns on what real possibilities exist for coordinated and collective action. The means for such action lie in organization: what Coleman calls (1990: 313) 'investments in social capital', that is, fixed and routinized forms for cooperation between people. When linked to the small family unit, such institutionalized networks are commonly referred to as 'primary associations'. When the organizing in question extends beyond this level, we may speak of 'secondary associations'. It is networks of the latter type, as a rule, to which the term 'civil society' refers: the organized activities taking place in the social zone between the family and the state (Hadenius and Uggla 1996; Diamond 1999).

As regards the individual dimension of democratic citizenship, there is little need here for any far-reaching analysis. The qualities in question have been subjected to close examination in research on political attitudes and behaviour, and they would seem to be well-known. The causal context must also be judged to be fairly well-documented. The attitudes and political resources characterizing active democratic citizens are to a high degree related to social standing and educational level; these correlations have been demonstrated by a good many studies from several countries (Verba, Nie, and Kim 1978; Petersson, Westholm, and Blomberg 1989; Verba, Schlozman, and Brady 1995).

We shall now concentrate rather on the second dimension of citizenship, that having to do with people's collective potential. As we have seen, there are two aspects here. The first has to do with attitudes: feelings of affinity, trust, and solidarity between people. The second is a question of resources, that is, the existence of fixed forms for coordinated action. In Putnam's (1993: 171) view, these two aspects of social capital—what he calls 'trusting' and 'joining'—are likely to be mutually reinforcing. People who trust other people find it easier to organize themselves. Conversely, widespread participation in associational life may help, on account of the routinization of contacts between people it entails, to strengthen feelings of affinity and trust.

In broad empirical testing, however, this relationship has proved more tenuous than Putnam presumes (Newton 1999). As will be demonstrated later, it is only under certain conditions that joining and trusting, in ways that promote democracy, are likely to go hand in hand. To the extent there is a relationship, moreover, the identity of the driving factor—that is, the direction of causality—remains unsettled.[2] Let us therefore consider the two alternatives to see what they represent in a wider sense. If we focus on the emotive component, on attitudes, we link up with the genre known as political culture.[3] According to this approach, differences in preferences and in organizational structures between different societies—the unit can be an ethnic group, a nation, or an entire continent—are explained on the basis of the overarching belief systems characterizing the unit in question. It is often assumed that such predominant beliefs are historically inherited and passed on through a continuous process of socialization. Some scholars have argued, for example, that the various great religions—Confucianism, Christianity, Islam, and so on—have fostered distinct patterns of political attitudes within their respective regions (see, for example, Pye 1985).

If, on the other hand, we focus on collective resources, it is primarily the distinctive organizational features that attract our interest. It is the associational patterns of a given society that we notice: how they are configured, how they form the basis for coordinated collective action, and how they affect the prevailing identities in society. The organizational 'buildings' that people create are seen, in this perspective, *both* as means for realizing certain preferences *and* as frameworks for shaping prevailing preference systems (March and Olsen 1989: 162ff; North 1990: 22).

It is the latter approach which furnishes the point of departure for the following analysis. This does not mean, of course, that I regard attitudes as unimportant; it means simply that I believe political attitudes are governed by organizational context to a higher degree than organizational context is governed by political attitudes. In other words, I argue that joining drives trusting more than the trusting drives joining.[4]

---

[2] In his study of Italy (1993: 180), Putnam takes the view that the question of the direction of causality is meaningless: it is to ask whether the chicken or the egg came first. Since then, however, he has apparently changed his mind: he discusses the matter of causality, albeit briefly, in his study of the United States (Putnam 1995: 665).

[3] Lucien Pye (1965: 7) gives the following definition: 'the notion of political culture assumes that the attitudes, sentiments and cognitions that inform and govern political behavior in any society are not random congeries but represent coherent patterns which fit together and are mutually reinforcing.'

[4] Empirical support for the causal conjecture suggested here is provided by John Brehm and Wendy Rahn (1997). In a study of civic engagement and interpersonal trust in the US, they find a reciprocal relationship, but also a quite asymmetrical one. Organizational participation generates interpersonal trust in a much higher degree than interpersonal trust generates organizational participation.

It bears stressing that the focus in this chapter on certain patterns of organization does not mean that I regard such patterns as the most important precondition for democracy. Their importance, relatively speaking, depends on the circumstances at hand. First of all, it has to do with the distribution of power resources generally in society. The more that other resources, of a more individual kind, are lacking, the greater is the significance of collective capacities. The latter can compensate, as Verba, Nie, and Kim (1978) have shown, for disadvantages in terms of individual-based resources. Therefore, the group-based capacity is normally most important for marginalized and unprivileged segments of society. Second, the special nature of organizational life plays a role. This is a question of the internal structure of the units in question, of the inter-relationship between the units, and of the terms of relations with the state. To a high degree, I will argue, it is these special traits of associational networks that determine their significance for democratic development.

Organizations Matter

In what ways, we may ask ourselves, is this business of organizational networks important? And why, to put the point in converse terms, should the absence of such networks be a loss for the citizens?

To begin with, *external strength* is achieved most effectively when people act together in a coordinated manner. Organization facilitates this. 'An association unites the energies of divergent minds and vigorously directs them toward a clearly indicated goal', says Tocqueville (1969: 190). A modern researcher in this field, Michael Bratton (1994: 233), puts it like this: 'Power—the ability to secure compliance to one's will—is difficult for individuals to obtain when acting alone. To mount a credible bid to exercise power, individuals must combine with others; thus power is accumulated and exercised in the context of political organization'.

Entering a fixed structure for coordination reduces uncertainty about how others will act: an uncertainty which will otherwise restrict each individual's incentive to contribute to collective action (North 1990: 25). The reform-minded individual who wishes, in a threatening context, to step forth and protest is typically reluctant to do so if there is reason to fear he or she will be left standing alone 'in the square'. One's willingness to act is affected, in other words, by one's judgement of how others are likely to act themselves: 'When protesting politically it is safer to be a member of a crowd.

The implication is that coordination is essential to the politics of reform. Knowing that others have acted or will act decreases the perceived risks of acting' (Bates 1994: 23). Organizations may be regarded, against this background, as cartels for guaranteeing a certain community of preferences and a collective potential for action. This enhances the political clout of the people involved.

The foregoing is illustrated by a report by Christine Sadowski about events in formerly communist eastern Europe. One of the important factors sustaining the system was 'the barriers of fear used to control, direct, encourage or prevent certain forms of activity among citizens' (1994: 162). It was only when autonomous and reasonably cohesive groups started acting openly that the collective paralysis cultivated by these regimes began to wane. This provided role models and showed that collective action was possible. As a result, the great mass of formerly alienated and marginalized people got politically involved. A repressive and passivizing coordination from above was successively replaced, and at an increasing rate, by active coordination from below.

The development of organizational structures involves the establishment of stable and routinized networks for extended coordination. This has two dimensions. In the first, individuals begin working together with others of the same sort, given some identity, who are located elsewhere. When this happens, a national network for coordinated action is created. Actions taken within such a framework do not, consequently, appear as a series of scattered and isolated local events—which would make them easier for the authorities to cope with. Sidney Tarrow indicates how matters can proceed when protests remain scattered and uncoordinated. He points to the failed attempt of the French republicans, who had pushed through the revolution of 1848, to resist Louis Napoleon's assumption of power in the early 1850s. They were numerous and, at the local level, fairly cohesive, yet they proved an easy prey for Napoleon's troops. This was because the various local groups were not coordinated with each other. Despite an abundance of that spirit, then, which Mill believed crucial for the defence of democracy—a willingness among citizens to sacrifice themselves for the sake of popular rule—the efforts of the republicans ended in disaster. For they lacked a critical collective capacity: that of organizational upscaling. They had not succeeded, that is, in establishing networks linking centre and periphery. Although numerous and highly committed, the French republicans lacked the intermediary organizational structures needed for coordinated national action (Tarrow 1994: 136ff).

The second dimension has to do with what opportunities exist for people to establish contacts with those of another identity than their own: for example, when farmers and workers interact, or religious and professional groups join forces. This type of extended community between different segments of civil society can be extremely important for resisting repressive tendencies in political life. The following events in Guatemala in the early 1990s may serve as an illustration. The sitting president, George Serrano, tried to carry out a coup by suspending the constitution, dissolving Congress, and dismissing the courts—all for the purpose of staying in power. There was nothing unusual in a Latin American context about this. What *was* unusual was the effective mobilization of civil society, which succeeded in blocking Serrano's drive to establish a dictatorship. The joint action of civic forces can be attributed in large measure to the existence in Guatemala of a nationwide umbrella organization—the National Forum for Consensus—which embraced a wide range of associations. It had been founded in order to provide a forum for dialogue between different social sectors. This body coordinated the civic resistance, and proved 'the key catalyst for reversing the coup' (Villagrán de Leon 1993: 122). A less dramatic role, though not a less important one, has been played by the Catholic church in such settings. In many countries, in Africa and Latin America especially, the church has served as an arena in which popular organizations can establish contacts. This has reinforced the cohesion of civil society[5] (Beremo 1992).

Beyond this, as a wider form of extended coordination, cooperation may be established with groups outside the country (Whitehead 1986). Such international contacts can be a great asset, for they make external support in various forms possible: for example, international pressure on the domestic regime, or direct efforts on behalf of the group in question. To this end, as indeed with all extended coordination, a network of fixed organizational structures is needed.

An effective popular organization functions as a structure for the exchange of information and the activation of preferences held by a circle of people. It is, moreover, possible, through organization, to build up a *store of resources* for the activities conducted. Such resources may be both material and professional in nature. The classic example is probably the strike funds accumulated by trade unions for members involved in industrial disputes. But it may also be a question of training members, providing legal support,

---

[5] For other examples of civic coordination promotive of democracy, see Diamond (1999: 230, 235ff.).

exerting political influence through lobbying, and so forth. An organization commanding such resources undeniably constitutes 'capital' in one obvious sense of the word. It may be of interest here to recall the doctrinal struggle which took place at the time of the outbreak of World War I between the reformist socialist Eduard Bernstein and his antagonist Rosa Luxemburg. The latter argued, in a traditional Marxist spirit, that the propertyless working class had nothing to lose but its chains, and so should focus its efforts on direct revolutionary action. Against this viewpoint, Bernstein maintained that the workers in fact had something to lose if such actions failed. Up to that time, the workers had been building up national organizations with a great many members, and these organizations administered considerable resources which their members could use. The workers had thus acquired property, of a collective kind, which they ought not lightly endanger (Rothstein 1992).

This brings us to another type of resource, or property, which organizations can develop through activities of long duration. I refer to certain capacities of a qualitative nature. Through repeated action, an organizational memory is created, a store of experiences which enables the organization in question to interact more effectively with its environment. Thus an experienced leadership comes into being, which by its capacity has acquired legitimacy with the members. It consists of leaders who are capable not just of taking the offensive and getting people on board, but also of restraining and disciplining members if needed (Öberg 1994). Organizations which possess, at one and the same time, the ability to activate and to discipline have the capacity to negotiate effectively, and to conclude agreements with public bodies and other organizations (Nordlund 1996).

The Chinese student movement of 1989 may serve to illustrate what happens when such an ability is absent. The radical mass movement which had emerged so rapidly attracted, as we know, a great deal of attention in the international media, and for a time it seemed to have the initiative in the struggle for power in Peking. But we also know how it ended. The fundamental weakness of the students lay, according to Yanaki Tong, in their deficient organizational capacity:[6]

6 As Per Nordlund (1996) shows in a study of African politics, this organizational weakness, together with the tendencies towards escalation that it feeds, would seem to be a general problem among student movements. The underlying problem seems to lie in the uprootedness of their members—as Kornhauser would describe it—and in the brevity of their enrolment; these have the effect of limiting the collective repertoire sharply. Such movements can take the lead temporarily with sudden aggressive outbursts, but not much more.

On the surface, the movement appeared to be organized and under control, such that violence and criminal activities rarely occurred. Beneath the surface, however, the lack of organization was reflected in the fact that the student leaders were unable to demobilize the demonstrations when it proved necessary to do so. The massive movement became more and more emotional and uncontrolled. Radical tendencies among the rank-and-file students prevented their representatives from making compromises in their dialogue with the government. Moderate student leaders were replaced by more radical ones. The highly moralistic and personalistic attacks on the party and the state leadership created an emotionalism that made demobilization impossible. In turn, the inability to demobilize the mass movement led to the final confrontation with the hardliners that ended in bloodshed. (Tong 1994: 334)

Tong compares this pattern of action with the strategy of Hungary's reform movement during the 1980s. Chastened by the lessons of 1956, when demands for political change had been crushed by Soviet tanks, the Hungarian reformers of the 1980s sought with success to restrain the most provocative demands of their followers. They concentrated instead on building up a civic, and superficially non-political, network of organizations. When the repression was eventually relaxed, these clubs, circles, and associations for the promotion of various purposes formed the basis of the emerging democratic opposition. In other words, those involved had learned from experience that collective power requires, if it is to yield the effects desired, a long-range effort to build up an organizational network, together with an ability to coordinate, when needed, in a moderating and disciplining direction (Tong 1994: 346–7).

Through organizational endeavours, we have seen, people can exert external influence. Once well established, however, an organization tends to have internal effects as well. It can contribute to the formation of a *normative identity*, that is, a common ideology, of a looser or firmer sort, which facilitates coordination. 'An ideology', says Coleman (1990: 320), 'can create social capital by imposing on the individual who holds it the demand that he act in the interests of something or someone other than himself'. As an example, he adduces religious schools in the US, where the dropout rates are significantly lower than at secular schools. A similar example may be seen in the strikingly high levels of activity—far above the norm—within religious congregations in Sweden (Petersson, Westholm, and Blomberg 1989). A strong normative identity strengthens the affinity which members feel with their organization. It increases their motivation to participate and to make private sacrifices for the common good (Tarrow 1994: 22–3). An organization is not just an aggregate, in other words, of individual preferences which it would mirror, so to speak. Organizations have an active role in constructing the identities held by their members. Persons who form part of a fixed collective, and thus interact regularly with a group, find their preferences affected in a certain way. They develop joint interests and a sense of community (March and Olsen 1989).

The creation of an identity is normally a feature of the first stage of organizational development. This process can at times be fairly troublesome and protracted, particularly when an organization is being created 'from scratch'. It may involve extensive deliberations, many of them marked by contention and conflict between factions holding different views. Groups which do not pass through this initial stage successfully will face constant problems in performing their tasks. Unless such groups settle the basic issue of who 'we' are, their members will experience little in the way of common 'belonging'. The feeling of involvement in a larger unit will be weak (Fish 1996: 81–2).

This in turn affects the activity repertoire of the unit in question. As we have seen, for example, relationships marked by trust and legitimacy must exist between members and leaders if bargaining is to be accomplished. For such bonds of loyalty to develop, it is usually necessary that members have a long-term connection with their organization.[7] Time—that is, the duration of enrolment—plays a role on two accounts. On the one hand, it reinforces the process of socialization into the culture and norms upheld by the unit. Organizational involvement affects the formation of preferences. Long-term interaction strengthens group identity. On the other hand, it increases the capacity of members to 'screen' their leaders and to hold them accountable. Viewing this interaction as a principal-agent relationship, we could say that, with the passage of time, the principals stand a progressively better chance of selecting agents that share their goals and are competent and reliable (Moe 1984). On both accounts, trust in the relationship between leaders and members is boosted. This enhances the collective repertoire of the unit in question.

Involvement in cooperative action, moreover, develops *certain abilities* among the actors involved. It equips people with organizational skills that can be used in a variety of undertakings. This is a point emphasized by Tocqueville. Participation in collective endeavours of a social or economic character endows people with attitudes

---

[7] As Gary Miller (1992: 186) notes, it has been clearly documented in behavioural research that advanced forms of cooperation are most likely to arise in organizations of very long standing.

and resources that can be profitably applied in public life. Verba, Schlozman, and, Brady (1995) accordingly report that people involved in church activities in the US are more prone than others to be politically active. Through organizational engagement, they gain skills which can be utilized in the political sphere. Similarly, trade-union members in South Africa have often been heavily involved in community activities (Torres 1999).

But it can also, as Tocqueville noticed, be the other way round: people trained in political activities can use their organizational skills to promote associational pursuits in the social or economic realms—for a recent example, see Tarrow (1996) on Italy. The 'recycling' of collective abilities can, however, take other forms as well. Developments can take such a course that an organization which had been established for a certain short-term purpose becomes a lasting organization, and takes new and changing tasks upon itself. In other words, a seed of social capital can take root, and the coordination capacity thus created may then be turned to another purpose (Diamond 1999: 231; Fox 1994a; Rueschemayer 1998). A transformation can also take place whereby organizations with a narrow initial agenda—of a strictly professional nature, perhaps—successively change their character, and come to address broader social questions. They take the step, as Yanki Tong (1994) puts it, from a managerial, non-critical public sphere to a political and critical one. It is in the latter role that they may come to challenge state power directly, and thus to serve as a societal check. Or in Elinor Ostrom's (1990: 190) more general terms: 'Success in starting small-scale initial institutions enables a group of individuals to build on the social capital thus created to solve larger problems with larger and more complex institutional arrangements.'

Facilitating Conditions

Organization, when it gets going, can yield palpable effects on political life. How, then, does it get started? Certain strategic parameters here are known. When Robert Axelrod conducted his famous game experiment, documented in *The Evolution of Cooperation* (1984), he found that repeated play, that is, a *continuity* of interaction, was a fundamental precondition for reaching a favourable pattern of coordination. Interaction under the shadow of the future—the knowledge that they shall meet again—makes the players less inclined to cheat or to take advantage of each other, for they know they can get paid back in the same coin next time round.

In addition, regular contacts within a group bring the advantage that the actors involved have better information about one another. They know each other's preferences and behaviour, and they learn whom to trust and whom not to (North 1990: 56).

It is thus critical that there be meeting-places making continuous interaction between individuals possible. Such *arenas* can be of many different kinds. Karl Marx claimed, for example, that the typical workplaces of industrialism—the factories—had the advantage, despite everything, of bringing people close to each other, thus endowing them with collective resources in the form of improved opportunities for organizing. Repeated interaction was an important precondition here. But the factory system had a further effect as well: those working in it had very similar social and working conditions (Tarrow 1994: 11).

If regularity of intercourse and homogeneity among participants are an advantage, it will be easier as a rule to establish cooperation in groups consisting of a *small number* of persons. Here the probability is greater, obviously, of a repeated interaction between individuals; furthermore, it is easier in smaller and tighter units to internalize certain behaviours and norms. This helps reinforce identity within the group in question. A smaller collective is easier to coordinate, other things being equal, than a larger one. The sense of community—a feeling of 'we'—is strengthened still more if there is a *common enemy*, opposing the group in question (Diani 1992). Likewise, cooperation is easily achieved among people who remain for a long time in the same area and live under the same conditions. In other words, geographical and social *immobility* breeds consent. Hence, a static society, where people live enclosed in well-defined segments, marked by mutual animosity, provides favorable conditions for group coherence and organization (Dahl and Tuft 1973: 13; North 1990: 12, 56; Ostrom 1990: 95, 211; Kornhauser 1960: 182; see also Sartori 1987: 228).

Special incentives may also be important. The opportunity for obvious economic or other material gain has often supplied a rationale for collective action. Thus, Vivienne Shue (1994: 79) shows from the example of China that the many new organizations, typically in urban areas, which have been able to establish themselves in recent years have often had an economic or related purpose: to promote commerce, make use of new technology, and so on. Similar patterns, albeit in a pronouncedly agrarian context, may be seen in Africa. Bratton (1994: 248–9) reports: 'Farmer associations arise because of difficulty faced by individual households in pursuing the "peasant option" alone. For small farmers seeking income from agricultural sales, economies of scale in commodity circuits are most accessible through combination.' Support for this conclusion may also be derived from the so-called rotating credit associations which have been formed in many different parts of the world. Such networks for economic collaboration, which function as collective investment and insurance systems, have in many cases constituted a first foundation stone for the build-up of social capital (Putnam 1993: 167ff; Uphoff 1992). More generally, it would seem, collective action receives a boost, especially in its early stages, if an element of selective and interest-related incentives is clearly present (Coleman 1990: 317; cf. Olson 1965).

Finally, it may also happen that organizations come into being through *spillover effects*, that is, by means of diffusion. Adducing the democratization process in Latin America, Alfred Stepan (1985: 336) calls attention to 'the horizontal dimension' of associational life. He shows how organization and activation in one sector of society has a tendency to stimulate similar initiatives in other sectors. Mobilizations in the religious sector, for instance, have facilitated similar developments among trade unions. Thus a cumulative process may get under way, in that new organizations draw others along with them; these latter then stimulate others, and so on and on in a virtuous circle. We have reports of a similar diffusion process in the democratization of eastern Europe (Sadowski 1994). There is also extensive documentation, thanks, not least, to the efforts of Ostrom (1990), of organizational spillover effects among popular organs for self-administration in various parts of the world.[8] Such effects can appear, Ostrom shows, when leaders and activists who have gained their places in such organs establish new ones, or function as sponsors and advisers. Yet personal connections need not always be present. The stimulus often spreads through pure diffusion, that is, through the power of example, so that people on their own initiative follow a model that has worked well elsewhere.

When these preconditions—or at least some of them—obtain, a potential basis exists for the broader organizational dynamic earlier described: a process which can result in a strengthened collective capacity in society. The existence of networks connecting people enhances their potential of taking joint action. There is an abundance of examples, ranging from Montevideo to Warsaw, from Seoul

---

[8] Ostrom's example, like the others I take up here, has to do with cooperation at the level of small groups. In principle, however, the same conditions apply to organizing on a 'higher' level. In studies of international integration, for example, a comparable logic, in the form of spillover effects, is applied within the framework of so-called functionalist and neo-functionalist theory.

to Djakarta, of how mass demonstrations and other collective activities have spurred the collapse of authoritarian regimes (Diamond
1999). As Ronald Inglehart (1997: 204) demonstrates, moreover, the
number of associational ties within a society can be of great importance in a process of democratization. For the maintenance and
healthy functioning of democracy, however, it is reasonable to argue
that is not the mere existence of organizational networks that
makes the difference, but the special nature and quality of these
networks.

Autonomy and Inclusion

Having begun with the lessons of group and game theory, we have
been able to state certain preconditions for the initiation of organization. When these obtain, a potential exists for a mounting pluralist diffusion of power in society. In order for such a diffusion of
power to be established, however, one fundamental condition must
be fulfilled: the associations in question must be autonomous from
the state. What then are the criteria by which the degree of autonomy may be ascertained? As I see it, the following three aspects are
most relevant:[9]

1. Policy autonomy: the organization must be able to choose both
   the goals and the means of its activities independently.
2. Staff autonomy: the organization must be able to choose its leaders and the rest of its staff independently.
3. Resource autonomy: the organization must be financially and
   administratively independent, in the sense of controlling the
   resources requisite to its operations.

A characteristic feature of regimes with totalitarian aspirations
is that they deprive such organizations as they permit to exist of
autonomy in all three of the mentioned respects. Trade unions in
the former Soviet Union were a clear example of this. Their tasks
were subjected to strict regulation—meaning, among other things,
that wage negotiations, strikes, and so on were out of the question—
and all persons in leading positions were handpicked by the governing party. All critical resources, moreover—given the activity
in question, which was to distribute certain benefits to workers—
were wholly under external control, that is, by the enterprise, the
party, and the state (Crowley 1994). Authoritarian regimes of a less

---

⁹ For a somewhat different ordering of similar criteria, see Bratton (1994) and
Nordlund (1996).

totalitarian sort normally restrict themselves to using one or a few of the possible means of control. The government in Kenya, for example, has controlled the trade unions, primarily through the device of choosing the leader of their peak organization.[10] In other cases, the trade unions' lack of political autonomy has mainly arisen from their resource-dependence on the state, as, for example, in a good many countries of Latin America (Mouzelis 1986; Collier and Collier 1991). There is reason indeed for authoritarian regimes to curtail the autonomy of popular organizations. The existence of independent associations, as we have seen, is a threat to the survival of such regimes.

For the success of democracy, once it has been inaugurated, the independence of social forces is an essential condition. Autonomy, Bratton (1994: 237) states, is 'the cornerstone of power; it lies in the heart of struggles between state and society'. It goes virtually without saying that, if civil society is to be capable of acting as a check upon the power of the state, it must in its various components be independent of the actor to be checked (Dahl 1982; Gellner 1994; Diamond 1999). Just as individuals must be independent as political actors if they are to be capable of defending their interests, collective units must be too. Yet this is only the one side of the matter.

While I have stressed the importance of functional autonomy on the part of civic organizations, this does not imply complete isolation from the state. If the activities and opinions of civil society are to have any impact on the operation of the state, there must in a democracy be various linkages between civil society and the public sphere (Rueschemayer 1998: 13). Turning to this aspect of the state-society nexus, then, we must address the issue of inclusion.

Organizations which are active in the social and economic spheres can contribute to the downfall of an undemocratic regime. But when the task at hand is that of democratic consolidation, as Juan Linz and Alfred Stepan (1996) remind us, an effective political sphere is necessary. This means, first and foremost, political parties. These bodies play a special intermediary role between the state and civil society, in that they aim at achieving representation

---

[10] The unions present a list of names, from which the government chooses one. When, on one occasion in 1993, the sitting chairman opposed the policies of the government even so, he was dismissed (Hadenius 1994a). We find a similar example in this report from Egypt: 'a powerful president of the General Federation of Trade Unions . . . described as "out of line" with respect to the government's open-door economic policy, was removed a few years ago at the instigation of the minister of manpower and training and replaced by the secretary of trade union affairs within the [ruling] National Democratic Party' (Al-Sayyid 1993: 238).

within the leading organs of public decision-making. Through the electoral and parliamentary processes, political parties channel social interests and express popular demands. In accomplishing these tasks, political parties normally—in a developed democratic polity, at least—serve a broad aggregating function, integrating the multitude of conflicting demands from society into workable packages. Parties help transform political demands into concrete policy accomplishments; at the same time, they serve as the principal organs of representation and political accountability (Huntington 1968; Sartori 1976; Roberts and Wibbels 1999). In addition to parties, furthermore, a wide range of associations geared at the promotion of specific interests—usually of a narrower or more exclusive nature—try by various means to influence the decisions of the authorities.

From the standpoint of the autonomy of popular organizations, interacting with the state can represent a delicate balancing act. This problem is naturally most pertinent in the case of political parties, as these are represented in the governing bodies of the state. It should be recalled, however, that the party-associated persons who direct the state apparatus hold their positions as individuals, which means that the parties, as popular associations, can preserve their organizational autonomy. There must be, in a democracy, a clear separation between the functions of the state and those of the governing party or parties.

As far the pressure groups that seek to influence public policy are concerned, contacts with the authorities may at times be of a fairly stable and intimate sort. So-called corporatist arrangements constitute the most institutionalized mode of inclusion.[11] Such relations can be manifested in two ways. In the first place, state organs may take part in direct bargaining with important pressure groups, in order to achieve some kind of agreement. Such practices have been most common in the area of labour relations. In the typical practice, the government cooperates with business and labour organizations, normally for the purpose of restraining wage increases—to control inflation—and limiting labour conflicts. Corporatist bargaining is not necessarily confined to 'hard' issues like the economy, however. In certain countries, for example, negotiations of a similar sort have started taking place in recent years between the government and environmental organizations (Dryzek 1996). Corporatist relations may also manifest themselves through

---

[11] I am referring here to democratic corporatism: what Schmitter (1974) calls 'social corporatism'.

representation, whereby the associations in question are offered seats in various advisory or decision-making bodies in the administrative branches of government.

The risk of being 'captured'—of losing autonomy as a consequence of the intercourse with the state—is normally greater when the associations involved are fragile, with little popular support and a meagre organizational capacity (Mouzelis 1986). This capacity is generally more developed when the organizations are rooted in the surrounding society. Studies of political parties have shown that parties which maintain close links with other civic associations tend to be the most successful in establishing a broad membership. Such contacts also tend, on account of the legitimacy in the target group which they help to create, to pay off well at election time (Crewe 1981; Diamond 1999). Well-established parties—those with a developed party 'apparatus' and a firm foundation in the surrounding associational life—are also far more capable of implementing their policies effectively upon entering the halls of government. Being in want of this capacity—Atul Kohli (1997) reports from India, where these linkages have diminished—parties face great problems in getting things done. This has turned political life into an arena mainly featuring grand proclamations with little effect in terms of actual 'delivery'. More generally, in the words of Steven Fish (1996: 78), "stabilizing the system of representation" . . . requires formation of genuine, institutionalized links between the state actors on the one hand, and social groups that command sufficient membership, following, or influence to serve effectively as agents of intermediation, on the other'.

Yet it is not just political parties that can benefit from such contacts; it can also be a two-way street. In his study of the early American republic, Tocqueville found that political parties often contributed to the establishment of civic and other associations: a nurturing function that has also been reported from other countries and later periods (Foley and Edwards 1996). Institutionalized connections with the political sphere may naturally afford social and economic organizations the opportunity to influence public decision-making, in the interests of securing selective benefits or advancing some more general agenda. Whatever the purpose of seeking a say in political life, the result tends to be an improved organizational capacity. Effective connections with the political sphere have in many cases proved an asset in building up a broad membership base and in attracting support from other social circles (Hadenius and Uggla 1996). The lack of such links can prove an obstacle to organizational development. This was the fate, in the judgement of

Fish (1996), of many new movements in Russia at the close of the
Soviet era.

Keeping to the Russian example, it is reasonable to recall a
metaphor Richard Rose used to illustrate the patterns long prevailing in that country, but having a wider bearing too. I refer to the
notion of an hour-glass society:

In an hour-glass society there is a rich social life at the base, consisting of
strong informal networks relying on trust between friends, relatives and
other face-to-face groups. Networks can extend from friends to friends too.
At the top of the hour glass, there is a rich political and social life, as elites
compete for power, wealth and prestige. In the vast Russian state, cooperation within and between elites and institutions is the normal way for individual officials to secure their own goals. Such a society resembles a civil
society insofar as a number of informal and even formal institutions are
tolerated and now legally recognized by the state. Yet the result is not a
civic community but an hour-glass society, because the links between top
and bottom are very limited. (Rose 1995: 35)

Such are the main arguments in favour of inclusion: strong democratic citizenship presupposes the existence of linkages between the
political system and other spheres of society. This objective must
always be balanced, however, with the need for autonomy; and this
is a consideration, *nota bene*, that poses restrictions in both direc-
tions. On the one hand, the political organizations, especially the
parties, must enjoy a significant degree of independence from other
associations in society. It is only through this relative 'insulation'
from the various social forces that the political system can uphold
its aggregating and moderating function, serving as a transmission
belt, as it were, between organs of the state and actors in society.
The 'game of politics', Linz and Stepan (1996: 10) remind us, is
marked by a specific culture of interaction and a particular mode of
decision-making. This game is sometimes held in contempt, but it is
nevertheless a necessary instrument of coordination in a consolidated democracy.

The converse condition must obtain as well: associational life cannot be permeated, directed, and 'used' by the agents of the political
sphere. Alongside their dealings with the state and with intermediary political units, societal groups must be able to maintain a high
degree of autonomy, with regard, as outlined above, to policy formation, staff recruitment, and resources. If this is not the case, the
political linkages in question will reflect not the interaction of
independent units but dependency and top-down dominance. The
existence in society of social and economic spheres which are largely
independent and which include a wide variety of basically apolitical

associations—the type on which, indeed, Putnam focuses—is an indispensable condition for a vital and properly functioning democratic order. These independent spheres are the 'habitats' for the formation of new identities and the fostering of new issues which the prevailing political system has neglected, or maybe even tried to silence. Through this latently critical and dynamic function, politically independent civil spheres serve as a source for the renewal of public discourse. They place new topics on the agenda and provide a check to the political establishment. They help thereby to impede tendencies towards rigidity: an ailment which afflicts the political system constantly (Foley and Edwards 1996; Dryzek 1996).

The Internal Arena

Assuming associational life as a whole meets the criteria just mentioned, and can strike a suitable balance between them, it can contribute to the articulation of different interests in society, and thus provide a basis for the dispersion of power required for pluralism. The existence of a multiplicity of intermediary groups constitutes a defence against despotism and monism in political life. Naturally, this is an important precondition for democracy. Yet it is not a sufficient one.[12]

To begin with the basis, so to speak: it is easy to see that not all social capital is equally advantageous from a democratic point of view (Booth and Richard 1998). Even crime syndicates like the Mafia in Sicily, or terrorist units like the Red Brigades and politically aggressive Nazi groups, represent an indisputable element of social capital, inasmuch as they embody a form for coordinated collective action. A further specification of concepts is therefore in order: we are interested here in organizations which, at least potentially, represent *democratic social capital*. This means we should not, when observing a particular country, take account only of the existence or non-existence of autonomous associations, or the capacity which in an outward sense these may possess. We must also include a series of qualitative aspects in our judgement: aspects having to do with the internal life of the associations in question (Diamond 1999: 228; Rueschemayer 1998). It is to this side of the matter that we now turn.

[12] As a concrete illustration, it bears mentioning that civil society can to some degree fill, according to Illya Harik (1994), the pluralist counter-power function in certain countries of the Middle East. The organizational life found in this region does not, however, satisfy the other qualitative criteria considered here.

When Tocqueville described the democratic vitality of the American republic, he attached great importance to the abundance of organizational networks. These intermediary associations facilitated collective action and served as powerful agents of civic counter-power *vis-à-vis* the state. But he also stressed something else. The civic spirit and active political culture which he found in such abundance among common people in the young United States, in contrast to the situation in his homeland, was, as he saw it, the result of a process of learning and socialization. Through their participation in self-governing organizations, citizens had been schooled in a democratic process. Through mutual interaction and intercourse, they had acquired a broader capacity for coordination, and developed more tolerant and open attitudes too. In the language of modern institutional theory, the preferences of citizens had been endogenously formed through interaction created by the organizational context of which they were a part (see, for example, Wildavsky 1987). Mill considered this dynamic and fostering function to be the strongest justification for democratic decision-making: only through popular responsibility and participation in public affairs can a suitable civic spirit grow forth (Lewin 1970). Democratic practice serves, moreover, to advance certain skills which can be employed politically.

From a democratic perspective, in other words, it is advantageous if the organizations forming the framework for collective action are themselves democratically structured. In this way they become, to begin with, more representative of the collective to be represented; they function better in their role as channels for the opinions found among their members. Alongside this plainly desirable quality, which we can call the channelling function, organizations also have a role as meeting-places and arenas. It is this latter role—the arena function—that we have in mind when we claim that organizational structures have a socializing and fostering import, in the sense that they develop collective resources and leave their imprint on the preference systems of the participating actors.[13] Briefly put, democratic citizenship is promoted by democratic practice.

From the standpoint of both these functions, it is desirable that organizations be characterized by pluralism and openness in their

---

[13] Evidence supporting this tenet is found in Verba, Schlossman, and Brady (1995). Comparing the impact of enrolment in different churches—churches constitute the most important organizational factor in the US overall—the authors discover a distinct difference between Protestants and Catholics. The former group is more skilled, democratically speaking, than the latter. This finding is attributed in turn to differences in internal structure. The Catholic church is marked by hierarchy, whereas Protestant churches are fairly 'flat', and they often encourage

internal life, and that there be developed forms through which members can hold leaders accountable and take part in the running of affairs. We know from experience that this can best be accomplished under certain conditions.

These preconditions are most easily created, to begin with, in so-called *horizontal* associations, that is, those organized by individuals together with their peers. These units are homogeneous, which as we saw earlier facilitates cooperation. But they also entail—and this is the important thing here—equality in one special respect: that of social and political resources. Why is this so important? Because, quite simply, it is only in this way that the individual autonomy so vital to democracy can be guaranteed. It is only when our dependence on each other's participation in some form of interaction is of a mutual character and an equivalent degree that we will treat one another as equals. Furthermore, it is only when resources are spread fairly uniformly throughout the group that there is a general capacity to hold those in leading positions accountable. When this is not the case, as in so-called vertical associations, in which the 'grass roots' command inferior resources and are more dependent on their superiors than the latter are on them, the likelihood is great that information, influence, and sanctions will systematically flow more in the one direction than in the other. Under such conditions, Putnam writes, 'only a bold or foolhardy subordinate, lacking the ties of solidarity with peers . . . [would] seek to punish a superior' (1993: 174). Within an organization, then, equality in terms of individual resources, which is normally associated with socioeconomic position, is, as Rousseau and Tocqueville assumed, advantageous from a democratic point of view (cf. Dahl 1989).

Autonomy and a reasonable measure of equality must prevail within organizational life. There must be *internal arenas* in which groups of members, and mid-level leaders too, can gather independently to discuss matters, spread information, and act in common. Only in this manner can pluralism—the checks and balances needed for a functioning democracy—be upheld. It was the abundance of such sub-structures within the American typographers' union which, according to Seymour Lipset, Martin Trow, and James Coleman in their famous study (1956), had made possible the unusually vital democracy prevailing within that union. Jonathan Fox (1994a: 27) reaches a similar conclusion in his study of

extensive participation on the part of their members. For the same reason, Afro-Americans, who are usually Protestant, are better equipped democratically than Latinos—normally Catholic—despite the fact that they are scarcely better-off economically or educationally.

trade-union life in Mexico: 'Participatory subgroups are crucial for leadership accountability. In their absence, leaders of large associations need only deal with atomized individuals who lack systematic opportunities to share information and to generate alternative options, counterproposals and contenders for leadership.'

In a later study of associational life in Mexico, the same author points to another factor of importance: the possibility of organizational upscaling. Popular involvement must not be limited to the locality. *Intermediary structures* must also be present, in order to facilitate interaction among the local units and to strengthen their capacity to exert joint pressure on the leadership:

Scaling up is especially important for representing the interests of dispersed populations since they have the greatest difficulties defending common interests and are more vulnerable to 'divide and conquer' efforts from above. If they do not develop scaled-up organizations, they are among the most vulnerable to the 'iron law of oligarchy' since dispersed populations have little capacity to monitor the activities of their leadership and therefore have little capacity of holding them accountable.[14] (Fox 1997: 124)

Conversely, leaders wishing to promote atomization and powerlessness among members would be well-advised to eliminate potentially competing arenas and intermediary structures within their organization. One can accomplish this, as Lenin did, by depriving subordinate party organs of all autonomy and right of initiative. With the instituting of so-called democratic centralism—which meant that subordinate organs could only take orders—and the prohibiting of factions within the party, the relations of power were soon cast in concrete. One can also do this, as Goebbels did, by ensuring that the leadership, and the Leader in particular, interacts with the members only in well-directed mass meetings, or through the electronic media. In this way, it was guaranteed that vertical communication went only in a single direction, while horizontal communication—between members—was restrained.

Kornhauser, for his part, summarizes the matter as follows:

the lack of a pluralist structure within organizations, like its absence in larger society, not only discourages membership participation. It also discourages the formation of an informed membership, the development of new leadership, and the spread of responsibility and authority, so that a wide gap between the top and the bottom of mass organizations tends to be bridged by manipulation. (1960: 98–9)

[14] What is needed most especially, according to Fox, are strong regional organizations. Regional bodies have the clout to offset concentrated elite power at the national level, as well as the ability to keep close ties to the local base.

In the interests of democracy, then, it is desirable that the organizations of civil society possess a vital and pluralistic internal life. This is critical both for channelling member opinion and for fostering a democratic spirit. Yet this ambition is not problem-free, of course, especially since it may collide with another obvious organizational purpose. A major aim of many associations is to exercise influence *vis-à-vis* outside actors. Internal conflicts may be a source of weakness in this regard, especially if they are exhibited clearly to the outside world. Unity, the absence of dissonance, and action in unison all contribute to effective action *vis-à-vis* rival actors. This is military logic, the logic of battle; and it dominated Lenin's perspective entirely. In the pessimistic judgement of Robert Michels, this contest between the requirements of internal democracy and the logic imposed by conflicts with rival organizations can but issue in a single result. Hence his famous words: who says organization, says oligarchy. Even if we refrain from endorsing his categorical statement—perhaps his pessimism would have softened a bit had he made the acquaintance of the American typographers' union—Michels' aphorism illustrates an important point: the internal and external arenas may present such conflicting demands as to require a trade-off of some sort. Sidney Tarrow puts the point thus: 'organizations must fulfil the function of coordination required for effective collective action while maintaining the autonomy at the base needed to provide participatory incentives for supporters' (1994: 149).

In his account of the political movements that emerged during the twilight of the Soviet system, Steven Fish describes a situation in which this balance was not achieved. These new movements displayed, Fish avers, a 'hyperdemocratic' mode of operation. They developed no clear lines of responsibility and authority, and they practised a collective leadership, shunning all forms of hierarchy. Party and trade-union conferences were 'anarchic marathons' marked by heated debates over all kinds of procedural matters, which often left little room for discussing central policy issues. Such meetings were normally well-attended, and important decisions on these occasions were usually taken in full session, or even by a direct vote of the entire membership. At the same time, the local branches of these organizations enjoyed a great deal of autonomy, with the result that decisions made on the national level could be completely ignored if they were considered inconsistent with local views. This state of affairs reflected a lack of coordination capacity on the part of these organizations. For want of loyalty, which takes time to develop, these *ad hoc* units had a very restricted repertoire. Unable to serve as organs for regulated collective action, they were poor instruments not only for 'getting things done' but also for representing their members and advancing solidarity and unity among the scattered local groups. On the one hand, Fish remarks, these practices clearly satisfied the Tocquevillian ideal of cultivating the habits of democratic participation and competition. Yet the new associations could not, due to their lack of an authority structure setting some clear limits to the discretion of their sub-units and of their individual leaders, muster any real organizational capacity (Fish 1996: 56–7, 67–8). A community without a regulated internal hierarchy—that is, some sort of delegation of authority—can hardly function as a forceful organization. As regards this elementary sense of 'oligarchy', Michels was certainly right.

This brings us to the question of the nature of the linkages between people in different sorts of groups. In certain spheres of life, our bonds with others tend to be fairly informal and simple. This is the case, for example, in our relationships with friends, colleagues, neighbours, classmates, fellow parents, and the like. Yet some of these relationships can also be of a formal or semi-formal sort: in the case, for instance, of fraternities, professional associations, or neighbourhood communities. At the other end of the scale, as we know, a multitude of units of a highly formal nature can be found in many countries. These have fixed operating procedures and rules of membership, as well as a developed organizational structure involving a hierarchy of leadership and extensive administrative functions. The advantage of the informal and semi-informal units, briefly put, is that they are more accessible. Their structure of authority tends to be 'flat', and more participatory in character. Their drawback lies in their normally restricted outreach—they tend to be locally bound—and their limited activity repertoire. Formal associations usually offer much wider connections out in society, both nationally and internationally. It is only organizations of this kind, for the most part, that can provide us with a rich store of 'organizational capital'. In the ideal world, from the point of view of collective capacity, people would of course be strongly involved in networks of both formal and informal kinds. Yet, on balance, the more formal and organizationally elaborate mode of group activism seems to be of principal importance. In a study of democracy and the engagement of civil society in Central America, John Booth and Patricia Bayer Richard (1998) find that membership in formal groups—trade unions, cooperatives, professional associations, and the like—is strongly correlated with political information, political involvement in various forms, and support for democratic norms. The same does not hold, however, for people engaged solely in local activism. These individuals are in general both less informed and less supportive of democratic norms, and their repertoire of political involvement is more restricted. Both forms of group activism are positively correlated with the capacity to contact public officials, and, to a lesser extent, with voting in elections; but in other respects, as noted, the effects were democratically positive only in the case of membership in associations of the organizationally more developed type.

Inter-organizational Relationships

So far the emphasis has largely been on the mobilizing side of collective activity. In this perspective, networks of different sorts are seen as means of expressing demands and bringing pressure to bear in society. For the vitality of democracy, of course, this function is essential. Democracy is government by the people. The existence of strong collective capacities in society makes this ideal more likely to be met, inasmuch as ordinary people are able in such a setting to exert political influence. This mobilizing and expressive capacity is not, however, the only function of importance. Democracy also implies the peaceful resolution of conflicts. It presupposes an ability to deal with people whose goals and attitudes may be very different from your own. In a democracy, one might say, you have to live together with your foes. Sometimes, in fact, you have to work closely together with them. If this is to be accomplished, an atmosphere of reconciliation and accommodation must be developed, entailing an ability among contending parties and groups to reach compromises and to establish some kind of common ground in matters of controversy. If this conciliatory potential is lacking, the exposition of conflicting views presupposed by democracy can result in a spiralling process of conflict aggravation, which may eventually render the democratic interplay of different groups impossible.

Two democratic capacities, therefore, should be developed side by side: the mobilizing function and the conciliatory one. There is, however, a latent tension between these two. That is why democracy can be so hard to establish. Mobilizing people means getting them organized, involving them in collective endeavours. Such a process means raising group demands and thus strengthening distinctions between people. One drawback of civic associations is that they are apt to build on particularistic identities of some sort. They contain a potential, accordingly, for exacerbating segmentation in society (Dahl 1982). Certain observers, therefore, from Rousseau to

Mancur Olson (1982), have tended to see civic organizations largely as dangerous special interests.

Civic organizing does not just coordinate existing opinions and interests within a given group. The preferences and identity of the individuals in question may in considerable measure be formed precisely by the association to which they belong. Indeed, it may only be after the persons in question have become organized that there is reason to talk about them as a 'group'. In this lies an instrumental function: if you want to enhance the strength of the organization, you should emphasize the special collective features of the group. Often this means, especially in political life, that organizations work to clarify and reinforce various differences that may exist within a population. Sometimes organizational 'entrepreneurs' play a critical role in constructing highly antagonistic group mentalities (Widmalm 1997).

In principle, of course, the activation of popular cleavages is a legitimate pursuit. As Dankwart Rustow (1970) has pointed out, the existence of differences within a population, in the sense of a variety of identities and ideas, furnishes democracy with nourishment and vitality. Without this, the vital force of pluralism is lost. That multiplicity, division, and the formation of factions are present within the '*demos*' is thus to democracy's benefit. At the same time, however, this polarization must be of a moderate and manageable character, making conciliatory solutions possible. As Rustow strongly stresses, democracy requires for its existence that there be, among the various groups in the population, a unity and concordance superseding other loyalties. The problem is that this unity sometimes does not exist; rather, it is the particularist and divisive loyalties that predominate (Pennock 1979: 246).

We may call this the problem of *encapsulation* (cf. Kornhauser 1960 and Gellner 1994). Where this tendency is far advanced, the members of different organizations are so segmented, so divided on the basis of particularist loyalties, that the spirit of solidarity and affinity central to the republican project cannot exist. What is missing is the sense of belonging to *one* overarching public sphere. Instead there is, as Peter Ekeh (1975) claims is the case in many African countries, a large number of closed and local public spheres. Within these sub-systems, a highly developed spirit of mutual obligation and trust binds the members of the group, coincident, that is, with a strong feeling of suspicion and estrangement *vis-à-vis* other groups, as well as *vis-à-vis* the national unit represented by the state. Under such circumstances, there is a high degree of interpersonal trust, but of a constrained, particularistic kind. The general interpersonal trust which signifies a broad sense of community in society, and which is required for democracy, is lacking.

Such tendencies are aggravated when the pattern of interpersonal relationships is one-dimensional and closed along segmental lines, so that people are encapsulated within their respective networks and do not mix with others, with the result that just one sort of identity is emphasized. This was the case with the old social segments in Belgium, the Netherlands, and Austria, as Arend Lijphart (1977) has shown. Citizens in these countries took part in a comprehensive social life; however, their activities were tied to networks of a closed nature—to so-called *familles spirituelles*, *zuilen* and *Lager*—defined by linguistic and religious identity. This meant that people of different 'sorts' lived systematically separate lives. This indeed makes organization easier, since it strengthens ties of trust and loyalty within the group. But it is a type of organization which strongly tends, on account of its closed nature, to reinforce group distinctions. Movements with an uncompromising and fundamentalist viewpoint have often sought to develop a separatist and all-embracing organizational culture, the better to control and socialize their members, and to protect them from outside influences (Diamond 1999: 223). In the more pronounced cases, as with some Muslim brotherhoods today, attempts have been made to create networks accompanying the faithful all the way from the cradle to the grave (Muslih 1993; Ruedy 1994).

To the extent that a process of increased trust and understanding at the mass level is to be encouraged, the organizational structure should sooner resemble the context surrounding 'modular man,' as described by Ernest Gellner (1994: 100):

Modular man is capable of combining into effective associations and institutions *without* these being total, many-stranded, underwritten by ritual and made stable through being linked to a whole inside set of relationships, all of these being tied in with each other and so immobilized. He can combine into specific-purpose, *ad hoc*, limited association, without binding himself to any blood ritual. He can leave an association when he comes to disagree with its policy, without being open to an accusation of treason.

A modular man, in other words, is an individual with relatively flexible and partial organizational affiliations. He can join associations of various sorts, and he can also leave them. When he does sign up, moreover, he does so only in a limited sense. The activities of the organization embrace just a part of his life. He has other identities too. Otherwise put, the collective framework should not be too exclusive and dense. Our network affiliations should be characterized, as Mark Granovetter (1973) puts it, by a multiplicity of weak ties, so that an overlap—what Granovetter calls bridges—is created between the different segments of society. What he has in mind is the phenomenon known in group theory as cross-cutting membership, or multiple affiliations. This means that, as citizens, we participate in many varied communities, and so associate with persons whose identity partly differs from our own.[15] This requires that organizations generally apply a fairly open policy in respect of the admission of new members, and that they have a restricted agenda: that they refrain, in other words, from any ambition to control or totally to enclose their members (Kornhauser 1960: 78ff; Lipset 1960: 74; see also Chazan 1994: 273) In other words, it is not organizational life *per se* but the special nature of associational ties that matters. As noted by Kenneth Newton (1999: 171–2), the important thing is whether or not voluntary activities bridge different groups and cut across social divisions. 'Closed groups which do not bridge social cleavages may create trust internally among their own members, but distrust externally with other groups and the wider society. Organizations which cut across social cleavages may help teach tolerance and understanding, and thereby create the "habits of the heart" . . . associated with trust, reciprocity and cooperation' (see also Gutman 1998: 358).

The desirable impact of this state of affairs is commonly thought to lie in the fact that social intercourse helps to dampen conflict. When we participate in several different contexts, we are confronted with a broad array of people from another background than our own. At the same time, we are socialized into a greater number of identities—each of which is therefore weaker. As a result of the cross-pressures generated by multiple affiliations, we become more understanding and tolerant of the views and behaviour of others. Thus we learn how to handle and to cope with the divergent preferences arising from pluralist processes. And not only that. With the broadened interaction arising hereby, a gradual harmonization of preferences can come about. Through social intercourse we become more integrated; we widen our public sphere; we extend our sense of belonging, responsibility, and trust. Thus it becomes easier to

---

[15] Seymour Lipset (1960: 31) analyses this factor in the following way: 'a stable democracy requires a situation in which all the major parties include supporters from many segments of the population. A system in which the support of divergent parties corresponds too closely to basic social divisions cannot continue on a democratic basis, for it reflects a state of conflict so intense and clear-cut as to rule out compromise.' Empirical support for the basic tenet that demographic and other diversity within associations boosts interpersonal trust is provided by Stolle (1998).

apply democratic procedures for decision-making on an overarching societal level[16] (Lipset 1960; Rae and Taylor 1970; Offe 1997).

Democracy presupposes interaction on a broad popular level: something which an open and multi-faceted organizational life promotes. Associations function, in this scenario, as arenas for meeting and intercourse. Thus a process of interaction from below is set into motion in society. But, it has been argued, where harsher conflicts between social segments obtain, such a process cannot get started. Popular mixture in such settings leads not to increased reconciliation and mutual understanding, but rather to open conflict—consider the behaviour of supporters' clubs at certain soccer matches. Such were the conditions, as we know, in the segmented societies studied by Lijphart. For the sake of social peace, different groups lived segregated from one another, each enclosed within its separate sphere of identity. The problem with encapsulating conflicts in this way is that they are held intact, and indeed may be reinforced. There is always a latent risk that open conflicts will flare up, thus reinforcing existing antagonisms—with notorious spiral effects as a consequence, as we have seen in Northern Ireland.

Lijphart avers that the solution to this dilemma has been found in collaboration at an elite level. The leaders of opposed segments have joined forces and established an agreement to promote cooperation. The basic logic is that cooperation is more easily achieved among a small number of actors. Such elite pacts, resulting in a 'consociational' form of democracy, are contingent on a number of conditions. One essential factor, according to Lijphart, is the determination of the central actors to push the conciliatory option; another is their skill in finding unifying solutions. Such solutions must involve extensive power sharing. When actors who do not trust each other come together for coordinated action—as in the case of the Prisoners' Dilemma, where the first preference of each participant is to thwart the other—it is important to bring about a structure of decision-making which is as inclusive as possible, both procedurally, in respect of participation 'at the table', and substantively, in the distribution of the goods on the agenda, so that everyone is guaranteed 'a piece of the pie'. Put differently, collaboration under the shadow of estrangement and suspicion requires finding a form for coordination

---

[16] This is the conventional pluralist view. It is based on the belief that fraternization furthers trust and understanding between people. In most cases, that is, under 'normal' conditions, this appears to be true. But there is an important exception to be borne in mind. If open hostilities between popular groups actually break out, the consequences tend to be worse where people are integrated and live close together (Hadenius and Karvonen 2001).

which is marked by *strategies of reciprocity and consideration*. How such strategies can be applied is illustrated in the consensual modes of decision-making described by Lijphart: the application of proportional representation, segmental autonomy, governments of national unity, and mutual rights of veto. The underlying logic is that, by such means, all of the players are able to safeguard themselves against political outcomes that would severely challenge the interest of their segment. No actor, Adam Przeworski (1986) points out, willingly takes part in a political game in which the probability of suffering losses is high, especially if such losses come in areas of great sensitivity to the actor (cf. Lewin 1985). The game must therefore contain some sort of security against outcomes which the actors find extremely unwelcome. Hence, they agree to apply a collective maximin strategy. This means they guarantee themselves against the worst outcome: losing in questions of critical importance. The way to ensure that such results are avoided is to work out an operational code of reciprocity and consideration, so that no one runs the risk of losing big—which means that no one can *win* big either. By this means, an agreement can been reached which serves to enhance mutual trust and identity among the players. The sense of community thus established at the elite level is supposed to trickle down to the mass level eventually.

The problem, which Lijphart also shows, is that the elite actors cannot always reach this solution. Even in cases where leaders have genuinely sought to apply such a formula, the results have sometimes been unhappy. In seeking to explain this fact, Lijphart points to certain critical conditions. A long history among different population groups of defence against a common enemy from without can serve as a facilitating factor. The feeling of affinity among the parties may also be enhanced if the country in question is relatively small. In addition, the segmental composition can have a great impact. When one segment is much larger than the other(s), he argues, the prospects for successful collaboration are slim. Instead, he claims, the appropriate composition is one in which a handful of groups more or less equal in size confront one another. In this Lijphart is probably right. However, the problem to which he points can be given a more general formulation. The difficulty arises when the parties are not sufficiently equal *in terms of resources*. As a result, the one side can have its way over the other easily and regularly. Lijphart sees this as a question of the number and relative size of the groups. If the matter concerns the clash of forces in democratic elections, and in subsequent parliamentary processes, Lijphart's presumption is of course altogether in order. But political resources are not just a matter of electoral capacity. They may also reflect, depending on circumstances, which faction has control over the state apparatus, or the support of military circles, or the favour of powerful economic interests;[17] and the distribution is skewed most heavily, of course, when the various resources are *all* concentrated in the same hands. With this modification, we may join Lijphart in concluding that a diffusion and relative equality of resources provides an important incentive for cooperation.

Yet even if this precondition is met, together with all of the others mentioned, a further obstacle may remain. What we have discussed hitherto is coordination on the elite level; however, getting the 'deal' accepted by one's own segment can be tricky. Sometimes such agreements are simply rejected: the members do not accept the agreed-upon conditions. At this point, yet another capacity must enter the picture. The integration from above described by Lijphart presupposes the existence of a special *organizational repertoire* among the segments in question (Barry 1975). Concluding elite agreements successfully, and ensuring that they are implemented, requires that a stable coordination capacity has been developed within the various groups. If this is lacking, negotiations and agreements at the 'summit level' are scarcely meaningful.

To be able to make deals with other actors, the organization in question must have an all-encompassing character, that is, a position of dominance within its field of recruitment. Furthermore, there must be clear centres of decision within it. Loosely composed, 'confederative' associations find it very hard to conclude agreements on their members' behalf. A capacity for negotiation necessitates a substantial element of hierarchy: that is, the existence of a leadership able to act on behalf of the organization. Only a leadership enjoying solid support from below can afford to expose itself to the risk of repudiation which agreements with outside actors always involve (Haggard and Kaufman 1995; Przeworski 1991; Öberg 1994). This applies especially when agreement has been reached with an actor traditionally viewed with distrust or even downright enmity. What makes it possible to take such risks is the existence of a high degree of loyalty within the organization. It is loyalty, according to Hirschman (1970), that prevents members of an organization from leaving it, notwithstanding their displeasure with the policies

[17] The Whites in South Africa are a telling example. They compose 12 per cent of the population. At the same time, they dominate the economic sphere completely, accounting for 60 per cent of the total national income (Torres 1999: 122). They have a political importance, accordingly, which far exceeds their demographic and electoral position.

pursued. The members of such an organization identify strongly with it, and they have strong confidence in its leadership. The establishment of such bonds results in a strengthened coordination capacity. In such a case, the organization is not just an offensive instrument, that is, a tool for mobilizing support and publicizing demands. It is also equipped to function as an effective actor within a game of negotiation. Such a game may consist of protracted piecemeal engineering, and it may sometimes require the organization in question to take a step backward in order to be able to move forward later. Such a game can demand much of the trust and patience of members. An organization without a stable fund of loyalty will find it hard to play.

Organizational ties of this type, as we know, are most easily developed in a context of close encapsulation. Lijphart argues in favour of segmental separation at the popular level. Communication between the groups should take place primarily at the elite level; the followers should be held apart. To uphold the mediating role played by leaders, the model presumes a substantial degree of segmentation in society. In other words, the top-down approach recommended by Lijphart seems to presuppose a kind of popular division, the consequences of which it aims to mitigate. Hence this approach has a conservative leaning; it may preserve the division it is meant to cure (Hadenius and Karvonen 2001).

As Lijphart and other students of democratic transitions have argued (see, for example, Higley and Gunter 1995), committed elite actors can pave the way for a process of reconciliation. If strategies of reciprocity and consideration are introduced, prevailing hostilities between different political camps may be moderated. The elite-pact approach has a limited democratic reach, however. It may be useful at an early stage of transformation. Due to its top-down logic and its encapsulating import, however, it cannot qualify as a permanent solution.[18]

---

[18] This was also Lijphart's view, originally. Although in the short run consociationalism could strengthen the segmental character of society, it would create sufficient trust at both elite and mass levels to render itself superfluous, he argued (1977: 233–4). In later publications, however, he has tended to regard the consociational scheme as a fully acceptable model, democratically speaking. In a recent work (1999), in fact, he portrays this model as one of two basic paradigms of democracy. It should be observed, however, that consociationalism has become fused over the years in Lijphart's writing with a broad and fairly indistinct notion of consensus democracy. The pros and cons of the elite approach are discussed in Hadenius (2001).

3

Weak Citizenship

A rich and developed network of civic organizations can, under favourable conditions, promote political pluralism, social integration, and the democratic socialization of citizens. This capacity is found in far lesser measure, however, in the social condition that Kornhauser calls 'mass society'. In such a society, citizens are largely atomized and unconnected to each other, for the collective resources embodied in civic organization are but weakly developed. Society thus lacks a structural firmness, and little exists in the way of a civic coordination capacity. A society of this sort falls victim to manipulation and oppression more easily, for it does not possess a highly developed capacity for self-government. Of course, uncoordinated groups of citizens can take to action in large numbers, in the form of riots, rebellions, and often spontaneous movements of protest against injustice and oppression. Sometimes, as we know from history, such convulsions have had a great and legendary impact. But these are exceptional cases. Rarely have such mass actions achieved their goals.

Owing to their lack of social capital, in the sense of a routinized coordination capacity, mass movements have an extremely limited potential for taking part in negotiations. Such movements are too loose in form and too lacking in the discipline and tenacity needed for a long drawn-out game of pushing and pulling. Their actions tend therefore to have an 'all-or-nothing' character; they are not the agents of small and gradual improvements (Nordlund 1996). For the same reason, such movements have a tendency to fall apart completely when they fail in accomplishing their mission.

In an historical perspective, unorganized uprisings by oppressed people, typically slaves or poor peasants, are the token of such tendencies. Some states of a more or less despotic character—for example, imperial China, tsarist Russia, monarchical France—had a long record of upheavals which at times shook society to its very foundations. More commonly, however, the long-term effects were meagre. After a period of turmoil and disorder, the outcome, due to

an insufficient organizational capacity, was the restoration of the
status quo ante. Yet in some cases, where the regime's 'muscles'
were severely eroded, such popular insurrections succeeded. These
are the moments—when 'the Bastille' is assaulted—that are reckoned among the great turning points in history.

In modern times too, mass actions of this sort have demonstrated
their potential for achieving radical political change. The east
European revolutions of 1989 were to a large extent the result of
popular revolts of a mass character. Furthermore, the subsequent
wave of protests which brought down many African regimes, and
which were often directly inspired by the events in eastern Europe,
were in a high degree spontaneous in character (Bratton and van de
Walle 1997). Notwithstanding its uncoordinated form, mass action
is not, as these examples show, without impact on, and dangers for,
the holders of political power. Yet it suffers from the defect that, in
order to succeed, it requires a powerless adversary. A regime which
falls, or makes large-scale changes in its policies, on account of mass
protests is usually one which is seriously weakened already, due to
internal division, deficient repressive capacity, and so forth. When
the 'attack' is aimed at a reasonably potent regime, by contrast, the
odds of success tend to be low: the result often resembles that seen
in China in 1989.

On account of its lack of organizational solidity, moreover, mass
action suffers from an incapacity to attain its objectives over the
long term. Its strength lies in its—often unexpected—eruptive
power, with which it can bring down or at least paralyze those in
possession of political power. Once the 'shock' has had its effect,
however, the enterprise easily loses direction. The substantive
results have thus often, even in the case of relatively successful
actions, been modest. Sidney Tarrow (1994) provides an illustration
of this dilemma in his description of the after-effects of the French
student revolt of 1968. Paralyzed by the widespread riots, in which
students joined forces with striking workers, the government under
de Gaulle promised far-reaching changes in the university system.
This apparent success had the effect, together with the large wage
increases granted to the workers, of bringing the direct actions to a
close. The reforms that had been promised then became the object
of treatment in the regular political and administrative process. In
the absence, however, of an organization equipped for such tasks—
the 'movement' was soon but a memory—the leaders of the revolt
were unable to exert any substantial influence. The reforms that
were eventually introduced must be judged very modest, at least in
comparison with the changes originally demanded and the pledges

made by the government. Once conventional politics resumes, in short, the leaders of mass actions find it hard to accomplish their goals.

As a major pattern of social life, mass action takes place mainly in despotic societies, that is, societies in which the state represses and retards autonomous popular organizing, at least in such forms as might be thought to possess political potential. Outbreaks of popular protest in such societies take the form of recurrent but atomized reactions to the prevailing order. Mass tendencies can arise in more democratic settings as well, of course, but they are usually restricted to marginal groups within the population (Kornhauser 1960).

Undeniably, then, the expressive forms of mass society analysed by Kornhauser have had real, and sometimes highly tangible, counterparts in the political life of a good many states. But where the political system is more open, so that autonomous popular organizing has the opportunity to emerge, organizational networks of a firmer and more structured sort are typically established. This is normally the case under democratic regimes and, to some degree, under regimes of the type termed 'authoritarian', as distinct from 'totalitarian', by Juan Linz (1975).

Between the strong citizenship examined earlier and the weak and atomized form described by Kornhauser, three common intermediate forms can be discerned: clientelism, populism, and 'social movements'. It is to these that we now turn.

Clientelism

Clientelism involves a vertical and hierarchical type of organizing in which people of unequal resource capacities combine. It may be regarded as an institutionalized form of dependence. Its basic logic is as follows: persons finding themselves in a vulnerable position seek out the support and protection of an individual—the 'patron'— who controls certain resources of importance. These may include work opportunities, political and administrative contacts, and the like. In exchange for his loyalty, the subordinate party—the 'client'—can gain access to these valued resources. Loyalty from below is exchanged for 'friendship' from above, that is, the allotment of certain favours. To this extent, the relationship is often reciprocal. The patron, for his part, is dependent on popular support for his social and political standing, which proves most useful at election time in particular.

As the relationship is commonly of this personal and 'intimate' sort, it is also typical that the geographical distance between the parties is small. The system is normally constructed, in its political form, on the basis of pyramidal networks. The base level consists of local brokers, each of whom controls his respective home area: a city district, a village, or the like. This control means, as a rule, that the broker can 'deliver' a block of votes at election time. These local patrons are tied in turn to a higher-level patron who controls a larger area. The latter is subordinate to a patron of still higher rank controlling yet a larger territory and greater resources. The system may thus contain several layers of 'middlemen' between the central leadership and the local base. In this way, it can function as an institutionalized link between centre and periphery. Clientelism is a means of connecting the local civil society with the political sphere. As a form of organization, it has often proved to possess lasting strength.

The links in question are largely, in terms of their content, of an instrumental nature. There is not much basis, normally, for a community of values between client and patron, for their relationship is one of dominance and subordination. Their interactions are founded essentially on the benefit each can derive from the other. For the patron, this means being able to exhibit his popular appeal—an appeal which can be 'exchanged' for political influence. For the client, it means being able to garner some of the 'spoils' generated by the patron's position in the political system; these may include work opportunities, benefits of various kinds, assistance in encounters with the authorities, and so on. Clientelist politics are not normally characterized, therefore, by clear ideological distinctions between different camps. The political parties are often strikingly bereft of programmes. They are not held together by a common identity permeating the organization. They function primarily as cartels for the distribution of the advantages, often of a material nature, which the occupancy of public offices can bring (Clapham 1982; Mouzelis 1986; Theobald 1990; Roniger and Günes-Ayata 1994; Widlund 2000).

The clientelist organization, or the 'machine', as it has been called in the United States, can be seen, in other words, as a system of distribution which furnishes the basis for a certain, instrumental, type of political legitimacy. Certainly, the distribution of benefits within the organization is not an equal one. Those in the top positions obtain the largest share. Still, some of the spoils must make their way to the base if the system is to function. The political loyalty 'invested' by clients must meet with a tangible reward. This exchange constitutes the *raison d'être* of the organization; it is for this that clients enter into relations of dependence and subordination. When a patron somewhere in the chain is unable to deliver, for example, his subordinates tend to establish relations with another and more capable patron instead. Changes can take place, in other words. The actors involved sometimes move about, and the key roles at times acquire new occupants. The underlying logic of the organization, however, remains the same.

A classic example can be seen in the era of the political machines in the United States. This began in the mid-1800s and lasted in some places, especially in and around Chicago, for almost 100 years. The early part of this period coincided with increasing mass immigration. Within a brief space of time, the US took in great many new citizens, of whom the majority were poor, inexperienced in the ways of democracy, and little able to orient themselves in the administrative and political context they had entered. In general, this mass of 'uprooted people'—to use Kornhauser's term—possessed meagre political resources; thus they had little in common with the citizens which Tocqueville, just a few decades before, had described as the very basis of the democratic American form of government. Not infrequently, the inclusion of these new citizens took the form of clientelism. Local machine bosses were able, through their connections, to offer the new arrivals access to social networks providing help in dealing with the authorities, gaining access to housing, and acquiring work. These networks furnished the major—in some areas the only—base for the parties' organization. By working up a loyalty among large groups of voters, and garnering their votes thereby, the machines were able to control nominations and elections to strategic public positions, thus making possible a far-reaching division of spoils. The more successful political entrepreneurs were able to establish veritable political duchies in some localities. As long as the machine was intact and yielding spoils, their position was practically unassailable (Theobald 1990; Shefter 1977).

We find similar patterns of organizational and party life in many corners of the world. Clientelism is a decidedly contemporary reality in many parts of Africa, it remains an important element in many countries of Latin America and Asia, and it plays a role in certain parts of southern and eastern Europe (Chalmers 1977; Eisenstadt and Roninger 1984; Roninger and Günes-Ayata 1994). As noted earlier, this system is first of all grounded in the needs of persons living under straitened and insecure conditions, and possessed of weak social networks. To acquire safety and protection, such persons establish contacts with individuals holding a position in the politico-administrative apparatus. These contacts are personal in nature: assistance and benefits are not claimed as rights, or obtained on the strength of general rules; rather, they are granted as a discretionary personal favour. Such a system presupposes that the prevailing legal and administrative systems are imperfectly developed. Public decision-making under clientelism is not characterized by the regularity, predictability, and neutrality enjoined by a state operating in accordance with the rule of law. Citizens confront a 'soft' and particularistic public apparatus: it gives an applicant his 'due' only when he has contacts; when he does not, the applicant is 'through'. In a system with such rules—or, more precisely, without real rules—it is rational for an actor commanding minimal resources to seek out a patron with connections in the public apparatus. The actor in question can thereby acquire the means for a reasonably secure and stable existence (Blomkvist 1988; Theobald 1990). He gets access to a measure of social capital. His position may be a weak and subordinate one, but at least he is not altogether excluded and destitute.

Clientelist organizations provide actors at the base level with a channel into the political sphere. From a democratic standpoint, however, this connection is a weak one. It builds on relations founded on the unequal distribution of political resources, and it is exercised through a discretionary—non-rule-governed—form of decision-making. These circumstances restrict the ability of subordinate actors to exercise influence and demand accountability. The vertical and personal character of the relationship means that clients have little in the way of links with each other. It is the patrons who occupy the points of intersection within the organization. It is through them, and thus indirectly, that clients relate to one another. This makes horizontal organizing, in which persons occupying the same position have direct relations with each other, more difficult. In its instrumental orientation, its hierarchical structure, and its passive form of organization as far as popular participation is concerned, clientelism offers little space for the sort of political practice promoting civic development recommended by Tocqueville and Mill.

Clientelism may be characterized as an initial stage of popular organization: a first step towards political inclusion and centre-periphery linkage. It tends to emerge during the phase in which mass politics, that is, the existence of reasonably open channels for popular participation, first makes its appearance. Clientelism is easily established, as it seldom threatens prevailing structures of social and economic power; indeed, it is often based precisely on such structures. Through its instrumental nature it possesses, moreover,

an impressive capacity to bind social segments together that traditionally were sharply separated. For clientelism does not require
much in the way of a common identity; its rationale is primarily commercial in character. The result is that parties and other associations of this sort can have a fairly heterogeneous base, and be
marked by a considerable internal division and factionalization. The
requisite cohesion is facilitated by the low rate of participation and
the indirect nature of contacts between different actors, whereby
persons of differing identity do not confront each other directly.

Political organizing has often started in clientelist forms. When
educational levels are low and opportunities for communication
limited, clientelism offers a functioning method by which reasonably stable contacts between the political centre and the periphery
can be created. Its advantages include a relatively low level of
conflict. Its agenda is restricted to the allocation of short-term
advantages, often of a material character; it is frequently stamped,
therefore, by an instrumental and business-oriented logic. In such a
system, entering compromises and concluding political deals is
fairly easy. Cooperation is also facilitated by the fact that the system is structured in a markedly hierarchical manner: a small group
of actors is normally in charge.

When a pluralist order is to be introduced, or new population
groups are to be incorporated into the political process, clientelism
furnishes a simple formula for getting the process going. It is easy
to establish, and its accommodative capacity is relatively high. Its
drawback lies in its extremely limited mobilization potential. Those
forming the stratum of clients, that is, the great mass of the population, are assigned a passive and subordinate role. It is around the
patrons that most everything revolves. Clientelism is also closely
tied in its practice to the state: it is from there that the spoils comprising the *raison d'être* of this form of organization come. For this
reason, as well as on account of its hierarchical structure, clientelism often becomes a source of political domination. Social relations in a clientelist context can reflect a pronounced dependence on
political entrepreneurs. Civil society thus lacks autonomy. It has
links into the political sphere, to be sure, but it largely lacks an
organizational capacity of its own.

Populism

Clientelist patterns have been an abiding phenomenon in certain
countries. In many cases, however, they have been replaced by

organizational forms of a *populist* kind. In this form of organization, the link between centre and periphery is less mediated. The stratum of so-called middlemen, who constitute the connecting links in the clientelist model, have here been replaced by organizational ties directly linking the local level with the national political sphere. This means that political leaders do not need the support of local 'entrepreneurs' in order to reach out to their base and acquire the electoral support that they need. They have an apparatus of their own for this purpose: an organization which they themselves control, and which performs this linkage function independently of local brokers (Kornhauser 1960; Mouzelis 1986; Widlund 2000).

Populism is characterized, then, by direct interaction between people and elite. This linkage, however, is of an essentially personalist sort. In the foreground stands a political leader who is able, through a special personal capacity, to build up an organization around his or her person. The leadership exercised by this figure displays, in Weberian terms, an element of charisma. The collective identity represented by the organization is based largely on trust in a central individual. It is this person who shapes the policy, and who is able, usually on a fairly autocratic basis, to appoint and remove the important members of the staff, and to control the organizational apparatus more generally (Mouzelis 1986: 78ff; Kohli 1990: 287ff).

An illustration of this may be seen in Partido Unico, a party created by Juan Peron in Argentina at the end of the 1940s. It was built up extremely rapidly, through the direct mobilization of new urban working-class groups in particular, who were attracted by Peron's personal appeal; he had acquired an image, as minister of labour in a previous military government, as progressive and highly effective. Partido Unico became a party wholly in Peron's hands. Through his strong charismatic appeal to the mass of members, he was able to outmanoeuvre the competing groups within the organization which had initially existed. Peron's leadership style emphasized a direct personal appeal coupled with a strong ideological charge. But he was not an organizer. His political apparatus was a loosely composed 'movement' the various branches of which were controlled by the leader. All candidates for political or union office were chosen by Peron and the executive councils he led (Mouzelis 1986: 80–1; Skidmore and Smith 1989: 86ff; Collier and Collier 1991: 344ff; Brooker 1995: 170ff).

Due to its focus on the leader and its control over communications with the base, the populist mode of organization is more centralistic than the clientelist form. The latter type of association is indeed hierarchically structured, but it is also less monolithic. It has a degree of pluralism built into it, inasmuch as the connecting links of the system—the middlemen—enjoy a certain autonomy. The middlemen can be strong enough, in fact, as to possess a genuine power of negotiation in an upward direction. Indeed, it happens at times that subordinate patrons cancel arrangements with their superior and transfer the network under their control to the patronage of another. This internal pluralism—or factionalism, as it sometimes turns out—means that clientelist organizations contain 'checks and balances' of a sort. They offer subordinates a means, which they typically lack in populist organizations, of holding leaders accountable. In populist organizations, by contrast, the functionaries are directly subordinate to, and dependent on, the top leaders. These are organizations borne up by subalterns.

In their political profile too, populist movements commonly exhibit a distinctive character. It is normally through appeals strongly emphasizing identity that they are able to mobilize the masses. Populism's appearance is usually associated with an increase in politicization at the mass level. The message spread by populist leaders frequently bears an 'us-against-them' stamp. Often it is question of representing the common—oppressed—people against the governing elite. But it can also be a matter of activating conflicts between different segments within the mass of the population, along religious, ethnic, socioeconomic, or regional lines, or combinations thereof. Thus populism bears the seeds of a polarized and antagonistic political culture. Its representatives often criticize the prevailing order harshly and demand far-reaching political changes. It is precisely herein that a large part of their popular appeal lies. When mobilizing their followers, they commonly politicize prevailing or latent antagonisms in society. These divisions may be of an ethnic and communalist kind, but they can also have a class character, inasmuch as populist leaders often present themselves as the champions of underprivileged, marginalized, and neglected social groups. As far as integration is concerned, populism thus has an effect opposite to that of clientelism. While the latter contributes—as long as the 'machine' is working—to the maintenance of calm and the dampening of conflict, the former leads as a rule to the exacerbation of social tensions (Canovan 1981; Mouzelis 1986).

A populist organization is based on the want of collective resources among its followers. Lacking an independent coordination capacity of their own, they are brought together from above. By this means they can join a community and take part in a collective identity. This may have a highly emancipatory effect. But such a community is tied in a high degree to a particular leader. It is this person who holds the group together. Populist organizations are weakly institutionalized, as a rule: without ordered procedures for the division of responsibility and competence, and with no developed forms for holding leaders accountable. The structure of local and regional branches is often but weakly developed. The organizational apparatus is tied to its leader and treated almost as his or her property. Not surprisingly, the leader usually has no desire to institutionalize the organization, for this might undermine his or her power position. The followers, for their part, are too atomized to be capable of exerting effective pressure in such a direction. As a consequence of the weak organizational structure, and the lack of autonomy for the various sub-units, there is a lack of arenas and intermediary structures facilitating internal checks and balances. Members and sub-leaders enjoy little opportunity for developing an independent capacity of coordination. The populist 'grass roots' are linked primarily upwards, to the leader; their links with each other are but weakly developed (Kohli 1990).

The movement formed by Juan Peron proved to be lasting, mainly because of its strong roots in the trade union movement, but it is otherwise typical that organizations built on a populist basis are short-lived; they come and go with the leader at their head. As mentioned, their organizational structure is frequently weak. This means, according to Atul Kohli, that populist politics performs badly in terms of governance. In elections, populist leaders often make sweeping promises to carry out reforms and improvements. But once well in power, they usually have but limited prospects of accomplishing anything substantial, if indeed they have any interest in so doing. For one thing, the electoral platform presented by such leaders is often diffuse, and perhaps unrealistic in some respects; for another, the organization they have behind them is too weak to supply the permanent and active support from among the population groups concerned. The type of popular organization built up by populist leaders is capable of achieving the degree of mobilization needed for electoral success. Such organizations are too fragile, however, to supply the capacity needed for successful decision-making and implementation over the long term. As Kohli puts it in reference to populist rule in India: 'without an instrument to systematically link the state and society [that is, a well-organized party], personalistic power enabled centralization but did not generate power to achieve goals' (Kohli 1994: 101; see also Kohli 1990: 45–6 and 399ff).

In many countries, the emergence of populist movements marked a new stage in the development of mass politics: a phase during which an earlier clientelist order gave way to a substantially broader popular mobilization and a higher degree of politicization. Often, such movements have expressly reacted against the closed, conservative, and corrupt boss-rule represented by clientelism. In Latin American history, an initial 'oligarchical' period can be discerned, spanning the 100 years or so following national liberation. This period was succeeded, in many countries, by a rising populist tide in the 1930s and 1940s. Presidents Vargas in Brazil and Peron in Argentina are emblematic of the change in political culture (Eisenstadt and Roninger 1984; Collier and Collier 1991). As Nicos Mouzelis (1986) has shown, a similar development took place in Greece and in several other countries of southern and eastern Europe in the early part of the twentieth century. India is a later example. After national liberation in the late 1940s, the dominant Congress Party developed increasingly into an organization founded on a clientelist logic. The patronage structure had first been established on the local level. Subsequently, it spread upwards in the apparatus. When Indira Gandhi assumed the party leadership in the mid-1960s, she found at her disposal an unwieldy party divided by factionalism and the rule of political 'barons'. In order to change this state of affairs, she attempted a clean sweep of the old organization. In an effort to bypass the existing structure of middlemen and factional leaders, she tried to build up a base of her own through direct contact with the rank-and-file. Her approach was pro-poor and anti-establishment. This led to a split in the Congress Party in 1969. The old guard kept control of the organization, thereafter calling itself Congress (O). Indira Gandhi, meanwhile, took over most of the party's members and sympathizers. In subsequent elections she had resounding success. Yet her new party, Congress (I), never built up a proper internal organization, particularly on the local level. Congress (I) became a centralist and highly personalist electoral apparatus, and, for quite a while, an extremely successful one (Frankel 1969; Brass 1984; Kohli 1990; 1994).

On the popular level, joining a populist movement involves a more active political decision than that involved in joining a clientelist organization. It also usually leads to an expansion of the political agenda, inasmuch as it means that people demand more far-reaching political changes. Populism often means breaking loose from narrow local political bounds; it indicates a capacity to develop wider political identities. But it leads to democratic citizenship of a weak variety. It involves organization from above, and it leaves little room for influence and control on the part of members. The involvement offered by populist movements is normally of a mass and *ad hoc* character: for example, rallies, demonstrations, marches. Seldom are such organizational arenas established to promote permanent and autonomous participation on the part of members. Populist organizations are directed from above, and they leave little room for the development of a coordination capacity from below.

The members of a populist organization function primarily as support troops for short-term mobilization. Critical organizational resources, therefore, are not built up; that is, such resources, of a material and qualitative nature, as make a more advanced and lasting collective capacity possible. The absence, in large part, of a developed internal organizational structure means such organizations achieve but a limited external strength: their action repertoire is narrow, and they can be used only for efforts of a brief duration, typically at election time. In other words, the organizational characteristics which pose an obstacle to the influence of members also undermine the capacity of such organizations to interact forcefully with their surroundings.

It is when they go on the political offensive that the strength of populist organizations is most evident. In 'ordinary politics,' however, with its piecemeal engineering and its compromises, they usually have less to offer. Populism is first and foremost expressive in character. It is unsuitable, however, for purposes of political negotiation. It is too unstable in its organizational structure for such a use. Populist organizations are usually formed quickly, in support of a particular political leader, and they tend to stand and fall with the fortunes of said leader on the political scene. Their members are strongly linked to the leader through bonds of affection, often of a charismatic kind. The ties members have with each other, however, are weak.

Social Movements

Turning now to those organizations usually grouped under the heading of 'social movements', we meet with a sharp contrast to the populist pattern. Social movements are marked by flat and non-hierarchical structures, and they make great efforts to promote the participation of members and to apply democratic methods. They place a great stress on local roots. It is from the base level that these movements are normally built up, and it is there that a large part of their activities are conducted. The participatory approach, with popular commitment and involvement, is typically a central part of the repertoire. At the same time, social movements are often characterized by an unclear leadership structure. Executive organs are usually granted but a limited competence, and collective leadership is often applied.

Social movements are often grounded in a strong identity that brings their members together: often an identity of a broad and universal nature, such as, for example, the promotion of human rights, peace, social justice, or environmental protection. Together with this orientation at the level of principle, such movements often exhibit a suspicion of, and antagonism towards, established politics and institutions. In their anti-establishment attitude, such movements resemble their populist counterparts, which give voice to the marginalized and excluded masses. Populism, however, aims at inclusion in the political sphere. Social movements, by contrast, commonly stake out the position of outsider. In the balance between autonomy and incorporation, they usually show a marked preference for the former.

This reluctance to be incorporated into the regular political sphere is combined with a predilection for 'alternative' types of activity. Demonstrations and other expressive activities are often preferred to such traditional methods for exercising influence as negotiating with the authorities or taking part in representative-democratic processes. Social movements call for direct popular action and cherish the spontaneous and the unconventional. They also seek to resist the 'cooptation' that can result from interacting with the representatives of public power (Hellman 1992; Dryzek 1996).

The organizational structure of social movements is often loose and open. Many such organizations operate on an *ad hoc* basis (Tarrow 1994; Cooper 1996). Their actions focus in large part on directing the attention of the public to the problems they want to see publicized. Their attempts at influencing public opinion often take the form of events capable of attracting the attention of the public, and of the media in particular. Actions of this sort—marches, occupations, and so on—often bring together people who can be reckoned, due to their participation in related and partly overlapping networks, as members or as sympathisers: a distinction without a difference, sometimes.

The tendencies here described are often considered characteristic of the 'new' social movements which have emerged in modern societies, especially those that have entered the post-industrial stage.

The peace, environmental, and women's movements are typical examples. The sweeping and often radical demands for social change put forth by these groups are often thought indicative of a new ideological orientation, one marked less by interest politics and more by moral and non-materialist values (Inglehart 1990). That these movements often have such an orientation cannot be doubted. It is not correct, however, to regard social movements as in all respects a new, post-industrial phenomenon. As Paul D'Anieri, Claire Ernst, and Elisabeth Kier (1990) have shown, there are examples earlier in history of popular organizations with a similar profile. They point in particular to the Chartist movement which began in England in the 1830s and remained active for some decades. In both their orientation and their organizational structure, the authors contend, the Chartists had much in common with the 'new' social movements of today.

Nor need social movements—in the organizational sense primary here—be oriented exclusively to such 'elusive' and moral values as those mentioned above. In Latin America, a large number of organizations have been established over the last 30 years which may be described, and which often describe themselves, as social movements. Some of these, certainly, exhibit an orientation resembling that of the most characteristic movements in North America and western Europe. Many, however, take a concrete, interest-oriented, and materialist approach. The neighbourhood organizations which have emerged in many places, urban centres especially, may be adduced as an example. They have been established to address the problems confronted by citizens in housing areas; it may be a matter of social and economic problems, of roads, or of water supply, and so on. Such associations are distinguished by strong local roots, a non-hierarchical structure, and an emphasis on popular participation. They often assume the role of critical outsider *vis-à-vis* the political and administrative establishment. A further characteristic feature of such organizations is that, parallel to the many concrete questions they pursue, they devote attention to certain fundamental problems in society as they experience it: problems often having to do with the distribution of benefits and of power (Escobar 1992).

As far as the fostering of democratic citizenship is concerned, there is undeniably much to be said in favour of social movements. Their local and participatory practices resemble those observed by Tocqueville in the young United States. Due to their loose and open form of organization, moreover, they are able to function as a forum for assembly and intercourse between different population groups. But combined with these merits are some evident weaknesses in connection with certain other qualities desirable from the stand-point of democratic citizenship. The localist orientation, together with the stress on retaining autonomy and remaining outside, means that such organizations tend not to establish links with the political sphere. Such links must be regarded in a democratic polit-ical context as highly desirable. It is by this means, through exten-sive links between centre and periphery, that democracy as a national project can be kept alive and vital. The fragile form of coor-dination displayed by social movements also leads easily to the result that very little in the way of 'organizational capital' can be established. Members' ties to their organizations are often weak and temporary. As a result, social movements are seldom able to accumulate the fund of resources that would enable them to take part in a broad spectrum of political interaction. Their political repertoire is restricted often to the occasional performance of demonstrative activities. The collective coordination capacity of these associations, in other words, is limited (Roberts 1997).

It can happen, however, that social movements develop a more elaborate organizational structure. As Claus Offe (1990) has shown, this is typically a three-step process. In the first phase, the move-ment functions primarily as a spontaneous and informal coalition, and its activities are marked by a high degree of militancy. In the following period, that of consolidation, more robust organizational structures of one sort or another are built up. A specialization of functions is introduced, and executive organs and positions are established. Thereafter, as a third step, the organization enters into regular relations with the state as a pressure group or negotiating partner, or by reconstituting itself as a political party, independ-ently or together with other groups. In this way, a movement that was loose and informal at the start comes successively to be insti-tutionalized. A shift towards more conventional forms of political action usually takes place at the same time.

A classic example of this pattern of development may be seen in the transformation, in several west European countries in the 1980s, of so-called green movements from loose coalitions of envir-onmental activists into political parties. As we know, these initi-atives were successful. The new parties achieved legislative representation, at both local and national levels, in several coun-tries. Another example, illustrating a different social and political context, is provided by an urban popular movement in Latin America. I have in mind the one which has emerged in Mexico. It was started, mainly by students, as a radical protest movement at the end of the 1960s; and the regime largely succeeded, with the help of repressive measures, in eliminating it in the 1970s. But the seed of social capital that had been planted took root, and soon began sprouting new leaves. In the early 1980s, many of these local coalitions re-appeared, and a national umbrella organization was established as well. This new organ has provided a forum for the exchange of information and for debates on strategy, and it has served as a link between the central authorities and the local groups. Its agenda features two main points: improving conditions for residents in the areas—usually very poor ones—where the organization has its base, and working for increased democracy and respect for human rights. The organization does not present itself as a political party. It sees itself mainly as a pressure group and negotiating organization (Bennett 1992).

Institutionalization of the sort considered here is not always possible, however, nor is it always desired by those involved (Piven and Cloward 1979). One of the objections usually raised is that a movement which becomes institutionalized loses its original profile, and forswears its role as an exponent for a critical and alternative outlook. In addition, institutionalization, and the specialization of functions that accompanies it, automatically brings with it the application of more hierarchical methods of work and of decision-making. The danger of which Robert Michels warned is written on the wall! These admonitions are no doubt relevant. For institutionalization changes an organization in a fundamental way: in the end it is a social movement no longer. It has instead crossed the line into the category, in itself a broad and internally variegated one, of 'ordinary' political organizations.

It bears recalling, however, that it was just in this way that many established political parties and interest organizations emerged. The European labour movement, for example, went through the transformation here described in the years around 1900. Protests and warnings of the kind mentioned here were heard also then; I have in mind the anarchist critique in particular. The anarchists claimed precisely that institutionalization and cooperation with the state could have only corrupting and inhibiting effects. With such an approach, they argued, the movement would lose its original radical vitality and become part of the despised established order. Indeed, it would serve in the end to support and legitimize said order (Tarrow 1994: 140–1).[1] From the standpoint of those seeking to achieve an immediate and far-reaching change in the social order,

---

[1] Much the same controversy can be seen in the struggle between 'fundos' and 'realos'—fundamentalists and realists—within the contemporary green movement.

this is of course a logical conclusion. Institutionalization presupposes an embrace of reformist methods and a faith in the possibility of playing a meaningful role within the bounds of the existing system. Where such opportunities are thought to be absent, the course of development tends to be different.

As we saw, social movements often emerge in protest at an elite-dominated political order. In contrast to the organizational forms characteristic of clientelism and of populism, social movements are distinguished by an extremely 'flat' structure. They leave considerable room for popular participation and grassroots influence. They are also heavily oriented to mobilization. This is mobilization of a sort, however, which is often paired with an 'outsider' political perspective. Because of this, and due to their characteristically high membership turnover, social movements often lack both the desire and the capacity to take part in 'ordinary politics'. Sometimes, however, an evolution takes place. It happens at times that such movements decide to redefine their role and to broaden their agenda. From having been active in the social and economic spheres solely, they take the step into the political arena. With their popular roots and democratic structure, associations of this sort can contribute substantially to strengthening democracy's foundations.

4

Democracy and Development

As Samuel Huntington (1991) has shown in detail, democracy had advanced over time in three waves. The first began in the mid-nineteenth century and extended to the years immediately after World War I. It started in the United States. The suffrage had been extended in that country during the 1840s to include all white men. After the civil war of the 1860s, black men were included as well. At about the same time, voting rights were being greatly broadened in the United Kingdom. There had long been a vital parliamentary tradition in that country. Yet even after the famous Reform Act of 1832, the electorate consisted of no more than 10 per cent of the male population. By the end of the nineteenth century, however, the suffrage was universal—but only for men. The first country to introduce universal and equal suffrage for both men and women was New Zealand, in 1889. The process of democratization then spread, in the years after the turn of the century, to several countries in Western Europe, as well as to the so-called dominions of the British Empire. Progress could also be noted in certain Latin American countries, Uruguay and Argentina being pioneers in this regard.

World War I, which was fought to 'make the world safe for democracy', as the President Woodrow Wilson put it, had an enormous impact. A few years after the Treaty of Versailles, upwards of 30 countries had adopted constitutions that were democratic, at least largely so.[1] Above and beyond the geographical areas mentioned, a large number of states in central and eastern Europe had become democratic too. Many of these were new nations, which had come into being as a result of Versailles. It was thus natural for them to link up with the prevailing democratic spirit. The trend spread from Estonia in the north to Albania in the south. This was a time of great hopes for the

[1] The criteria are the existence of political freedoms and of a democratically based legislature and executive. The suffrage in the early 1920s was limited to men in certain countries, as in France, where women first got the vote in 1945. Literacy requirements and other competence standards were also applied in many countries. Regarding the basic criteria of democracy, see Hadenius (1992a).

future of democracy. In his famous work, *Modern Democracies*, which describes the events here noted, James Bryce (1921: 24) depicts the spread of democracy as 'a general trend of social progress'.

Had Bryce experienced the period that followed—he died shortly after completing the book—he would surely have been disappointed. For the tide now started to shift. A counter-wave was beginning to take shape, and would gradually gather more and more strength. The 1920s and 1930s would be marked by far-reaching democratic setbacks.

The new trend was already visible in Petrograd in 1917. The Bolsheviks' overthrow of the republican regime, and their closure of the democratically elected *Duma*, in which the Bolsheviks had won less than a quarter of the seats, was a source of inspiration for radical leftists in many countries. Their dream was to seize power and to install a new government in accordance with the communist model. Usually such efforts failed. In a few cases, however, revolutionaries were able to take power and to hold it for a brief time, as in Hungary and parts of Germany. This method of gaining power was more successfully employed, however, by right-wing nationalist forces. Benito Mussolini, who had learned much about political strategy from Lenin, assumed the leadership of a group of Italian Fascists, as they called themselves, and marched on Rome in 1922. He encountered little resistance, and was able to oust the elected government and to make himself dictator. This was, it was later to prove, very much a trend-setting event. No less than the German Nazis were greatly inspired by Mussolini's daring. For Hitler, 'Il Duce' was long the example before others. Democracy now fell victim to usurpers in a great many European lands. By the end of the 1930s, authoritarian governments of various stripes has assumed power in virtually every country of central and eastern Europe, Czechoslovakia being the exception. Developments in southern Europe were similar. Italy we have mentioned already; Spain and Portugal followed. The anti-democratic trend was powerful in Latin America too. In as good as every state that had introduced a civilian and tolerably democratic regime, a shift to military rule took place in the 1930s. The sole deviating case was Colombia. When Hitler and Stalin concluded a pact in 1939, allowing each to expand within his respective sphere of interest, democracy's prospects undeniably looked bleak. The democratic system in Czechoslovakia had been abolished by armed German assault. The same fate soon befell Denmark and Norway. The Netherlands, Belgium, Luxembourg, and France were next. Meanwhile, the Soviet army attacked Finland. When the outlook was darkest, in the first years of the 1940s, the democracies of Europe could be counted on the fingers of one hand. In the world as a whole, the number of democracies came to about ten. Autocracy seemed to sweep all before it.

At the war's end, however, the 'course of history' shifted direction once more. A second wave of democratization, yet more powerful and far-reaching than the first, now followed. It stretched roughly from 1945 to the early 1960s. The Western allies established a democratic system, more or less by imposition, in the states that had been defeated in the war: Japan, Italy, and Germany—that is, in that part of Germany occupied by the US, Britain, and France. Similar attempts, less successful, were made in South Korea. Democracy was restored in those countries of northern and western Europe where it had been destroyed by the German occupiers. Moreover, civic and popular governments were re-established all over Latin America, and democratic institutions were introduced in certain countries of the Middle East, namely, in Turkey, Lebanon, and Israel. These latter cases arose partly as a consequence of the decolonization process now under way. This process affected Asia as well: for example, democratic institutions were installed at this time in India and Ceylon—now Sri Lanka. By the late 1950s and early 1960s, moreover, the principles of popular rule had seemed to advance yet further. Enduring democratic institutions were re-established in Colombia and Venezuela in 1958, following a period of harsh military dictatorship. The new states of Africa, which had been liberated after years of colonial domination, also attracted great attention. Most of these states introduced democratic government upon gaining independence. This was, once again, a time of great hopes regarding democracy's prospects.

Fairly soon, however, a process of unmistakable retrogression set in. In Latin America, military juntas again took the helm of government in the mid-1960s. The formative event was the coup of 1964 in Brazil, which was followed by similar seizures of power throughout the continent. By the early 1970s, military rule had become the dominant pattern. True, such things had happened before. What was new, however, was the naked brutality exhibited by these rulers. The world was shocked by the use—by regimes in such countries as Chile and Argentina—of murder, 'disappearance', and torture. In Africa, the new democratic governments had been toppled over well-nigh the entire continent. In many cases, only a few years had passed before some form of autocracy had been introduced, usually in the form of one-party or military rule. These regimes too proved capable, in many cases, of an astonishing degree of repression.

In other words, in a short space of time—little more than a decade—the picture had radically changed. The early 1970s were a time of pessimism where democracy was concerned. Dictators seemed to be the men of the hour. This applied particularly outside of Europe. Yet authoritarian regimes could be found there also. In the years after World War II, the Soviet model had been installed throughout eastern Europe, and there were no signs that this system would change. Autocracy had also long prevailed in Spain and in Portugal, and the overthrow of democracy in the late 1960s by the Greek military attracted great attention. Yet it was here, in southern Europe, that a new trend would shortly begin.

The third wave of democratization began with the fall of dictatorships in Portugal, Spain, and Greece in the mid- and late 1970s. The same thing then happened in Latin America, and with astonishing speed. Within the course of a single decade, every military regime in the area was replaced by a popularly elected government. A trend toward democracy was also evident in East Asia. A widely noted shift of regime took place in the Philippines, and in such countries as Taiwan and South Korea—long under autocratic rule—distinct changes in a democratic direction took place. Most striking, however, and for the majority of observers most surprising, were the changes that happened in eastern Europe. The emblematic event here was the fall of the wall in Berlin that had sealed off communist East Germany; this took place in 1989. The process had started in Poland and Hungary, and it spread quickly throughout eastern Europe. Within the course of a single year, all of the communist one-party states from the Baltic to the Balkans fell like dominoes. Soon it was turn of the Soviet Union, the state from which autocracy in the eastern block had originated. The old regime in Russia was abolished in 1991. Here, as in other countries of the region, changes in a democratic direction commenced.

The changes in eastern Europe had immediate repercussions in Africa. This was a continent dominated by authoritarian governments at the end of the 1980s. Of the 45 states south of the Sahara, more than half had some form of one-party rule at this time. To this must be added the military regimes that held sway in ten of these countries. Multi-party systems obtained in the remaining ten or so states—often, however, with restrictions of various kinds. Only four countries—Botswana, Gambia, Mauritius, and Senegal—practised forms of government meeting basic democratic criteria. But this picture was shortly to change. When the 'third wave' reached Africa, it penetrated widely. The changes had started already in 1990. Francophone west Africa was affected first. Within a short time, however, dictatorships over the entire continent were toppled. Africans could look to examples from afar, especially to eastern Europe, for the demise of one-party regimes. But there was also an example closer to home: the dismantling of the *apartheid* system in South Africa in the early 1990s, which was a great source of inspiration. The one-party regimes were all abolished within a few years, and the majority of military regimes disappeared as well. Across a broad front, multi-party systems were introduced and more or less free and fair elections held.

The states north of the Sahara have been much less affected by this wave of change. The same goes for the rest of the Arab world. There was an opening in Algeria at the beginning of the 1990s. The military regime in that country arranged to hold free elections, but abruptly terminated the experiment when it became clear that a Muslim fundamentalist party was going to win. This set off alarm bells throughout the region. A degree of progress, from a democratic standpoint, has been registered in such countries as Jordan and Kuwait; and in Lebanon an old consociational formula, combined with strong external influence, has been reinstituted after years of internal strife. Viewed as a whole, however, the area is dominated by authoritarian governments. In the Far East the situation is more varied. Significant progress has taken place in, for example, Thailand and Singapore. Improvements have also been made in Bangladesh, Malaysia, and Indonesia. But the tendency in these countries is quite uncertain. On the other hand, dictatorship remains firmly ensconced in a good many countries, China being the most prominent example. Such highly autocratic states as North Korea, Burma, and Afghanistan bear recalling here as well. Somewhat lighter forms of authoritarianism prevail in many of the central Asian republics which became independent when the Soviet Union dissolved. The same can be said of Pakistan, a country which for a long time has oscillated between semi-democratic forms of government and military rule; since 1999 the latter form has prevailed.

As we have seen, the third wave has had a varying impact in different parts of the globe. Its effect has been very limited in certain regions, or even absent altogether. And where its effect has been felt, a subsequent tendency in the opposite direction has in many cases appeared (Diamond 1996; 1999; Zakaria 1997). This is especially true in Africa, where dictatorial governments, often of a military type, have re-appeared in a number of countries. Gambia and Congo-Brazzaville are examples. In addition, the transition to a multi-party system has in many cases been rather half-hearted. In several countries, the previously dominant one-party system has been replaced by an arrangement that might be called a 'one-and-a-half-party system'. Here, opposition parties are allowed in some measure to operate and to take part in elections—in which, however, they have no real chance of challenging the regime. Kenya and Namibia illustrate this pattern. There are also several important countries, Sudan and Congo-Kinshasa, or Zaire, among them, in which an old autocratic order has in all essentials been retained. In several of the countries which previously formed part of the Soviet Union, moreover, the movement towards democracy appears to have been halted, and developments have moved in another direction. The Ukraine and Belarus belong to this category, as do several republics in the Caucasus and central Asia. It should be kept in mind as well that many of the new democracies in Latin America and elsewhere exhibit a far from ideal record in the area of political liberties. Alongside with fairly open and fair elections there may be considerable human rights abuses, intimidation of the press, and so forth. Countries such as Colombia, Peru, Turkey, and Sri Lanka illustrate this 'illiberal' tendency.

Yet we must conclude that, in a longer historical perspective, far-reaching changes in favour of democracy have taken place over the last century. Periods of progress have indeed been succeeded by times in which developments have proceeded in the opposite direction. The long-term trend, however, has been steadily positive. Each new wave of democratization has embraced a greater number of states, and exhibited a wider geographical scope, than its predecessor. And although the democratic experiment has in some cases been of short duration, it has usually been 'profitable' as an investment for the future even so. For as Huntington has pointed out, participation in an earlier wave of democratic advancement has been a good predictor of participation in a later one. Even when the result is a failure, a seed of democratic experience is sown. When new democratic efforts are later undertaken, this seed may take root and grow into a vigorous plant. At the close of the twentieth century, almost half the world's countries could be classified as democratic.[2] Of course the trend can shift; it has done so before. But if the earlier pattern holds, such that an investment in democracy pays off, if only in the form of delayed returns, then the present high-water mark may be said to constitute evidence for the optimistic assessment of democracy's prospects once ventured by James Bryce.

---

[2] In the 1999 Freedom House survey, 44% of the independent states of the world are rated as 'free', that is, democratic (Karatnycky 2000).

Precondition I: Socio-economic Conditions

As we have seen, democracy has made great advances. But its progress has been neither even nor uniform. Democracy has rather, in the manner of waves, advanced and retreated, and advanced and retreated again. Conditions in different parts of the world have varied greatly. Certain regions were affected early on, and in such areas it was often possible to stabilize democracy, though not always. Other areas have been affected first in recent years. In many countries, moreover—indeed, entire geographical regions— little or nothing in the way of democratic practices has developed. How can these varying patterns be understood?

One place to search for the answer is in democracy's economic and social preconditions. This has been a very common approach within research in this area. The paradigm which has dominated thinking in this area is that devised by the theorists of the 'modernization school', who developed their theoretical programme during the 1950s, and whose heyday came in the 1960s. Where political analysis was concerned, their theory was rooted in the behaviourist political sociology dominant at the time. The main idea was that political-institutional changes in the direction of democracy are the consequence of transformations in economic and social life. The processes meant here were industrialization, urbanization, and economic growth, as well as other changes linked to these. The developed Western world set the mould. In the West, such processes had gone hand-in-hand with political development in the direction of democracy. The same thing would now take place in other parts of the world, the modernization theorists reasoned.

The idea was that economic transformation would have profound social and political consequences. Modernization marks a break and a liberation. The traditional life patterns of agrarian society are abandoned. People break free from their old closed and hierarchical environments. A new political culture, one characterized by activity and mobilization, grows up. With economic development follows an increase in national wealth. Large-scale investments in popular education become possible, and competence on the mass level can be greatly enhanced. The supply of information improves too, as a consequence of economic and technological development. Common citizens thus acquire greater knowledge and a broader outlook. They also obtain better resources for defending their interests. Improved education and information affect attitudes, as do increasing mobility and social intermixture. The general frame of reference becomes more rational and open. Individuals become more tolerant and understanding of the beliefs held, and the behaviour displayed, by members of other groups. Barriers of estrangement and mistrust between different segments of the population, which have often prevented peaceful and democratic cooperation in traditional societies, can be broken down. In young and divided nations, modernization encourages feelings of 'brotherhood', and makes for a greater sense of affinity between citizens. Greater unity and integration also follow from the fact that, with a higher rate of economic growth, a larger 'pie' is available for sharing. Distributive conflicts thus become easier to handle. In the Western world, moreover, modernization had paved the way for a new social layer. A middle class of great economic and political importance was formed during the modernization phase. Since Aristotle the view has been common that the existence of a politically powerful middle class is a precondition for a functioning democracy. The idea is that this class can serve, due to its intermediate position, as a mediating link between upper and lower classes, and as a moderating factor in political life generally. Social and political polarization diminishes with the emergence of the middle class. The peaceful resolution of conflict presumed by all pluralist government is facilitated thereby (Lerner 1958; Lipset 1960; Deutch 1961; Inkeles 1974). The modernization school presented two broad theses, which seem to work well in combination. The first was a theory about the strengthening of political resources at the mass level. With the spread of modernization, the common people, who had been excluded from politics earlier, acquire the ability to defend their interests. As increasingly competent and well-informed citizens, they demand the right of participation in the political process. Those who had been passive now become active and demanding. Development is followed by heightened political involvement. This can lead to increased tension and confrontation, but such need not be the case, according to the theorists of the modernization school. For their other thesis bears precisely on the reduction of conflict. Through mobility and intermixture, integration takes place at the mass level. Access to greater resources also serves to dampen conflict—when there's lots of hay in the stable, the horses don't bite—and with the increasing dominance of the middle class, a social element now exists in political life that can mediate between warring parties and formulate functioning compromises. Such development had taken place in North America and western Europe. Similar results should ensue when growth and industrialization take off in other parts of the globe, argued the adherents of the modernization school. Economic development brings forth democracy.

Is there empirical support for this thesis? Do any correlations of the predicted sort appear? In brief, the answer is 'yes'. Few theories in the area of comparative politics have been subjected to such thorough examination. In studies from the 1950s onward, various indicators of modernization—per-capita GNP, literacy levels, circulation of media, and so on[3]—have proved to be positively correlated with democracy. A common method has been to take the degree of democracy prevailing in various countries at a certain time, as measured on some scale, and match it against per-capita GNP, energy consumption, or literacy. A clear correlation almost always appears in bivariate analyses, and a substantial correlation remains even after other factors of significance have been controlled for (Bollen 1979; Hadenius 1992a; Vanhanen 1997; Inglehart 1997) The mentioned factors also usually stand out in studies of the democratization process, as well as in studies of democracy's rate of survival once established. Thus can Huntington (1991) state that, in the transition from autocracy to democracy, the degree of economic development is an important factor. At a certain stage, which in the mid-1970s came to a per-capita GNP of between $US1,000 and $US3,000, countries enter a 'political transition zone' in which democracy is often instituted (see also Inglehart 1997: 160). In cases where democratization has already taken place, the risk is great that, as Adam Przeworski *et al.* (1996) have shown, the effort will fail if economic conditions are unfavourable. In their study of political conditions in 135 countries over 40 years, beginning in 1950, the authors note that the probable life span for a democratic regime at a low level of per-capita GNP—under $US1,000—is substantially lower than that for a democratic regime at an intermediate level—$4,000–$6,000 dollars.[4] And if a country's per-capita GNP exceeds this intermediate level, experience shows, it is highly unlikely that democracy will fail. At this economic level, the success of democracy seems assured. These observations link up with findings made by Ronald Inglehart (1997). In a study of some 40 countries he can demonstrate significant relationships between, on the one hand, democratic duration and, on the other hand, economic development and social traits—well-being and interpersonal trust—which he sees as part of the modernization syndrome.[5]

---

[3] It should be noted that the different indicators of modernization have proved to be internally correlated in a high degree. This suggests that such indicators are exponents of a coherent cluster of social change (Hadenius 1992a).

[4] All in terms of 1995 dollars.

[5] It should be noted, however, that well-being is a factor that can legitimize any regime, including an authoritarian one. As for the other factor, which has to do with

Yet it is clear that per-capita GNP and other indicators of modernization cannot explain as much of democracy's presence or absence as once it seemed. For all too many deviating cases can be found on the map of the world. On the one hand, there are poor and relatively underdeveloped countries where democracy has been introduced and where it has proved to be highly stable: for example, India and Botswana. On the other, there are some extremely wealthy countries, like the oil states of the Arab world, which have remained deeply authoritarian. It is furthermore clear that the theory is unable to explain the great swings in democratic fortunes—the great waves back and forth over the course of the 1900s—described earlier. Especially peculiar, from the standpoint of the theory, were the setbacks suffered by democratic regimes in Latin America beginning in the mid-1960s and continuing for another ten years after that. These setbacks took place in countries which had achieved a relatively high level of development. Many found themselves in the $4,000–$6,000 dollar interval, as measured in 1995 dollars; Argentina, in fact, had exceeded the $6,000 dollar level by the time of the coup in 1976. This pattern of development— in which virtually an entire continent fell, within a brief span of time, under the sway of military juntas, many of them horribly brutal—seemed unintelligible in light of the precepts of the modernization school.[6]

Despite the correlation between economic development and democracy demonstrated by modern research, it is clear that the explanatory power of this theory is limited. As indicated above, the theory contains two main propositions. The first of these, that

trust, it is not clear from Inglehart's investigation whether this is a cause or a consequence of democracy. On the latter matter, see the findings made by John Sides, discussed on p. 86 below.

[6] In order to explain this anomaly, as well as others mentioned here, an alternative theory was launched in the 1970s. It took its point of departure in a country's degree of dependence on the international economy. When applied historically, it was called 'world systems theory'; when applied to contemporary conditions, it was known as the 'dependency school'. A high level of foreign investment and a pronounced concentration on international trade, in certain goods and with certain partners, were viewed as indicators of dependency. Dependency undermines development, the theory averred, for it involves exploitation by foreign interests. And it is an obstacle to democracy too, for the foreign interests in question prefer obedient, authoritarian governments. In systematic empirical tests, however, this theory has found little or no support (Hadenius 1992*a*). Dependency theory was an attempt, I dare say, to provide an explanation in the spirit of the grave pessimism for democracy's prospects that prevailed in the 1970s. When the trend turned and the third wave swept forth, developments took a direction at odds with the theory's predictions—not least in Latin America, to which the theory had applied most especially.

having to do with the diffusion of power resources, has much to recommend it. With economic development and increased national wealth, greater resources are available for raising the general educational level. As many studies of power and democracy have shown, education is a very important political resource. This applies both in poor countries, where literacy is a strategic factor, and in rich ones. Studies of political participation in the US today show that education is the most important variable governing whether or not citizens vote or otherwise engage in political activities (Verba, Schlozman, and Brady 1995; Diamond 1992; Hadenius 1992; see also Petersson, Westholm, and Blomberg 1989). By contributing to education and improved information, economic development makes citizens politically stronger and more competent. The common people acquire resources with which to take part in political life. Demands are raised for broader participation. The result is a vitalized and more inclusive system of popular rule.

The tenability of the second thesis of the modernization school, however—that concerning integration and the dampening of conflict—is more doubtful. With industrialization, new fractures are created in the population, and these can be graver, especially at first, than those which had obtained in the old agrarian society. Social and economic inequalities increase, and serious political strains may result.[7] Economic development can, furthermore, take place very unevenly within a country. It can take off within certain geographical zones and leave others untouched; and it can affect certain portions of the population and not others. A strikingly dual society can thus arise: a society in which certain delimited 'modern' centres are surrounded by a stagnating traditional sector (Evans 1979). In addition, worsening class divisions within the population can accentuate older segmental conflicts of an ethnic or regional character. Cleavages which compound each other tend to complicate democracy's operation. Instead of cross-cutting cleavages, which according to pluralist theory are to be preferred, mutually reinforcing cleavages are created. In addition, Samuel Huntington (1968) has pointed to the fact that religious and political fundamentalism often arise when modernization makes its entrance. The cause of this, he avers, lies in the threat to an old way of life posed by the new social and economic conditions. The habitual patterns of traditional society

---

[7] As Edward Muller (1997) has shown, economic inequality within the population is a factor which, *ceteris paribus*, undermines democracy's stability.

must now be defended with an increasing aggressiveness (see also Chirot 1994: 29ff). As noted by Inglehart (1997: 38), rapid economic and social change can lead to severe insecurity, resulting in an authoritarian reflex among the public. This may take the form of support for extreme, backward-looking ideologies and/or adulation of strong leaders.

It is socio-economic development, moreover, which tends to orchestrate the turn from a politically pacifying, clientilist mode of politics to a more mobilizing and expressive, populist form. Modernization creates new and different lines of conflict in society, and so encourages organizing on the basis of new identities, which often have a sharper profile. Communication and education also usually improve at this stage, particularly on account of the expansion of the print and electronic media. This facilitates the direct contacts between centre and periphery which are characteristic of populism. With this form of organization often follows a palpable heightening of the level of conflict in political life. Populism tends strongly to emphasize segmental identities, such as those based on class, ethnicity, region, or religion. It normally gives birth, accordingly, to a more ideologically profiled and polarized political culture.

In other words, 'the passing of traditional society'—which Daniel Lerner (1958), one of the foremost exponents of the modernization school, described as the relieving process—can produce a great deal of conflict and pain. Kornhauser (1960) makes a similar point. The eruptive and politically unstable mass society of which he warns finds its most fertile soil, he claims, in periods of intensive social and economic transformation. Popularly rooted movements of the twentieth century with a strong anti-democratic appeal, such as communism and fascism, have been expressive of these tendencies. Such movements have emerged, Kornhauser believes, as a consequence of and reaction to the revolutionizing social changes and 'uprootedness' accompanying modernization.

Modernization, in sum, can provide a basis for political competence and involvement: factors which strengthen the democratic resources and expressive opportunities of citizens. But such changes can take place unevenly within a population, and in other respects too, major economic and social transformation may aggravate tensions in society. If the latter tendency proves powerful, the practice of democracy may prove difficult.

According to another 'school', it is a particular side of economic development that has been critical for democracy's prospects: namely, the emergence of capitalism. As Charles Lindblom (1977) reminds us, no state which has pursued economic development in distinctly non-capitalist forms has succeeded in upholding democracy. Such an economic structure has always been combined with an authoritarian political framework—the Soviet system, and its counterparts elsewhere, being the clearest example. It is principally two arguments which are adduced in support of the thesis that capitalism has had a favorable impact on democracy's prospects. The one has to do with the dispersion of power. In a society characterized by a market economy and private ownership of the means of production, economic resources are dispersed into many hands. Monopolistic tendencies can be found in certain sectors, but competition and the 'circulation of elites' form the primary pattern. The pluralism and mobility in the economy then have repercussions on political life. The multiplicity of power resources in society means that pluralism in the political process can be preserved. In a developed capitalist democracy, neither the state nor any other actor can wholly dominate the political game. There are always ample sources of contestation. The dispersion of power in the economic realm furnishes a favorable basis for democracy in the polity (Hayek 1944; Schumpeter 1947; see also Usher 1981).

According to another line of argument, it is the emergence of distinct classes typically following in the train of capitalist development that constitutes the critical contribution to democracy. Democracy's introduction has usually meant the abolition of a more aristocratic or oligarchical form of government. A regime has then been instituted in which, owing to universal and equal suffrage, the decisive influence has been wielded by the lower strata of the population. The possession of political power by society's lower classes hence is important for the introduction and preservation of democracy. The emergence of a working class is held to be a critical factor here. The formation of the working class is a product of capitalism. Labouring in large teams in factories, and living densely in urban centres, workers have developed a horizontal identity involving a strong sense of unity against a common adversary: the owners of the means of production. This cleavage *vis-à-vis* the owners has formed, due to the shared identity to which it has given rise, the basis for common organizations possessed of powerful resources, both economically and politically speaking. These organizations, in the form of trade unions and political parties, have stood at the forefront of the fight for democracy in many countries (Therborn 1977; Rueschemeyer, Stephens, and Stephens 1992; Valenzuela 1989; Mann 1993).

These are the most common arguments for the thesis that capitalism has had a favourable influence on democracy's prospects.[8]
Comparative empirical research has indeed indicated the existence
of a correlation of the kind here indicated: countries stamped to a
high degree by capitalist forms of production are more democratic
as a rule than others. Political freedoms in particular—freedom of
the press, the right of association, and so on—are more highly developed in such countries. This lends support to the thesis that economic multiplicity promotes political pluralism (Hadenius 1992*a*).
Evidence that this is so has also emerged from studies of individual
countries. Taking his examples from China, Tong (1994) shows how
reprisals against portions of the press which have sought to maintain a certain independence have been parried, in some measure,
through contributions from sponsors active in the partially priva-
tized business sector. The same author also shows how, in Hungary,
voluntary organizations working for democracy could be maintained, during the final stages of the old regime, first and foremost
through private contributions. Reports from Africa, finally, have
shown how critical newspapers could be kept going, despite the government's efforts to starve them of funds, through economic support
from the independent business sector (Hadenius 1992*b*; 1994*a*).

It is none the less true—to return to the international pattern—
that a good many deviating cases have existed which complicate the
picture. As mentioned earlier, Lindblom (1977) shows that all democracies in the world have practiced capitalism in substantial measure. Yet there were a great many capitalist states, at the time of
Lindblom's study, which were authoritarian to a high degree, and
the same is still true today. From this we may draw the conclusion,
possibly, that capitalism, as an economic system marked by autonomy and diversity, is a necessary condition for democracy, but far
from a sufficient one.

Those who emphasize the importance of the working class for democracy concentrate on the period of industrial breakthrough. Only now
does a working class crystallize, which through numbers and cohesion
can exercise political influence. With its concentration on industrialism, this approach has basically the same focus as the theory
advanced by the modernization school. The degree of empirical accuracy seems also to be broadly similar in the two cases. A special causal
link, however, forms the centre of attention here. The theory emphasizing the role of the working class as a democratic vanguard is based

[8] Another argument focusing on the role of the bourgeoisie, advanced in particular by Barrington Moore and geared mainly to the early stage of pluralist development, is discussed in Part II, pp. xx.

on two assumptions. First, it presumes that the class in question is able to organize itself in autonomous and effective organizations. From a class *in* itself it must, in Marxian terms, transform itself into a class *for* itself. In practice, however, this has been done with highly variable success. Between a developed industrial capitalism and the establishment of cohesive class-based organizations, the relationship appears to be far from 'one-to-one'. Second, the theory presumes that organizations of this sort place the fight for democracy very high on their political agenda, and that—assuming this is the case—they are able to cooperate with other organizations on behalf of this goal. On account of their limited numbers—seldom have they constituted a majority of the population—the workers have been unable in a democratic system to conduct political decision-making on their own. In order to realize their objectives, therefore, they have had to conclude alliances with other groups, which requires a developed capacity for negotiation and compromise (Przeworski 1986; Rueschmeyer, Stephens, and Stephens 1992). These conditions have not always been present, however. In some countries, workers' organizations have been deeply divided in their view of democracy—Germany under the Weimar Republic being a pronounced example. Furthermore, and typically in connection with the circumstance just mentioned, labour movements have sometimes had great difficulty entering into the type of agreements with political opponents which are necessary to lay a stable basis for democracy. In many countries of Latin America and southern Europe—Spain not least—this was long a complicating circumstance.

The research done on the fall of democracies has pointed to a fundamental fact. Military juntas and other would-be coup-makers have seldom succeeded in seizing power when civil society has stood united in democracy's defence (Powell 1982; Linz 1978; Finer 1988). The actors concerned must have, as a common denominator, a willingness to conform to the principles for political action entailed in democracy. Democracy must have the status of a unifying 'overideology' (Tingsten 1971; see also Barkan 1997). If important actors in the political game are directly hostile to democracy, as in Weimar Germany, then the system is clearly in danger. But democracy's existence is also uncertain if large groups of citizens are indifferent to it, because would-be coup-makers will in that case be able to seize power without encountering serious resistance. As John Stuart Mill (1991: 83) puts it:

Representative institutions necessarily depend for performance upon the readiness of the people to fight for them in case of their being endangered.

If too little valued for this, they seldom obtain a footing at all, and if they do, are almost sure to be overthrown as soon as the head of government, or any party leader who can muster force for a *coup de main*, is willing to run some small risk for absolute power.

The problem is that this has often not been the case. The history of Latin America, in particular, is full of examples of dictatorial, usually military, seizures of power which have enjoyed the support of a good many political parties and organizations. These organizations have often had roots in the middle class (Veliz 1980). It has also happened, however, that workers' organizations have actively supported a shift to authoritarian rule; the support of the Argentine trade unions for Peron is a clear example here. Organizations whose primary strength lay in the bourgeoisie or in the working class have in many cases allied themselves, more or less actively, with the destroyers of democracy. From Mussolini's march on Rome to Pinochet's coup in Chile, significant business and middle-class groups have endorsed undemocratic seizures of power. And where workers' organizations are concerned, it bears recalling that not all have been of the reformist, social-democratic type. Labour organizations of an anarchist or communist orientation have, in many cases, opposed the principles of political democracy up until the middle of the twentieth century, and sometimes even later.

Adherents of the theory that capitalism has played a critical role claim, on the one hand, that this economic system contributes to political pluralism, and, on the other, that it creates the basis for collective mobilization by society's lower classes. An increased political diversity naturally can, together with a reinforced common capacity among society's lower layers—exactly those groups which have been shut out from influence over long periods—furnish favorable conditions for democracy. Certain qualifications must be borne in mind here, however.

As with other popular cleavages, socioeconomic distinctions enhance the prospects for organization. Through social homogeneity and shared interests, people become more inclined to take joint action. Such attempts may, however, issue in very different outcomes. Sometimes there is a close correspondence between prevailing cleavages, socioeconomic or other, and associational patterns of society, which strongly affects political life (see, for example, Lipset and Rokkan 1967 on the historical development of the European party system). At other times, however, such linkages are conspicuous by their absence: this, as we shall see, is the case to a high degree in Latin America.

It is not self-evident, in other words, that existing divisions in society will be manifested in correspondingly strong forms of organization. A developed urban economy of a capitalist type *can* result in social patterns bearing features of, if anything, the atomized society described by Kornhauser. Furthermore, it is not obvious that the pattern of organization, should it become effective and stable, will have consequences favorable to democracy. Not all social capital is, as we know, promotive of democracy. It should be observed, moreover, that the mere existence of a pluralist power structure, due to increased mobilization capacities among different groups in society, is not a sufficient condition for a functioning political order. Political pluralism can instead give rise to an accelerating process of irreconcilable conflict. The social and economic dynamic that generates pluralism and popular participation must be incorporated in forms which counteract the centrifugal tendencies of political life. Only if this happens will such dynamic be democratically fruitful.

Precondition II: Institutional Conditions

What makes popular government difficult to apply is the fact that extensive civic resources are needed for its successful exercise. In the absence of a society possessed of such resources, Tocqueville pointed out, democracy is difficult to maintain. As he saw it, moreover, the evolution of such traits is in turn a function of the way in which the state apparatus is structured. It was here that Tocqueville discerned the crucial difference between the two countries that were the primary object of his study. In the one case he saw a state which served, on account of its structure, to stimulate active citizenship. In the other, he observed a state with largely the converse characteristics.

In this Tocqueville was a forerunner of today's neo-institutionalist school of analysis. Institutions bear, according to this view, a double-edged relationship to society. On the one hand, they are created by society; on the other, they set the framework for it. Or, as March and Olsen (1989: 162) have recently put it: 'Political institutions not only respond to their environments but create those environments at the same time.' Institutions exist, in other words, in a reciprocal relationship to their social surroundings. For special historical reasons, certain institutional patterns arise which tend have a long-term structuring effect. It is this which is the source of the 'path dependence' discussed by North (1990). Institutions are recalcitrant structures. They can be hard to implant; and some are harder than others. Once well in place, however, they give rise, in interaction with their environment, to conservationist tendencies—which of course are not unbreakable. For they are able, in substantial measure, to form the society with which they interact.[9] This is because institutions, as regulative frameworks, provide incentives for certain kinds of social behaviour. In addition, institutional stability stems from a insider/outsider logic. Incumbent forces that benefit from the prevailing rules of the game are reluctant to tamper with conditions advantageous to their political standing. This in turn illustrates the fact that institutions are never neutral: they favour certain actions and inhibit others. It follows from this that institutions correspond, in their mode of operation, to certain vital social interests. Aware as they are of this fact, actors have in all times contended for the power to shape institutions. The victors in this struggle have left a heavy imprint on the course of development.

Where democracy is concerned, certain institutional parameters have proved to be crucial. Most important, I believe, are the following:

(1) a long experience with political pluralism;
(2) a separation of powers, particularly through substantial elements of decentralization; and
(3) a rule-governed state apparatus.

1. Democracy is a complicated collective game. It requires advanced coordination capacities on the part of the actors involved. Hence, in the view of Tocqueville, democracy is a process of learning. It is through learning, and being socialized into certain patterns of behaviour, that citizens acquire the collective capacity which makes it possible to practise democracy.[10] Repeated play, we have learnt from research into collective action, facilitates the evolution of cooperative strategies. In a complicated game involving many actors, such development tends to be a slow process. The practice of popular government needs to be developed over long periods of trial and error. The establishment of a stable democracy may take generations to accomplish. It is thus an advantage if some of the institutions on which this form of government rests are introduced early on in the history of a state.[11]

---

[9] As Putnam (1993) has pointed out, it is more meaningful to view the relation as an equilibrium than as a question of simple cause and effect.

[10] A similar idea is advanced by Dahrendorf (1990) and Di Palma (1990).

[11] In modern research, a similar thesis has been put forward by Brian Barry. The values that sustain democracy are sooner an effect of its practical application than a cause of its appearance, he claims (Barry 1970: 48ff; see also Diamond 1994: 13). Support for this thesis can be found in Stefan Szücs' dissertation on attitudes

Mastering the centrifugal forces latent within popular government is usually easiest when fixed organs for representation are available, creating arenas for interaction between different social groups. Interaction generates a capacity for resolving conflicts peacefully. Persons taking part in such contacts get, on the basis of experience, better insight into the intentions of the other side. This increases the predictability of the behaviour of other actors. Thus can trust between different social groups be increased, together with the willingness of participants to invest in more cooperation. Through the communication thereby established, moreover, a process of mutual influence can be initiated. Each of the parties becomes affected by the notions of the other side, and a convergence of values and perceptions may gradually come about. Institutional arenas of interaction have a potential for nourishing an atmosphere of increased confidence and understanding and hence, in the long run, a moderation of conflicts between parties (Diamond 1994). As a consequence, certain overarching loyalties may emerge. Initially, such a development of mutual trust and understanding may be limited to the elite level; but it may in time be transmitted to wider sections of the population.

The establishment of arenas for ordered and regular interaction can also eventually contribute, as a side-effect, to the formation of such group identities as provide a basis for popular organization. 'The English Parliament aided in the formation of an interlocal *national* bourgeoisie', Brian Downing remarks (1992: 31). The examples are many in which political organizations have had their roots in parliament. Groups of parliamentarians have formed political clubs, which then built organizations for gaining popular support. Even parties established in the opposite manner—so-called outsider parties, which have come into being in a bottom-up process—have in many cases had an existing parliament as a rationale for organizing. They have been formed, that is, to lend force to the demand for broader parliamentary involvement (Duverger 1954; Shefter 1977).

Regardless of how the organizations in question were formed, the existence of guaranteed rights in this area is a fundamental

among local leaders in different European countries: the longer a country's experience with democracy, he finds, the more prevalent are democratic attitudes within it. He concludes that the best safeguard for the development of democratic leadership is provided by the social capital generated by experience with democracy's functional features (Szücs 1998: 268). It should be recalled, incidentally, that the theory of democracy as a learning process does not bear on the *origins* of popular government, but rather on its *effects* once well it has come into practice, at least on some scale.

precondition. The time factor, moreover, is important in this instance too. It is a great advantage if free organizing can be practised over a long period. For the process by which the 'the art of association' is developed is often a gradual one. If the process is constantly interrupted—due to bans or other obstructive measures—this process will be very slow. The result is weaker forms of organization (Gallagher, Laver, and Mair 2001). An illustration may be seen in the case of the French republicans, whose inability to combine forces against Louis Napoleon's coup in 1851 was described above.[12] Due to the long periods of repression under monarchical regimes during the first half of the nineteenth century, together with the absence of national representative organs, there were very limited prospects for forming a cohesive organization at the national level. On the local level, elections were indeed held, albeit on the basis of a limited suffrage. This yielded an incentive for the growth of local republican clubs—clubs which found it difficult, however, to establish a functioning collaboration among themselves. The republicans, it has been said, were something in between a movement and a party (Aminzade 1995). After a few years of political freedom and electoral choice following the revolution of 1848, the repressive order returned under the empire of Napoleon III. It was first upon the monarchy's fall, followed by the convulsions of the Paris Commune, that a new constitution, in 1875, could lay the basis for a more developed party system (Aminzade 1995). Drawing on more recent experiences, Jonathan Fox (1997: 124) finds that, in Mexico, similar weaknesses in the form of local isolation are in large part the result of the prevailing authoritarian legacy: 'state actors have regularly used force to deny indigenous Mexican communities the opportunity to scale up and form organizations of sufficient scale to defend their interests.'

A lack of political pluralism also has mental effects on organizational patterns. The absence of arenas for influence and interaction, together with the lack of organizational rights, induces a sense of alienation and political estrangement. This can manifest itself in a marked hostility to the prevailing order. In such a setting, outsider groups have no aspirations of entering into, and gradually altering, the existing political order. Instead they seek, by any and all means, to overturn it (Lipset 1983; Foley and Edwards 1996; Booth and Richard 1998). It is no coincidence that the most aggressive variant of socialism, that most averse to the existing system, took root in states where autocracy had long held sway, such as tsarist Russia.

---

[12] See Part II, p. 22.

In countries with a long pluralist tradition such as England and Sweden, by contrast, the role of such currents has been insignificant (Tarrow 1994: 92ff; see also Birnbaum 1988). Nor is it any coincidence that, in the 1930s, both Germany and Spain had a strongly polarized and centrifugal party system. Extremist parties of the left and right were much stronger in these two countries than elsewhere (Sartori 1976: 163ff; Gallagher, Laver, and Mair 2001: 239; see also Lindström 1985).

An autocratic context, we may conclude, inhibits the development among citizens of both the desire and the capacity to take part in the form of conflict resolution required for democracy. In such a setting, autonomous organization is counteracted, and no arenas exist for interaction or for free conflict resolution. The tendency among actors to pursue their political objectives by uncompromising and heavy-handed methods is encouraged instead.

It is an advantage, in other words, if democratic government, or ingredients thereof, can be applied as early on as possible in a country's development. The project may fail. Yet critical 'seeds' may be sown even so. Experience with democratic practice yields a capacity that does not melt away all at once; it can be retained, at least in a latent form, through lengthy interruptions. Putnam's study of Italy (1993) points this out clearly. Huntington (1991) too presents facts indicating that such is the case. He shows that countries taking part in an earlier wave of democratization have a better chance than others of taking part in the next upturn. The first attempt yields, notwithstanding its failure, the potential for rebounding and succeeding the next time round.

Empirical inquiries into democratic attitudes and behaviour seem to substantiate the existence of a process of political learning at the individual level. In a broad international study based on interview data, John Sides (1999) finds close correlations between democratic institutions and social capital, that is, associational involvement and interpersonal trust. These matters are indeed reciprocally related, Sides concludes, but the causal arrow goes most strongly in the one direction: from the nature of institutions to social capital. These findings link up with observations made in studies on support for democracy. To a significant degree, democratic commitment is determined by people's concrete democratic experiences, of a positive or negative sort. Support for democracy among citizens is contingent on their democratic experience and on the internalization of democratic values (Evans and Whitefield 1995: 512–13; Diamond 1999: 174ff).

In all, these observations seem to support the tenet that popular government, through its practice, can reinforce its own preconditions.

As for the development of democratic values and resources in society, pluralist institutions do indeed provide a better context than authoritarian ones. Still, there are considerable differences in 'democratic stimuli', depending on the special nature of the pluralist institutions in question. One set of qualities, democratically speaking, has to do with the degree of power distribution in public life. This brings us to the next institutional parameter of importance.

2. According to Tocqueville, a considerable measure of decentralization is indispensable for a system of active popular rule. It was on this point that he discerned the major difference between his homeland and the United States. In France, with its strong administrative centralization, citizens were treated as the passive object of state policy. Without the opportunity to exercise local influence, citizens had become estranged from one another, and from the public organs which governed them. In New England, by contrast, much more favorable conditions obtained:

The New Englander is attached to his township because it is strong and independent; he has an interest in it because he shares in its management; he loves it because he has no reason to complain of his lot, he invests his ambition and his future in it; in the restricted sphere within his scope; he learns to rule society; he gets to know those formalities without which freedom can advance only through revolutions, and becoming imbued with their spirit, develops a taste for order, understands the harmony of powers, and in the end accumulates clear, practical ideas about the nature of his duties and the extent of his rights. (1969: 70)

By taking part in local government, American citizens learned the practice of democracy. This habituated them to resolving conflicts and holding leaders accountable, and gave rise to feelings of identification with the public organs. Citizens were included in the political sphere in a natural way. Furthermore, the civic skills acquired through participating in local public affairs could be utilized in other settings also. This yielded resources for the exercise of influence at higher political levels, and gave a strong impetus to civic organization. The close connection between local government and free associational life was, in Tocqueville's view, a fundamental feature of American democracy. The socializing impact of decentralized political activity emerges as a decisive factor in Putnam's study of Italy as well. The regions faring best, democratically speaking, had a common history of popular participation in local decision-making; those performing poorly tended to be marked by a legacy of centralization.

The existence of local arenas for decision-making makes it easier for common citizens to get involved in the political process. Local decisions touch on matters close to home, providing a natural incentive for participation. Through taking part in public affairs, citizens improve their ability to perform the tasks required by active citizenship (Diamond 1999: 121ff). A collective capacity is thus established at the local level, which can have significant side effects. This capacity endows citizens with a greater capacity to make their voice heard and to back up their words in a forceful manner. This in turn contributes to the growth of civic and political organizations with vital local roots. Thus common citizens enjoy, through the independent coordination capacity they have developed, the opportunity to exert a critical influence over common affairs. They are not simply the passive object of organizations. They are capable, rather, of taking part in the governance of such organizations themselves.

Decentralization entails a separation of powers in the political and administrative spheres. This breeds openness in public life. 'The greater the degree of decentralization, the greater is the degree of formal access. Decentralization implies multiple points of access' (Kriesi 1995: 175). In a system with many arenas and channels for the exertion of influence, the probability of being able to establish new popular organizations is greater. This has a double effect. Through the new associations, new opportunities for popular influence are created. This provides opportunities for new groups to work in the public organs. Tendencies towards political marginalization can thus be counteracted (Lipset and Rokkan 1967). At the same time, pressure on the established organizations increases, making them more responsive. Moreover, decentralized structures enhance the likelihood that political actors will advance conciliatory strategies. In a political order with many centres for decision-making, there are more political 'prizes' available for the taking. The winner-take-all character of the game is thus reduced. Not everything stands or falls with the occupancy of office at the national level. There are other offices of importance too, lower down in the system. These can become accessible to parties which have been unable to influence politics at the national level. A decentralized system also creates the conditions for removing certain sensitive questions from the national political arena. This is the idea behind the 'segmental autonomy' which is a component of the consociational method for dampening conflict (Lijphart 1977).

Certain qualifications must, however, be borne in mind. When we speak of the advancement of political capacities at the grass roots that decentralization can generate, this presupposes, to begin with, that the arenas established are characterized by democratic procedures (Crook and Manor 1998). Local autonomy has often served to create pockets of fairly undemocratic practice: for example, the 'fiefdoms' of local political strongmen. Such was indeed the case during the era of machine politics in the US;[13] and—to mention just one example—similar conditions prevail today in Russia (Stoner-Weiss 2000). Under such circumstances, the processes of popular political learning can hardly develop. Still, the prevailing separation of powers can contribute to inclusion and pluralism in the national political game. For this effect to ensue, however, local organs must enjoy a substantial measure of autonomy, in the form of their own resources and decisional competence (Diamond 1999: 133ff).

We have dealt so far with the vertical power distribution in public life—between local, regional, and central levels. To this should be added the horizontal dimension, which has to do with the balance of powers at each level. Especially important here is the situation at the central level. It concerns the extent to which the executive branch, where the essential power resources are prone to be assembled, is effectively counter-balanced by legislative and controlling organs. The conditions in this regard have repercussions both for the 'temperature' of conflict and for the organizational patterns of political life. The question now addressed pertains to the debate about the merits and drawbacks of presidentialism in contrast to parliamentarism. An historical rationale behind the introduction of presidentialism in many states is that the system brings with it a prime office of national unity. The presidential office and its occupant symbolize the state and hold the country together. Due to direct election, there is an identity between the leader and the people. In states marked by a low degree of coherence at the popular level, which has often been the case in new states, this could be considered a valuable asset. The lack of unity in society, one could say, is mitigated by a strong and unifying institutional arrangement.[14] Another argument is that the general traits of presidentialism—the separate election of the person in question, a fixed term of office, and the right of the office-holder to select his or her government—lay the basis for a strong executive power, which promotes political efficacy and gives legitimacy to the democratic system.

[13] See above, p. 53.

[14] As noted by Matthew Soberg Shugart (1998), there is often an inverse relationship between the strength of political parties and the strength of the executive at the moment of constitutional founding: the less organized and more fragmented the parties, the stronger the demand for a strong, unifying executive. Due to the choice of such an institutional design, however, the initial conditions for the parties tend to be maintained.

The problem is that presidential systems have on many occasions turned out to be too dominated by the executive, such that the president to a great extent directs the political game while the legislature and controlling bodies do not manage to serve as effective organs of counter-power. This has particularly happened in systems involving a high degree of vertical centralization—that is, a low level of decentralization—in political and administrative affairs, inasmuch as such systems greatly strengthen the power resources in the hands of the executive arm of government.[15]

Presidential systems, it has been maintained, set the stage for a zero-sum political game. Much tends to be at stake in elections in such systems, as far as power resources are concerned, and there is only one winner. This breeds an atmosphere of confrontation, and a conflict-ridden political culture. The logic of the system also has implications for the way political parties are organized. Since presidents are elected individually, they need not be supported, as in parliamentary systems, by a governing party or coalition of parties in the legislature in order to hold office. Party coherence, in other words, is not that important in presidential systems. In effect, political parties are apt to be more fractionalized in presidential than in parliamentary systems. This tendency is strengthened by the fact that presidential elections often have a highly personalistic character: people select an individual suitable for the office, not just a representative for a party. This adds to the centralist tendency of the presidential model. The fractionalization of parties decreases their capacity to serve as effective channels for popular influence. This in turn weakens the potential for parliamentary organs to stand up to the executive branch effectively (Linz 1994; Lijphart 1992).

It should be remarked, however, that such tendencies are mitigated in great measure in so-called semi-presidential systems. For the requirement here is that the head of government be not the president, but a prime minister, or the like, who is endorsed by the legislature. In this constitutional formula, in other words, a parliamentary mode of government is applied (Sartori 1994; Shugart and Carey 1992).

---

[15] This is in turn illustrates why decentralization is such a critical factor: in several ways, directly and indirectly, it affects the nature of political life, and at both the local and the national levels. The presence of this factor, I would argue, is a fundamental reason why presidentialism in the US has fared so much better, democratically speaking, than in most other countries, where presidential rule has been normally associated with a high degree of vertical power concentration. Cf. Riggs (1992).

In addition, the effect of electoral systems must be considered. As is well-known from the work of Maurice Duverger (1954) and his followers, electoral codes provide voters with different incentives, as far as the expression of their party preferences is concerned. In majoritarian systems, people tend to make a choice between a few big parties, the ones that stand the best chance of election. In proportional systems, by contrast, the threshold of representation is generally much lower. In consequence, people have an incentive to vote for small parties as well, should they wish to. In majoritarian systems, accordingly, the likely outcome is the formation of a two-party system, whereas multi-party systems are apt to prevail in countries applying the proportional electoral code (Tagapera and Shugart 1989).[16]

Overall, political access, that is, representation, is easier in proportional systems. These systems, accordingly, are more inclusive. They have an inclination therefore to be less confrontational. The proportional electoral formula is a principal ingredient in the institutional package of power-sharing advocated by Arend Lijphart (1977). This formula seems well-suited for societies marked by strong segmental cleavages, especially of an ethnic or religious nature. It may also in general be advisable, as Larry Diamond (1999) remarks, to offer a high degree of political inclusion in young democracies, where the level of trust between political groups may still be very low (see also Reynolds 1999).[17]

One obvious consequence of proportional representation is that it encourages the formation of a fragmented party system, especially when the threshold for representation is very low. The good thing about this is that it promotes cooperation among parties. No decisions in parliament can be made without the joint support of several

---

[16] It should be borne in mind, however, that the relationship between majoritarianism and a two-party system mainly holds for countries where parties attract a nationwide following: under these conditions, two big parties are indeed likely to sweep the polls. Consider, however, a country in which the political landscape is marked by cleavages of a regional character, while the parties are mainly tied to a certain geographical area, where they can win the lion's share of the vote fairly easily. In such a country, many parties may well be represented in parliament, even if the electoral system is majoritarian in character.

[17] Parties are sometimes extremely weak, moreover, in the early stages of democratization, such that they find it difficult to assert themselves in elections. This problem is evident on the regional level in Russia. Here, a large majority—some 80%—of representatives have no ties to parties; they run as independents. In regions which apply the proportional formula, however, the situation is normally better—from the point of view of the parties—than in regions where the majoritarian system is used (Stoner-Weiss 2000).

groups. And with many parties involved, shifting coalition patterns tend to ensue. This involves extended circles of cooperation among parties, and encourages the development a compromise-oriented political culture (Sartori 1987: 227). Yet there are also drawbacks associated with a fragmented party system. First of all, there is a risk, arising from unstable coalition patterns, of ending up with too fragile a system for decision-making, to the detriment of policy coherence. Consequently, the joint representative capacity of the political parties is weakened. This in turn negatively affects the political clout of legislative organs.

Majoritarian systems, to be true, have a strong bent towards political exclusion, and they are often more confrontational. On the other hand, the parliamentary parties are normally much stronger in such systems, and more capable of carrying out coherent legislative programs. In this way, they can serve as effective organs of representation, both in their own right as organizational channels for popular influence, and through the strengthening of the parliamentary bodies wherein they operate.[18]

For the strengthening of the representative function of political parties, a presidential system together with the proportional electoral formula stands out as the least attractive combination, as it spurs the development of many fairly small, and at the same time internally fractionalized, parties (Mainwaring 1993). If the objective is to dampen conflicts in society, on the other hand, the proportional formula looks clearly the most appropriate, especially in tandem with a parliamentary mode of government.

3. Another parameter of importance is the existence of a rule-governed state apparatus. This institutional feature sets the stage for the development of trust and reciprocity among political actors. Moreover, it impinges on the way popular organizations are formed and on the legitimacy of the democratic game. In short, the quality of governance affects the quality of democracy.

Involvement and interaction spur democratic cooperation, we have noted. But certain conditions must obtain for the result to be a happy one. As we know, social intermixture can also issue in serious conflict. An important parameter here is that set by the surrounding system of rules. Cooperation is easier to maintain if effective regulatory instruments are available. If association with others on the basis of trust is to be possible, there must be fixed

[18] It should be noted that, in both proportional and majoritarian electoral systems, the cohesion of parties is contingent on the use of such arrangements as preferential voting, open ballots, primaries, and the like, which ensure that it is not the party leadership that selects the representatives, but rather the voters.

rules for the dealings in question. It is our awareness of these rules, and of how strictly and predictably they govern our behaviour and that of others, which determine to a high degree what kind of cooperation, if any, we can have with those around us. In small and relatively uncomplicated settings, these rules can be of a purely informal nature; they are well-known and internalized among the affected persons even so. But the greater the number of people involved, and the more complex the matter to be treated, the greater is the need for codifying the rule-system in question and backing it with official sanction. In being codified, such rules are normally made clearer; this makes the system more predictable. With the sanction of the state, moreover, the efficiency of the system is typically increased, for the rules can be enforced through coercion. Finally, the official confirmation of certain legal principles can endow these with a special normative status; the British Magna Carta can be mentioned as an example.[19] Whether norms are formal or informal in nature, in other words, is not an insignificant matter.[20]

It may be worthwhile here to recall Elinor Ostrom's (1990) study of the micro-processes which have formed the basis in various countries for cooperation on behalf of certain common local objectives— the protection of water resources, for example. She shows, to begin with, that face-to-face interaction is a stimulating factor. But she also stresses something else. If the attempt is to be successful, there must be clearly stipulated rules governing the dealings in question, as well as organs that can enforce these rules in an impartial manner. In the absence of such features, the private actors have a strong incentive to engage in various forms of free-riding, that is, to exploit the system for their own gain. This undermines the cooperation which would favour everybody in the long run. The underlying logic is quite simple, actually: if I cannot count on the rules being effectual, I had better help myself before others do the same. In an institutional structure without fixed and effective rules, the actors have a strong tendency to make only short-term, speculative 'investments' in interaction. This has the effect of destroying the conditions for a form of interaction which would be more profitable over the long run. To bar such tendencies, certain regulatory instruments must be at hand. Forms for inspection and control must be built into the game. It must be possible to see who is playing by 'the

---

[19] See Part II, p. 169.

[20] This is a factor that neo-institutionalist theorists, like March and Olsen (1989), appear to overlook. Cf. van Caenegem (1992: 11ff).

code of cooperation' and who is not. There must be forms for resolving conflicts, and for punishing players who engage in strategies of deceit. Such forms must also be sufficiently effective, and at the same time neutral *vis-à-vis* particular players, to contribute to a general faith in the collective process. Ostrom puts the point as follows: 'monitoring and gradual sanctions are necessary to keep the rate of rule-following high enough to avoid triggering a process in which higher rates of rule infractions fuel subsequent increases in rates of rule infractions' (1990: 187; see also Axelrod 1984; Axelrod and Keohane 1985).

Trust in institutions enhances interpersonal trust (Brehm and Rahn 1997; Rothstein 2000). It is the existence of a functioning system of rules that makes long-term cooperation possible. This has an important implication: the worse the climate of cooperation is at the outset, the greater are the demands on the strength of the system of rules. Where there is little trust between the actors, a large increment is needed of the 'external support' which institutions can give. If you do not trust each other, you must trust the institutions. In societies containing far-reaching conflicts, it is particularly important that the legal and administrative structure upheld by the state be of a fixed and rule-governed kind.[21] If this is not the case, the risk is great that segmental interaction will intensify old conflicts. The actors will thus be taking part in a process of learning in which they learn suspicion rather than trust (Mo 1996).

Institutions must be constructed that work against group discrimination. This has to do with the functioning of legal and administrative bodies, and most fundamentally, with how law-enforcing units, such as the police and the military, operate (Diamond 1999). When confidence in such institutions is lacking, disastrous spirals of power abuse can be set in motion. Robin Theobold has described the Machiavellian inferno that can arise in a setting in which strong segmental divisions are present and effective neutral institutions are absent:

[21] The theoretical argument is advanced by Barry Weingast (1997: 253, 258). Cooperative pacts are established, he maintains, when basic procedures and norms are introduced which govern how politics is to be played. At the same time, however, universal rules of this sort are often difficult to apply where they are most needed— in societies marked by sharp ethnic divisions. In such societies, coordination problems arise due to legacies of mutual distrust and differences in values among the groups or due to the fact that one group actually benefits from the prevailing order, in that said order enables it to exploit others (Weingast 1997: 256–7; see also Horowitz 1991: 51ff; Weingast 1998). A discussion of how to deal with this dilemma is provided by Hadenius and Karvonen (2001).

An atmosphere of acute distrust prevails; politics becomes a ruthless zero-sum contest in which contending parties strive not simply to stay on top but to eliminate their opponents altogether. The political style is, therefore, conspiratorial: characterized by constant manœuvering, the making and breaking of alliances, carpet crossing, character assassination and sometimes physical assassination. Those in power use every means to hold on to it, for once out they believe, usually rightly, that they will never get back in. (1990: 93–4)

Such confrontational tendencies are enhanced in particular when the lack of rule-governed governance is combined with a high degree of political and administrative centralization. When there is much to win, and to lose, in a political game—in respect to both power and opportunities for personal enrichment—and when access to such gains is also greatly restricted, the stage is set for belligerent relationships between political competitors.

A 'soft' state—one characterized by the virtual absence of rule-governed governance[22]—affects the character of popular organizing as well. Where people cannot rely on the existing system of rules, they usually seek out, as a substitute, networks founded on personal contacts. If you cannot trust the official institutions, you must rely on your friends. This, as we know, is the logic of clientelism. This form of organization has in all times accompanied the soft state. It is the supply of spoils yielded by state position which constitutes the very 'fuel' of clientelism. Such a system is based on particularistic advantage: you will enjoy a favour only if you have the right contacts. Clientelist arrangements presuppose a state which leaves substantial room for nepotism and corruption, and in which the benefits of public policy can be targeted on supporters of the regime.

Another aspect of the soft state is that it contributes, as a rule, to a low level of political legitimacy. Corruption, nepotism, and the like are regarded by citizens with suspicion and contempt. Such an order also encourages a low level of efficiency in public administration, and indirectly in the economy too, thus generating discontent.[23] On account of both its mode of operation and its inadequate performance, such a state inspires very little popular trust (Holmes 1993; Della Porta and Vannucci 1997; Diamond 1999). It is in cases where such a system of predatory rule remains intact into the modernizing phase that a populist pattern of organization tends to emerge. Populism makes its appearance as a protest against the passive spoils logic of the old elite-ruled system. Wide-ranging

---

[22] On this, see Myrdal (1968) and Blomkvist (1988).
[23] This is discussed further in Part II, pp. 259–60.

demands for political measures to solve social problems are typically put forward. In view, however, of their deficient organization
and their weak capacity for implementation, combined at times
with unrealistic campaign promises, populist regimes often find it
hard to break the old order. Such regimes have had a tendency to
adopt an irregular and particularistic form of rule, which facilitates
the leader-centred personalist politics that populism involves.
Patronage politics continues, but in new and more centralized
forms, and with partly new beneficiaries.[24] In opposition to this
state of affairs, social movements with a strong anti-system appeal
have then tended to emerge, especially in more developed societies.
They aim their fire at the elite domination of politics, whether in a
clientelist or a populist form. On account of their fragile organization, however, as well as their status as political outsiders, such
movements have often had but small political influence, and a relatively brief existence besides. Spiralling shifts in organizational
patterns may thus take place. But it is a question of weak organizational forms throughout. Few changes occur in that area as long
as the institutional structure of the soft state remains intact.

A popular government based on soft administrative and legal
structures is a fragile creation. The organizations stimulated by
such a state normally display a weak coordination capacity. This
tends to give the regime, notwithstanding its electoral basis, weak
roots in society. In this setting, the feelings of identification between
citizens and the public organs—a core feature of the republican
idea—find an infertile soil. The 'love of the republic' regarded by
Montesquieu as the foundation of democracy, and of which
Tocqueville gave such ample report from the young United States,
is but little developed here. Citizens tend rather to turn their back
on the public organs. The citizens and patriots are easily counted
who, in the ideal of Machiavelli, are prepared with sword in hand to
defend their state. The low legitimacy fostered by the state, on
account of its abuse of power and its deficient manner of operation,
produces apathy and political indifference. The mass of citizens are
not necessarily anti-democratic in their sympathies, but they are
sufficiently indifferent to refrain from intervening if and when the
regime is threatened by undemocratic means. This makes it easy for
coup-plotters to set about their doings.[25]

[24] India's Indira Gandhi is a striking example here (Rudolph and Rudolph 1987:
127ff).
[25] There are also cases where apathy towards, and suspicion of, prevailing institutions has led to violence and rebellion. Sten Widmalm's (1997) study of the conflict
in Kashmir sheds light on such an instance.

This form of democracy is not, in other words, simply deficient. It also has a strong tendency, on account of its weakness, to pave the way for authoritarian rule—which naturally does not, in turn, improve democracy's future prospects. The civic capacities underlying popular government cannot easily develop in the midst of frequent swings between dictatorial and democratic government. Such swings have been common where soft legal and administrative structures prevail. Low quality of governance causes low quality of democracy; low quality of democracy spurs democratic fragility.

Democracy is promoted, in sum, by a long-standing practice of representation and by the maintenance of organizational rights. It is stimulated too by the existence of institutional structures based on administrative order and the rule of law, and by the separation of powers: by the presence, in particular, of local and regional organs of decision-making which are open to popular participation. If a stable democratic order is to be achieved, these conditions should be in place in substantial measure. Pluralist politics, with its electoral practices and political rights, tends to be very fragile unless accompanied by the other institutional reforms reviewed.

To this I would add two further comments. The one concerns the large state, the other the colonial state.

Does it matter whether or not the state undertakes activities of a broad scope, that is, whether or not it performs many of the tasks of social life? The answer is both 'yes' and 'no'. If, as I have claimed, a legacy of autocracy, centralism, and soft institutional structures creates a bad basis for democratic development, then these negative tendencies are strengthened if the state in question is also a large one. For, in such a case, society is more penetrated and imprinted by these negative traits. A totalitarian state—a state which suppresses all autonomous civil activity—is naturally a large state, with the ambition and capacity to control the various activities of society. If, on the other hand, the institutional conditions are more favourable, a large state can stimulate the development of the collective capacities that democracy needs in order to function. In many European countries, as Tarrow (1994) has shown, increased state activity has provided an impetus to popular organization. A state which conducts activities that affect people's living conditions is, naturally enough, an interesting target for the exertion of influence. If such influence can be exercised in free and ordered forms, a growing state can bring with it an enhanced social self-organization.[26] The experience of

---

[26] Organizations which have contacts with the state, and thus are able to exert influence, usually find it easier to attract members, experience proves (Hadenius and Uggla 1996).

modern welfare states in Europe has shown that a broad scope of public activity is compatible with a vital political democracy. There are limits, however, which cannot be exceeded. The state must not become so dominant as to crowd out that crucial autonomy which must be present in both the social and economic spheres if democracy is to stay vital:

A robust civil society, with a capability to generate alternatives and to monitor government and state can help [democratic] transitions get started, help resist reversals, help push transitions to their completion, help consolidate, and help deepen democracy. At all stages of the democratization process, therefore, a lively and independent civil society is invaluable . . . at least a nontrivial degree of market autonomy and ownership diversity in the economy is necessary to produce the independence and liveliness of civil society so that it can make its contribution to a democracy. Likewise, if all property is in the hands of the state and all price, labor, supply, and distributional decisions are the exclusive purview of the state in control of the command economy, the relative autonomy of political society required in a consolidated democracy could not exist. (Linz and Stepan 1996: 9, 11–12)

Let us turn now to the colonial state. States of this kind have seldom furthered democracy. The reason is simple: colonialism means that one country has supremacy over another. The people of the latter country thus cannot govern themselves. Colonialism is based on coercion, and it normally grants but a limited influence to those who are subjected to it. Yet the effects of colonialism can vary greatly, depending among other things on the following factors:

- External legacy. Colonial states often establish an institutional order bearing clear traces of the conditions obtaining in the metropolitan country. If these are marked by a high degree of autocracy, centralism, and so on, the colonial administration will likely assume a similar character. Naturally the converse applies as well.
- Internal legacy. The conditions obtaining in the colonized country can also be important. If a space for pluralism and popular participation has existed previously, elements of such arrangements can, under certain circumstances considered below, live on.
- The difficulty of achieving hegemony. If the people to be subjugated are numerous and cohesive, more extensive measures are needed to achieve control. This contributes, as a rule, to a more militarized colonial apparatus.
- The degree of penetration. If the colonial power initiates a large number of new activities in the colonized area, the need for

control is greater, and thus a larger and socially more penetrating colonial apparatus is necessary. This often leads to a higher degree of repression and centralization.

As we shall see in the following chapter, the colonial influence has varied quite substantially in these respects.

Three Cases

Popular rule presupposes certain qualities on the part of the people: this is the central idea in the republican tradition. Democracy needs democrats. There must be both a willingness and an ability on the part of citizens to practise this form of government. It is to this that we refer when we speak of democratic citizenship. It means citizens play the active and demanding role entailed in bearing the ultimate responsibility for public decision-making.

This, as previously stated, is a question of attitudes as well as resources. Moreover, a distinction can be made between traits we bear as individuals and those we bear as part of a group of one sort or another. Individual-level traits include our degree of political interest, as well as the degree of openness, rationality, and tolerance characterizing our political attitudes. But it is also a question of our actual capacity to defend our interests, to make our voices heard, to participate actively, and to exert influence. As research has shown, such qualities are closely associated as a rule with education and socio-economic position. Persons with longer schooling and a higher place on the social ladder are usually better 'equipped', democratically speaking, than others. The same pattern emerges when we compare nations as a whole with each other: in countries with a high level of economic development and general education, citizens' political attitudes and resources are usually better matched to democracy's demands.

On the collective side, we have mainly been taken up hitherto with the question of resources, in the form of coordination capacity in its several senses. The underlying idea is that organizational capacity strengthens the ability to take common action and gain political influence. We have furthermore assumed that the organizational context can have important spillover effects with regard to democratic norms and skills among the people involved. Through their internal structure as well as their external relationships, organizations may enlarge the spheres of tolerance and interpersonal trust in society and expand the circle of people in possession of essential political skills.

To serve a democratic function, the organizations in question should have deep popular roots, and a capacity to channel opinion from the bottom up. They should function autonomously of the state, yet they ought also to have links, directly or indirectly, into the political sphere. Alongside this mobilizing and channelling function, moreover, an ability to bridge divisions and to interact with people of another orientation must be present. This requires that, within the organizational sphere, there be a conflict-dampening capacity: an ability to moderate, to discipline, and to negotiate. In this regard, the social context can be more favourable or less. The conciliatory faculty is favoured by the absence of grave cultural or economic cleavages in society. It is furthermore an advantage if political and social identifications do not completely coincide. The more multiple and varied are our social networks, the wider are our contacts with others. This facilitates cooperation and the resolution of conflict. And to the degree that divisions into distinct population segments can be found, it is best if such segments are many in number, and more or less evenly matched in resources, so that no one group can dominate altogether.

In addition, institutional conditions play an important role. By nurturing certain civic capacities, state institutions can counteract and mitigate troublesome conditions in society. But it could also be the other way round. By their way of operating, institutions may undermine society's democratic potential, thus making prevailing difficulties even worse. The positive impact of institutions, as we saw, derives mainly from three general conditions: the long-term maintenance of a pluralist political order, division of power, and governance in accordance with the rule of law.

Given that democracy's health is a function of the combined effect of socio-economic and institutional conditions, we can distinguish four alternatives, as illustrated in Fig. 5.1.[1]

In what follows, I shall try to illustrate these alternatives concretely. Let us begin with the cases in which the preconditions are in balance, +/+ and - /- ; these correspond to squares 1 and 4.

Conditions are most favourable in square 1. In the societies found there, favourable conditions of both sorts are present in rich measure. So have conditions long been in North America and in many

---

[1] Democracy's preservation is not purely a function, of course, of the factors mentioned here. International conditions, for example, can play an important role as well (Whitehead 1986; Huntington 1991). I *would* claim, however, that the conditions bearing on internal prerequisites set the parameters for democracy's vitality to a high degree. As Joel Barkan notes (1997), democracy must be a home-grown product if it is to put down roots.

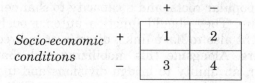

FIGURE 5.1: *Two kinds of explanatory conditions*

countries of western Europe. Industrialization and economic
growth started early in these countries, thus promoting popular
prosperity and great changes in the areas of popular education and
mass communication. These countries also saw the introduction,
albeit at varying rates, of several of these institutions that supply a
favourable soil for democratic development.[2] These circumstances
explain the relative stability of popular government in these parts
of the world.

Africa

The opposite situation, represented by square 4, can be said in
many respects to characterize conditions in Africa. The area south
of the Sahara has long been one of the poorest regions of the world.
In the mid-1970s, the per-capita GNP in this area was about
$US250, and in the majority of states less than 30 per cent of the
population was literate, as far as can be determined. Fifteen to 20
years later, in the early 1990s, per-capital GNP came to about $500,
while the literacy level was about 50 per cent (World Bank 1978;
1995). Thus the individual resources of citizens—political human
capital—are but weakly developed. As far as collective capacity is
concerned, certain observers took the view, when liberation arrived
in the 1960s, that an advantage lay in the fact that the African population, dominated as it was by small farmers, was economically
fairly homogeneous. The division into distinct classes characteristic
of other continents was not to be found in Africa (see, for example,
Nyerere 1967). Other cleavages, however, have proved all the
harder to handle. To be sure, the pattern of segmental divisions has
been highly pluralistic in character. Lijphart has portrayed a division into many groups as an advantage. This has not proved to be

[2] The 'take-off' in Europe is analyzed in Part II.

the case in Africa, however. Prevailing divisions have been primarily ethnic in character. Collective identities are to a great extent tribally and regionally defined and marked by a high degree of social and political encapsulation. In consequence, inter-segmental trust and solidarity is normally on a low level.

The institutional context, furthermore, has been far from favourable in Africa. Most of the states existing today were created by the colonial powers, who carved up Africa between them at the end of the nineteenth century. The borders then drawn were often wholly arbitrary, and took no account of demography. Colonial rule was established through coercion, of course, and it was often brutal at the start. The conquest itself, however, was typically a simple affair. In terms of military technology, after all, it was two completely different worlds that confronted one another. The local coordination capacity was very limited besides. Over large parts of the continent, states had not previously existed, but rather tribal societies, which were divided from each other. These were rapidly defeated and then easily incorporated into the colonial order. Once the territories had been penetrated militarily, it was usually possible to govern them with the use of a minimal administrative apparatus. The fact that, in many cases, the new territories contained no profitable natural resources made for a strikingly passive form of colonialism.[3] In the French territories, the centralistic administration practised in the homeland—the *intendant* model—was applied. The British, for their part, used a system of so-called indirect rule. This system was based, like its counterpart at home, on employing the local elite in the administrative apparatus. The method was to co-opt chiefs and other local potentates—who were assured a privileged position and a measure of autonomy within their areas—in exchange for loyalty and the payment of tributes. Dominance was maintained through predatory practices and strategies of divide and rule. For a long time, moreover, constitutional rights were conspicuous by their absence. Political freedoms and arenas for popular representation did not, as a rule, appear until the final phase of the colonial period. During this stage an expansion of the state apparatus often took place. Roads were built, schools established, health care provided, and so on. A kind of 'welfare colonialism'[4] in a paternalist and centralist spirit now took form. Where the rule of

---

[3] The whole of French West Africa, with a population of 18 million, was governed in the 1930s by about 4,500 officials; and this was at the height of the empire. In British-ruled Nigeria, with a population of 20 million, the corresponding figure was 1,400 (Jackson and Rosberg 1986: 6–7).

[4] The expression is taken from Young (1998: 106).

law was concerned, the colonial administration contained two con-
tradictory tendencies. Its mode of operation was often patrimonial
at the start: through the allocation of favours, the colonial power
sought to gain acceptance within the traditional elite. Gradually,
however, legal and administrative organs emerged which, in the
British territories especially, bore many characteristic traits of the
professional and rule-governed bureaucracy.

The states established after liberation continued the state-led
course of development begun in the colonial period. The difference
now was that they did so on a substantially larger scale, and on the
basis of other models. This was a time of great hopes. Development
assistance and other kinds of international support increased in
scale. Ambitions were high. The leaders of the new states believed,
as did the members of the international aid corps, in the possibility
of achieving a far-reaching social and economic modernization of
African societies. This could be accomplished, it was generally
thought, through active and purposeful measures on the part of the
state. The great progress that had been seen during earlier decades
in the Soviet Union and the communist states of eastern Europe
demonstrated, it was maintained, that a planned and state-led
course of development could yield rapid and effective results. In consequence, a sharp expansion of the state apparatus took place,
involving a high degree of centralization. The object was to direct
development from the top down. The state's radius of action
extended, furthermore, over a great many different social areas.
The number of public employees grew at an enormous rate.[5]

As liberation approached, democratic forms were introduced,
often in haste, by the colonial powers. In the great majority of cases,
these democratic forms survived only for a short time.
Authoritarian governments, especially of the one-party type, came
to predominate in Africa for a period of several decades. Judicial
bodies were made dependent of the regime. Organs charged with
inspecting and auditing state agencies were weakened or dismantled. Parliaments, inasmuch as they existed at all, were mainly rub-
ber stamps. Power was concentrated in the hands of the state's
executive branch. Indeed, it was often concentrated in the hands of
a single person: the occupant of the office of president. The new
regimes tried to govern mainly with the carrot and the stick. The
stick meant governance through coercion. Substantial efforts were
sometimes made in this area, and brutal methods were used

---

[5] It might be mentioned, for example, that state expenditures on public bureaucracy in Tanzania rose by 90 per cent just between 1972 and 1979 (Tangri 1985:
118).

against opposition of all kinds. But African states did not possess the repressive and administrative resources needed to sustain a functioning police state over the long run. Usually, therefore, the carrot had to be applied instead. By using the opportunities offered by the state apparatus for spoils and nepotism, the political elite sought to acquire legitimacy and social roots. The volume of the apparatus naturally afforded ample opportunities for patronage politics. As a result, the rational and regular elements present in the bureaucracy inherited from colonial times were largely washed away. The patrimonial administrative inheritance, rather, became the model of the day. With its heavy concentration of power and its soft mode of operation, the African state provided many opportunities for discretionary and personalist rule.

The typical African state was an authoritarian and centralized state bereft of the rule of law. It was of a far-reaching scope besides. African society was heavily dominated by the state. An institutional context of this sort hardly yields a favourable soil for the growth of the civic capacities required for a vital democracy. The vigorous popular organizing in autonomous forms seen during the struggle for decolonization came in most cases to an end. Such organizations as were allowed to exist were tied to the state through corporatist forms of dependence and control. If they wished to function openly they usually had to accept subordination to the governing party. The various formal and informal networks linking state and society displayed a clientelist logic. They served as channels for spoils. In the usual manner they were pronouncedly hierarchical in structure. Systems of this type have often shown a capacity to promote the peaceful resolution of conflict. Examples of this can be found in Africa too.[6] As a rule, however, African politics exhibited a remarkably high potential for conflict. One factor often adduced in explanation thereof is the heavy dependence on the state: the occupancy of state office has furnished the golden road to social and economic advancement, for which few prospects otherwise existed. Much is at stake, in other words, in political life. Such conditions pose an obstacle, to be sure, yet not an insurmountable one. But the actors involved have often had no interest in establishing the accommodating, 'consociational' forms of intercourse that might have dampened conflict (cf. Berg-Schlosser 1985). A fundamental difficulty has lain in the irregularity which has characterized African political life. Investment in cooperation has had a very meagre institutional support. Legal and administrative structures have been weak. In

[6] Kenya under Kenyatta and Senegal under Senghor may serve as examples (Zolberg 1966; Berg-Schlosser 1985; Barkan 1987).

combination with the strong segmental fractures in society, this institutional weakness has had serious consequences. In many cases, a political pattern marked by irreconcilable clan conflicts has emerged. The object is to seize power, and to keep it by any means. In a setting marked by uncertainty, in which power shifts hands through frequent coups and constant reshuffles—as was long the case in Africa—the aim of political activity is to keep competitors at bay and to help yourself to the spoils.

After some decades—by the 1980s, more or less—it had become clear that the 'African model of development' was in deep trouble. Administrative and fiscal mismanagement had produced grave economic deterioration. Public services had largely broken down.[7] The living conditions of the population had sharply worsened. There was no money left in the treasury for financing the spoils which had provided the system with a measure of legitimacy. The debt burden in many cases was enormous. The state had lost most of the governance capacity it had at one time possessed. A tendency towards social disengagement was the common result. Citizens turned their back on the state. As a consequence, the state became ever more marginalized. Aid-givers and international loan organs started demanding economic restructuring. The main changes sought were a liberalization of the economy and a reduction in the state apparatus. Such measures often increased the hardships faced by the population, fuelling dissatisfaction with the prevailing authoritarian order.

The many regimes that fell at the beginning of the 1990s were normally in this condition. In many cases, the popular protests were led by state employees who had not received their salaries for a long time. Students and teachers at the universities, which had deteriorated greatly in most cases, took active part in these often spontaneous actions as well. In some cases, moreover, trade unions and other organizations which had been under the regime's control earlier were able to break free and to help coordinate the protests. Demands were raised for political liberalization, including the release of political prisoners, the introduction of political freedoms, and the holding of free elections. Most of the regimes had to accede to these demands. There was little else they could do. Bereft of resources on account of the miserable economy, the state lost its governance capacity. The regime could no longer buy itself support among influential groups. The spoils machine had run out of gas. The final resort—outright coercion—was not a feasible option

---

[7] For a detailed account, see Grindle (1996: 18ff).

either. Lacking the needed revenues, and drained by extensive administrative 'leakage', many of the governments in question were unable to pay the salaries of their military and police. As a consequence, these latter groups, which had constituted the backbone of the authoritarian regimes, ignored the orders issued by their 'master' on several occasions. Sometimes they even sided with the protesters.

The subsequent political liberalization has produced, through the open elections and political freedoms to which it has led, a more favourable institutional context for popular organizing. Representative organs can serve as arenas for socialization into pluralist, and at the same time conciliatory, practices. On several occasions, moreover, the incumbent party has been voted out of office, so that a transfer of political power has been accomplished in a peaceful and orderly manner. These are important achievements. Steps towards increased decentralization are another positive tendency to be noted. But much remains to be done. Discrimination against political opponents is common, as are measures against the press. In many cases, moreover, elections have left a great deal to be desired where freedom and fairness are concerned. In several second elections, therefore, major opposition parties have decided not to take part. Furthermore, parliamentary organs generally remain very weak, and executive power continues to dominate. The prevailing model—presidentialism—exhibits many of its power-concentrating traits. Decentralization is in many cases more evident on paper than in practice: local governments exert a very restricted autonomy in matters of policy, and they lack economic and administrative resources besides. In reality, moreover, the functioning of the state apparatus has been little affected by the winds of change. A great many predatory practices persist in the political and administrative areas. Juridical institutions cannot easily gain autonomy or assert themselves, and the same can be said of organs of verification and control. The general and sometimes worsening tendency is for state institutions to be marred by extensive corruption.[8] In combination with a high degree of centralization, such conditions make the 'price' to be won—or lost—in the game of political competition extremely high.

As one might expect, popular organizations are but little developed in Africa. The parties are often highly elitist in character and stamped by a clientelist logic. Their efforts are focused heavily on

[8] In the corruption poll conducted by Transparency International (1998), which takes the form of a scale ranging from 1—a high degree of corruption—to 10—a low degree—the average level for the countries south of the Sahara is about 3.

the spoils to be gained from the occupancy of state office. In their popular roots they are often tied to ethnic and regional identities. Other bases of organization are normally conspicuous by their absence, particularly on the regional and national levels. Lively networks often operate at the level of village and neighbourhood, but coordination among these networks, in the form of an organizational scaling-up, has seldom come about. Weak links between periphery and centre—a characteristic feature of the hour-glass society—prevail in Africa still.

As for the design of electoral systems, it could be noticed that this does not overall make much of a difference in terms of voting behaviour. Whatever the formula applied—there are many examples of both the majoritarian and the proportional model—the outcome is normally a high degree of ethnic bock-voting with little reference to programmes and issues.[9] This has two implications. On the one hand, it is a token of the low frequency of cross-cutting cleavages, and the resulting low level of trust between segments, that signifies African political life. On the other hand, this voting pattern brings with it a generally high degree of proportionality—even in majoritarian systems—due to the geographical concentration of parties. In consequence, inclusiveness at the legislative level can be fairly good. But in other respects the prevailing system is marked by the common drawbacks of unifying presidentialism and proportionalism. There is normally a lack of inclusiveness at the government level, where the main resources are concentrated; and parties are marred by a strong propensity to internal fractionalization. The want of accessible offices of significance at the regional and local levels adds further to the weakness of political parties. Representatives of opposition parties are commonly doomed to a shadowy existence—a dilemma that is an invitation to floor crossing in parliament—whereas MPs on the government side are at the mercy of the president to gain political influence and access to resources.

Not only is the mobilizing capacity weakly developed in most African countries, but there is a want too of an advanced conciliatory capacity. Often, political life has the character a zero-sum game. Winner takes all. To explain this state of affairs, it has sometimes been alleged that there is no tradition of pluralism in the African political culture. An atmosphere of consensus, it is said, marked traditional society. There exists, therefore, no acceptance of

---

[9] This tendency is jokingly referred to in Africa as the 'yellow dog' syndrome: you would rather vote for a yellow dog than for a candidate belonging to another group (Reynolds 1999: 250–1).

political dissonance involving the expression of opposing views. Such cultural traits can of course be long lasting and put their imprints on political sentiments also in the modern setting. But other factors are of importance as well. We should remind ourselves, first of all, that the experience of plural politics is very short. At an early stage, an atmosphere of intensive confrontation tends to be the usual pattern; to work out strategies of trust and cooperation among competing parties normally takes a long period of trial and error to accomplish. In addition, institutional conditions can be more or less helpful. A lack of rule-governed practices in the administrative and political realm, which opens the floodgates for excessive patronage and embezzlement, in combination with a far-reaching centralization of powers, which strongly restricts access to the fruits of power, tend generally to lay the ground for a strongly confrontational political culture. To a great extent, these conditions explain the mentality of implacability, and the consequent difficulty of introducing strategies of reciprocity, that signifies African politics (Jackson and Rosberg 1982; Hydén 1983; Chazan 1994; Rothchild and Lawson 1994; Bienen and Herbst 1996; Gyimah-Boadi 1996; Bratton and van de Walle 1997; Young 1998).

In view of the situation here reported, involving unfavourable conditions in both socioeconomic and institutional respects, the preconditions for democracy in Africa over the short term cannot be seen as promising. It is unsurprising, against this background, that the wave of democratization which had swept over the continent at the beginning of the 1990s has in several cases been halted, and indeed transformed into its converse.

Let us return now to our two-by-two figure. Of particular interest, of course, are those combined cases in which the one type of condition is present to an essential degree but not the other. These cases are represented by squares 2 and 3 in Fig. 5.1. Let us begin with the first-mentioned combination, in which institutional patterns are not favourable, while in important respects matters are better on the socio-economic side. Latin America exhibits such features; many countries in that region have long displayed this imbalance.

Latin America

In the early years of the twentieth century, a striking economic upswing took place in many Latin American countries. In the early 1930s, such states as Argentina, Chile, and Uruguay were among the most developed in the world. Thereafter, to be sure, a degree of stagnation set in. In more recent years, however, these and several other states in the region have done relatively well in regard to both educational levels and economic growth. In the mid-1970s, the great majority of Latin American states belonged to the category of 'middle-income countries'. The average per-capita GNP of these countries was just under $US1,000 at the time. The corresponding figure for literacy, meanwhile, was around 70 per cent. In the 1990s, the latter figure reached 85 per cent, while the average per-capita GNP in the region came to about $3,000 dollars (World Bank 1978; 1995). In these respects, accordingly, conditions in Latin America have been fairly good in comparison with Africa and many other parts of the so-called Third World. This has not sufficed for popular rule, however; democracy has led a most uncertain existence on that continent.

Where social cleavages are concerned, common bonds of Spanish language and Catholic faith make for a high degree of cultural homogeneity. Problems of an ethnic character are found mainly in those areas, in the Andes and parts of Central America, with a large Indian population. Class divisions, on the other hand, are often highly salient; many countries in the area display grave social and economic fractures. These conditions have derived from the social structure of the preceding agrarian society. A *latifundia* system was established in many Latin American countries. Production took place on large estates—*haciendas*—on which the labouring population was harshly oppressed. A rigid social hierarchy, signified by pronounced class cleavages, has been maintained to a high degree even in modern times. In western Europe, as we know, such cleavage structure has laid the ground for the development of strong parties based on class identity. However, that has generally not been the case in Latin America, despite the fact that class divisions have overall been more pronounced in this continent. Latin America has been marked by weak popular mobilization and polarized and conflictual political tendencies. Prevailing institutional conditions have played a significant role in this regard.

The Spanish colonizers who arrived in what later became Latin America in the early 1500s encountered a society which was, for its time, remarkably well-ordered. Two large states dominated the area: the Aztec empire in the north, and the Inca empire in the south. Where administration and other infrastructure was concerned, these states were very well-developed and highly centralized. In terms of military technology, however, they were inferior, and so could be relatively easily defeated; the *conquistadores*, after all, had firearms and horses. The Spaniards took over a society and administrative structure marked by a high degree of hierarchy and autocracy. They continued in the same vein. Several factors contributed to this outcome. The society to be subdued was large and, in many areas, highly cohesive. An extensive military and administrative apparatus was therefore needed. Colonial penetration was prompted as well by the fact that great riches were available for the taking. Enormous quantities of precious metals, silver in particular, could now be shipped across the Atlantic to fill the coffers of the Spanish monarchy. The model for the colonial administration was in large part taken from the home country—in particular, from centralized and autocratic Castile. On the local level, to be sure, there were representative organs—*cabildos*—in which the Spanish-descended population could take part. But these were isolated in their localities: they had no links with each other, nor any channels for exerting influence upwards into the system. Their decisional competence, finally, was highly restricted. In many questions, even those of a purely local nature, it was the royal bureaucracy in Madrid that decided. As the Spanish empire declined in the 1600s, administrative control within the colonial territories declined as well. With the reorganization undertaken by the Bourbon kings in the eighteenth century, however, the centralized system took on new vigour. Not for nothing did Tocqueville (1969: 306) conclude that the rulers of Spanish America had provided their subjects with highly unfavourable conditions for self-government.

The decolonization that took place in the early nineteenth century required large-scale military efforts. In many areas, moreover, it was a long drawn-out process. At the same time, an era of institutional dissolution began. The new states that had been formed were often without clear boundaries, giving rise to protracted hostilities. In addition, the administrative apparatus within the various areas had more or less collapsed. The new centres had no control over their respective peripheries. In order to drive out the colonial power and establish law and order within and between countries, the leaders of the new states undertook a thoroughgoing militarization of the state apparatus. Military methods were also used internally. Control over the periphery was achieved to a great extent through coercion and repression, and subsequently upheld through a far-reaching political and administrative centralization. A culture of opposition and revolt emerged at the same time, this too taking a military expression. The *caudillo*—the man on horseback who sometimes seized power—attained the status of a popular hero. Hence centralization soon re-emerged, albeit with a more pronounced militarist flavour to it. Another pattern that was left over from the colonial order was the tendency of using the state as a milch-cow for personal gain, and thereby, in turn, as a means of buying political support.[10]

Rapid shifts of power and periods of civil war and chaos characterized political life in many of the new states for a long time. Not until the end of the century could a reasonably stable order emerge. This took the form of either a military government or a civilian regime of oligarchical type. In the latter case, a culture of elite cooperation could often be established. A gradual broadening of political participation could then, in a pattern familiar from Europe, take place on this basis. Argentina, Uruguay, Chile, and Colombia were the countries in the vanguard here, and they were followed by a good many others as the twentieth century got under way; on account of the pronounced cultural and linguistic similarities among the countries in the region, there are unusually favourable conditions in Latin America for 'snowball' effects in political life. The civil order established was based on clientelist patterns of organization. Local political barons were bound together in loose networks based on personal ties, and the system was 'nourished' in familiar fashion through access to political office. A soft and highly centralized state power furnished a suitable soil for this kind of politics. The softness of the state made it easier to use power for political ends. Centralization helped make the system closed and thereby easier to dominate. In its elitist form the system served to dampen conflict, but it provided little room, by the same token, for active popular participation.

The Great Depression of the 1930s hit many countries in Latin America hard. A long period of economic growth now came to a sudden halt. The effect on living standards was dramatic. This was also a period of heightened political mobilization. Increased urbanization, improved communications, and higher levels of education—all the fruit of the considerable economic development that had taken place—had provided the broad mass of the people with greater political resources. Passive and oligarchical forms of government became, under such conditions, ever more difficult to maintain. In

---

[10] Anthony McFarlane (1996: 61) makes the following remark: ' . . . one of the most important elements of Spain's social and political heritage to the independent Latin American states at the start of the nineteenth century was the tradition of weak and corrupt government . . . When Spanish power collapsed, and colonial elites seized power between 1810 and 1822, they inherited *ancien régime* societies in which public office was still widely regarded as an extension of the private person, and where the wealthy used their resources to create relationships which could be converted into political power.'

their stead, therefore, activist popular tribunes now took the stage. A 'populist era' began. When talking about populism it is important, where Latin America is concerned, to bear a terminological point in mind. In our presentation earlier, we used the term as a general designation for a certain type of popular organizing. In Latin America, however, the term 'populism' is used primarily to refer to policies of a certain type: redistribution on behalf of the broad popular masses, and state control over the economy. Populist policies in this sense can be carried out by both military dictators and elected leaders. Leaders of the latter sort have commonly acquired their position by mobilizing popular support on a populist basis.[11]

Populist policies consisted, to begin with, of an intensive use of the state treasury, in order to make jobs available and in order to provide the material basis for various social reforms. It also involved an attempt to increase state control over the economy, through the regulation of wage formation, the nationalization of companies, and the establishment of state production monopolies. These elements were typically accompanied by a strongly protectionist policy for the benefit of domestic industry. The consequence was a heavy expansion in the scope of state activities. In an effort to secure support, state leaders sought to tie trade unions and other organizations to the state through corporatist arrangements. The focus on the state as the rationale for organizing, which had been evident already in the oligarchical era, became yet more accentuated now. The dependence of civil and economic life upon the state became a major feature of Latin American life. This 'Latin American model' of political incorporation could be held together, on the one hand, by the extensive access to patronage that the big-cum-soft state made possible, and, on the other hand, through a high degree of political and administrative centralization.[12]

This combination of a distributive and a developmental state did not, however, produce successful economic results over the long run. Galloping inflation, heavy budget shortfalls, and declining international competitiveness were the common result. Moreover, the populist movements which emerged in many countries exacerbated

[11] Several of the foremost exponents of populist policies, such as Vargas and Peron—see p. 59 above—started out as members of a military government, or, in the case of Vargas, as the leader thereof. They then sought a popular mandate and got one.

[12] Claudio Veliz (1980: 283) in particular has stressed centralism as a theme uniting the various countries of the continent: ' . . . the governments of Cuba and Mexico; Chile and Peru; Brazil and Argentina are centralist not because they are left-wing, right-wing, capitalist or socialist, but because they are Latin American.'

political conflict. A high degree of polarization came to characterize political life in many of the states which had restored civilian rule after World War II. The typical consequence was military intervention. Now, as earlier, the military's assumption of power was a simple affair in the main. Democracy had few active defenders. Indeed, the tradition was for significant forces in civil society to support the putschists: at times it was the business world or the church which did so, and at other times the trade unions, together with parties connected to the one group or the other. Furthermore, many interest groups continued to cooperate with the state after the military had taken power. Government by the military was often considered a necessary transitional solution once civilian government had been stalemated. This was a token of a weakly developed conflict-solving capacity in political life. The parties could not themselves handle their differences. Instead, a third party had to step in and 'clean up the political mess'.

Military involvement was often of a caretaking, temporary nature. For the sake of the nation, corruption, economic mismanagement, and implacable party rivalry would be swept away. When the work of restoring order was done, civilian politicians would be allowed to resume control. However, the coups that took place in various Latin American countries in the 1960s and 1970s represented a change in mentality on the part of the military. Their ambitions were now much radical than before. The object in many cases was to cut off corporative ties to interest organizations and to put an end to the distributive policy that had burdened the treasury. A neo-liberal and highly market-oriented economic policy was applied. The goal was to remould economic and political life. This would be accomplished through an authoritarian and technocratic form of government. This 'revolution from above' was carried out by coercive means. It was for this reason that the methods now employed were unusually brutal. The project was often a failure, economically speaking. Corruption and mismanagement were rife. By the end of the 1970s, most of the economies run by generals were on the ropes, and the foreign debt was sky-high.[13] Nor was the attempt at political house-cleaning successful for the most part. Despite all the efforts made to free political life from collaboration with various particularistic interests, it had soon proved necessary to turn to such groups in order to get anything done. It was not easy to direct social and economic life with truncheons and rifles. Good old clientelism had often been more

---

[13] For details on the worsening incapacity afflicting most states in the region, see Grindle (1996: 21ff).

efficient. These setbacks led to divisions in military ranks. A process of disintegration paved the way for political liberalization. By the end of the 1980s, all of the military regimes had given up.

Political life under civilian leadership exhibits varying patterns in Latin America today. In Mexico, a hegemonic-party, in power for 70 years, has been able to shut out competitors through far-reaching electoral fraud and a clientelist incorporation of associational life. Similar arrangements have long applied in Paraguay. In both countries, however, a gradual breakdown of the old system of political dominance seems under way. The more democratic states, for their part, can in most cases be placed in one of two relatively distinct clusters at each end of a scale. In the one we find states which have established a high degree of cooperation at the elite level. Venezuela and Colombia have been the prototypical cases here. Following a period of heavy-handed military dictatorship, the leading parties, which had previously been at each other's throats, concluded a pact of cooperation and power-sharing. This took place at the end of the 1950s. Since then, the 'consociational' arrangement prevailing between the parties has gradually become more informal. Nevertheless, a high degree of accommodation has for long time dominated the picture in these two countries. Uruguay may also be said to fall into this category, for it too has had a long history of cross-party cooperation. The model in question is based, in accordance with Lijphart's prescriptions, on a hierarchical form of coordination. It presupposes that political elites are able to find a formula for sharing power, and that they are able to persuade their followers to accept that formula. This in turn presupposes solid organization and loyalties of long standing. Such has largely been the case in the countries mentioned. The parties therein have had faithful voters and relatively broad support. Electoral volatility has been low. The ideological profile of the parties is diffuse for the most part. These are catch-all parties, and they are often highly fractionalized. The organizations of civil society, moreover, are heavily incorporated by the parties. For a long time, this has applied particularly in Venezuela, where the two leading parties have controlled virtually all civic and economic associations of significance. This control, which according to one observer 'borders on obsession' (Coppedge 1994: 29), has been maintained primarily through clientelist policies. Economic and other advantages have been distributed strictly along party lines.[14] The preconditions hereof have been

---

[14] Coppedge (1994: 29) gives the following description: 'Sometimes party loyalists are sent to infiltrate a new organization and eventually elect one of their own as its

strong central control over political life, the existence of soft institutions, and an ample influx of resources, resulting from oil, into the
public sector.[15]

The opposite cluster is represented by such states as Brazil,
Ecuador, and Peru. Here the parties are very weak, both organizationally and in terms of membership. Electoral volatility is high.
The parties often have a transitory character, and they are functionally tied to a particular person. As is frequently the case where
populist forms of organization are involved, political life exhibits a
high degree of polarization and confrontation, with severe political
crises the result.[16]

Let us now summarize the picture. We may count on the positive
side of the ledger the fact that, in virtually all countries of the
region, democratic procedures, however constrained, have been in
operation for a period of some length: in many cases for about 15
years, and in some cases much longer. The constant military inter-
ventions of the twentieth century have inhibited the development of
parties in many countries. That pattern is now, perhaps, on its way
to being broken down. This yields a space for learning processes
which can strengthen democratic capacities in society. Generally
speaking, it is better for the future of democracy to maintain far-
from-perfect democratic institutions than to abandon them completely. The alternative—authoritarian rule—does not normally
provide a more fertile soil for the advancement of democratic values
and collective capacities in society (Linz 1997).

Another promising sign is the diminishing frequency with which
political opposition takes the anti-system expression that was earlier so common. Instead of rejecting the system or taking up arms,
many radical movements have decided to enter the regular political
process. Increasingly, democracy has attained the status of an overarching ideology. Yet, at the mass level, attitudes to democratic

leader. More often, a party will co-opt an independent with an offer of a position in
the government or a seat on a commission, in the party body, or in the Congress.
Because there are so few channels of influence outside the parties, few leaders can
resist these offers . . . If co-optation fails, parties create parallel organizations that
tend to attract more support than the independents because, having a party connection to the government, they achieve better results.'

[15] Recently, however, this elite model has collapsed and been replaced by a
purely populist mode of governance (Hadenius 2001).

[16] In Peru in 1992, the elected president carried out a coup together with the military, and the constitution was scrapped. Democratic freedoms were set aside for a
time. The presidents of both Ecuador and Brazil, meanwhile, were forced to resign
in the middle of their terms. Both presidents, it bears noting, had a pronouncedly
populist appeal.

procedures tend to be mixed. Survey research reveals that in Latin American countries normally some 85 per cent of the citizens regard democracy as the ideal form of government. When asked about the actual performance of democratic institutions, however, the response is not very encouraging. On average, no more than 30 per cent say they are satisfied with the way democracy is functioning in their homeland.[17]

A tendency with positive potential is decentralization. It was formerly common for local organs to be subject to heavy central control; mayors, for example, were often appointed by the president. Now, however, elections have been held in many countries for local and regional organs.[18] A greater openness in political life can be the result. Where there are numerous entry points into the system, the process cannot be controlled from the top so simply. New groups can gain entrance more easily. Access to local arenas, moreover, can stimulate organizing at the level of the base. This can provide the foundation over the long run for a stronger bottom-up influence in the system.[19]

But there are also less promising features. Among these may be reckoned a persisting dominance of the executive power at the central level. The prevailing constitutional configuration—presidentialism with a remaining high degree of vertical power concentration, combined with proportional representation—makes for feeble organs of counter-power. Policies of decentralization have often been pursued only half way: elections are held locally but essential economic resources are still controlled by the centre. In addition, legislative bodies are still in a weak position. The same goes for legal organs and auditing agencies, which are often the target of strong political influence and marred by ineffectiveness and

[17] Venezuela is a telling case. Interviews done in this country in 1993 demonstrate, on the one hand, an overwhelming support for democratic principles. On the other hand, 46% of respondents answered in the affirmative to a question as to whether coups could on occasion be justified. And a decisive majority—59%—held that the failed military intervention a year earlier, against a president accused of extensive corruption, had been justified (Myers and O'Connor 1998). It should be observed that Venezuela has a long record, by Latin American standards, of unbroken democratic government, as well as a relatively high level of economic development. A general account of democratic attitudes in Latin America may be seen in Lagos (1997). For an international comparison, see Klingemann (1999).

[18] In the late 1970s, fewer than 3,000 local governments in Latin America had elected leaders. In the late 1990s, the figure had risen to nearly 13,000 (World Bank 1997: 112).

[19] Venezuela could be mentioned as an example. Here, a programme of decentralization launched in the late 1980s seems to have contributed to the break-up in recent years of the old monopolistic party system (cf. note 14 above).

corruption.[20] On account of its soft character, the state, which in many cases remains large, provides a good deal of room for discretionary policies of a clientelist or populist type. In consequence, political parties normally display a strong elite dominance and have a fragile popular footing. Overall, civil society still remains politically dependent and weakly organized. Popular trust in prevailing institutions, moreover, is generally remarkably low.[21]

India

A single combination from our figure now remains to be considered: that represented by square 3. In cases of this kind, socio-economic conditions are not in democracy's favour, while the opposite holds true for institutional conditions. India may serve as an example here. This country has long suffered from poverty and underdevelopment. Its per-capita GNP in the mid-1970s was $US180. That figure in the 1990s came to $300—below the average for sub-Saharan Africa on both occasions. The literacy level in India in the 1970s, at about 35 per cent, was slightly higher than that in Africa, while the figures for the 1990s are about the same: roughly 50 per cent of the population is now literate in both India and Africa.

As for economic and cultural fractures, moreover, prevailing conditions would give rise to pessimism. The social structure is scarcely of the sort commonly considered to promote democracy. In religious and linguistic terms, India is a deeply divided society. In the social area, furthermore, a caste system specific to the country prevails. For thousands of years, this ascriptively based system has separated different groups of Indians from one another. Tocqueville saw in this religious system a contrast to the equality and monism characteristic of both Christianity and Islam. In India, people lived alongside each other, but in different societies. 'They are', he wrote of the castes, 'like different nations coexisting on the same soil' (Siedentop 1994: 111).

---

[20] Writing about the legal system in Latin America, Pilar Domingo concludes as follows: 'The prevailing image of impunity and corruption severely undermines regime legitimacy, and the lack of perceived rights and guarantees erodes the prospects for binding loyalties to democratic rule both within the political elites and at the societal level' (1999: 171). In the Transparency International (1998) rating, the average corruption score for Latin America is about 3 (cf. footnote 8 above).

[21] Haring (1975); Veliz (1980); Malloy (1987); Diamond and Linz (1989); Collier and Collier (1991); Castañeda (1994); Fox (1994b); Burkholder and Johnson (1994); O'Donnell (1994); Mainwaring and Scully (1995); R. Miller (1996); Diamond (1999); Roberts and Wibbels (1999).

Where democracy is concerned, however, India's record is far better than Africa's. Against the odds, not least from the point of view of the modernization school,[22] India has in the main upheld democratic forms of government since liberation in 1947. There was an obvious interruption, however: in the 1970s, Indira Gandhi ruled the country for two years under a state of emergency. It bears recalling, however, that this period ended when the sitting government was voted out of power in a basically free and fair election.

As we saw, there is not much to indicate that it is socio-economic factors which have endowed Indian democracy with its vitality. On the contrary, India has suffered from a distinct handicap in these respects. The success of democracy in that country must therefore be explained in some other fashion. This brings us to the institutional side of the matter.

While, on Tocqueville's account, many European states were overly centralized, India suffered from the opposite condition: excessive diversity and insufficient cohesion. However, he fastened as well on the well-developed system of local self-government conducted within the framework of the caste system; it was essentially through these village-level organs that social life was administered. (Siedentop 1994: 107ff).

Indian society, for the most part, was only weakly penetrated by the state. A range of regimes came and went. Governments collected taxes in order to be able to dominate their territory and finance an often enchanting royal court life. They did not, as a rule, accomplish much more. In administrative terms, the system of government was highly indirect. Society was largely self-governing. India, Karl Marx remarked, was a country of thousands of autonomous villages.[23] To begin with, the British, who had subdued the disintegrating Mughal empire in the 1700s, were simply one in a series of such 'marginal' rulers. For a long time, India was lightly governed by the British East India Company. For reasons of fiscal caution, the English government did not wish to become involved, contenting itself instead with a yearly tribute from the company. But a large-scale national insurrection in the 1850s changed matters in this regard. The revolt required a considerable military effort to subdue, thus demonstrating that the type of government

---

[22] The title of an international conference on democracy held in 1997, 50 years after the founding of the Indian state, was a telling one: 'Against the Odds'.

[23] Hall (1985: 59). Mahatma Gandhi gave a similar account. It bears noting that Gandhi, in contrast to Marx, made his statement with great appreciation: he saw the village republic, perhaps somewhat romantically, as the natural building block of state and society in India (Mitra 1997: 4).

hitherto applied—at once passive and discretionary—could not continue. India was made subject to the crown, and an intensive period of institution-building commenced. A system of high courts on the British model was introduced. These legal organs were staffed with professionals and guaranteed an autonomous standing. They came to function as an effective check on the colonial authorities. An administrative apparatus common to the entire country was set up; it was not, however, always uniform in its manner of functioning. This bureaucracy proved, in the circumstances, to be extremely efficient, rational, and well-trained. Its higher offices were reserved to Britons as a rule, but the number of Indian bureaucrats gradually increased. Representative organs were also established. In the 1880s, elected local bodies were formed. In the 1890s, provincial assemblies were set up in which Indian representatives could take part. In the 1920s, the door to Indian participation in provincial government was opened. A decade later, finally, the country acquired a constitution. It lay down a federative division of the country and increased the representation of the Indian population.

The British *raj* should not be idealized, of course. It rested on a substantial element of coercion throughout. The foreign rulers were sometimes extremely heavy-handed. In comparison with colonial practices elsewhere, however—on the part of the Spaniards and the French, for example, as well as on the part of the British themselves in other places, particularly Africa—the treatment accorded India was special. Freedom of the press obtained, as did other political freedoms. This furnished a favourable basis for efforts at popular organization. In addition, the colonized population was offered the opportunity, albeit long a limited one, to participate in provincial decision-making organs. Independent and relatively efficient courts were established too. In this way, India acquired uniform legal arrangements for the first time, thus facilitating national integration. The extension of the administrative apparatus over the entire country furthered integration as well. It bears noting, moreover, that this bureaucracy was manned almost entirely by Indian officials by the end of the colonial era.

The main Indian opposition movement, the National Congress, was formed in 1885. It demanded political reforms, including representation. Since these demands were met, at least in part, Congress representatives decided to take part in the organs in question. Already early on, then, reformist attitudes emerged, and a cooperative disposition developed. In social terms, the Congress had its base in the anglicized and well-educated middle class. It was federal and highly democratic in structure. Its governing organs were composed of elected representatives for the various provinces and regions. The movement had a powerful integrative effect. Since time immemorial, India had been characterized by a high degree of heterogeneity. Ethnically, linguistically, and religiously, the country was sharply divided. The same applied in the area of political geography. Colonial India comprised a myriad of provinces, regions, and surviving principalities—the last-mentioned under British suzerainty. Below these, an enormous variety of local units existed. With its strong organization, and its highly conciliatory approach in matters of a cultural and religious nature, the Congress succeeded in establishing itself as a national movement. It came thus to function as an intermediary structure both horizontally and vertically: it helped connect the different population segments with each other, and it linked the centre to the periphery. The networks created by the new popular movement helped, in combination with the increased local penetration of the British administration, to break down the local 'encapsulation' which had long stamped social and political life in India. The long-term goal of the Congress was national liberation, and it undertook an increasingly successful mobilizing drive to this end. Led from the 1920s on by the charismatic pacifist Mahatma Gandhi, the Congress made use of peaceful yet effective methods. Campaigns of non-cooperation and civil disobedience attracted a vast popular following. The question then arose: should the movement participate in the representative organs set up by the colonial power? Gandhi and his followers were hesitant on this point for a time, but they soon decided to take part in the representative process. Taking part, they thought, could demonstrate the popular roots of the party, and indeed reinforce them. Electoral campaigns presented a good opportunity for building up the party organization. A network of local party units could be organized in connection with elections. And, indeed, the Congress Party's dominant position was clearly demonstrated in the elections of 1936–7. The party now assumed full governmental responsibility in the majority of the country's provinces.

Liberation from the British resulted in only gradual changes on the institutional level. The suffrage was extended to the entire population. The federal order was retained, as was the legal and administrative structure founded by the colonial power. The constitution of 1950 strongly emphasized the principles of democracy and the separation of powers. The Congress Party was now, and for several decades would remain, the dominant political force. Judged comparatively, it was an unusually well-equipped party. It had a long period of organization-building behind it. It had led the fight for national liberation, and it was accustomed to conducting electoral campaigns and to exercising government power. The leader of the party after Gandhi's death was Jawaharlal Nehru. A man of democratic convictions, and a champion of conciliatory forms of conflict resolution, Nehru left a deep mark on the new state during its formative phase. It was the leaders of the first generation who had gone into the breach during the struggle for liberation. Among them, Gandhi's idealistic style of leadership was the example. Many of these leaders were convinced socialists, including Nehru. They had great faith in the capacity of the state to lead economic development and to redistribute wealth and income to the poor. A planned economy and a rapidly expanding state were the model.

Already at this time, a tendency towards clientelism began to spread in the party. At first it was mainly on the lower levels. Gradually, however, it moved upwards. After Nehru's death in the mid-1960s, the clientelist barons were ready to take charge. The party was directed for a while by 'the syndicate', a group of influential state ministers who had become highly skilful at exploiting the political advantages of incumbency. The party was growing more diffuse, programmatically speaking; it was being reduced to a cartel of political bosses who owed their position to their ability to allocate spoils, for which the large state offered ample opportunities.[24] It was this body of influential middlemen of which Indira Gandhi wished to rid herself when she split the party in the late 1960s. The new party mobilized support on a directly populist basis. Internal democracy, in the form of elections to various positions, had been retained in the old party, but little of it was left in the new. This was a party built around its leader. The extended network of relatively autonomous party units on the local and regional levels disappeared for the most part. The new party was directed from above in a discretionary manner by its leader. The allocation of spoils as a rationale for political participation did not cease with this. The main difference now was that spoils were allocated in a substantially more centralized fashion. Elections were held following the state of emergency, and the Congress Party lost power for the first time. Victory went to a loose coalition of parties know as the Janata Alliance, the components of which were united by a determination to defend democracy, and by a wish to strengthen the federal order. The Congress Party returned to office in the 1980s. Since then, however, it has steadily diminished

---

[24] Francine Frankel (1969: 458) describes the situation as follows: 'Indeed, local elites were attracted by the Congress precisely because it was the government party and could assure influential constituents preferential treatment in the award of loans, grants, contracts, licences, and supplies.'

in importance. Now it is one party among others. Elections in India have become much more intensive and open.

India remains deeply divided. At the same time, however, it is a society of mobility and dynamism. The identity of its members is often composite and mixed, and not nearly as immobile and closed as Tocqueville believed in his time. Great regional variations in the pattern of caste divisions, together with considerable heterogeneity and mobility within the castes, help produce striking fluctuations in the behaviour of voters and the coalition patterns of parties. Significant elements of consociational intercourse have also been established. Especially worthy of note here is the segmental autonomy that prevails, which takes the form of a developed federalism and a substantial autonomy in sensitive questions of religion and language. In Indian political life generally, there is a well-developed capacity for negotiation and compromise. This culture of mediation and consent can be traced to the spirit of tolerance and forbearance in the face of differing patterns of life which has characterized Hindu society historically. Yet this can scarcely be the entire explanation, for in all periods there have been serious antagonisms between different religious, and other, segments in the Indian population; indeed, these have flared into open violence at times. This has been the case between Hindus and Muslims not least. The fact that these tensions could be largely held in check may be ascribed in large part to institutional conditions. The relatively independent judicial institutions have served to dampen conflicts. In addition, the federal and decentralized structure has been very helpful, for it has afforded minority groups an opportunity for self-determination. Fewer 'conflict questions' have thus come up on the national arena.[25]

India practises the parliamentary form of executive selection, which is generally less conflict-prone. On the other hand, a majoritarian electoral formula is applied. In contrast to the 'normal' Anglo-American pattern, however, a high degree of fragmentation of the party system has occurred, due to an increasing appearance of regional parties. Through a significant share of small parties, along with larger ones, represented in parliament and also in government, India displays to a great extent the plural and inclusive traits associated with proportionalism. The access to elective offices of importance at the state level, and also further down in the system, reduces the winner-take-all character of the political game

[25] Federal arrangements have been facilitated by the fact that boundaries were changed on several occasions during the 1950s, so that the States came to coincide more closely with historically rooted linguistic and cultural regions.

even more. At the same time it strengthens the political clout of parties, as many of these, even opposition parties at the national level, can enjoy the fruits of executive power (Weiner 1989; Khilnani 1992; Hardgrave 1993; Sisson 1994; Lijphart 1996; Kulke and Rothermund 1997).

The 'Congress System' featured economic planning combined with spreading clientelist practices. These policies led to increased centralization and a softening-up of the state's administrative structure. These tendencies became stronger during the more populist phase that followed. Indian political life has increasingly developed, many have argued, in the direction of disintegration and decay. In many Indian States, and even in parts of the central bureaucracy, corruption is rampant.[26] An increasingly personalist politics has promoted top-down rule, and furthered the degeneration of administrative and organizational structures. Also the court system, which initially could maintain its independence and neutrality, has come under pressure; this was typically the case under the reign of Indira Gandhi. The consequence has been an increasingly expressive and conflictual pattern of politics. A clear sign of this may be seen in the growing success of regional and ethno-religious parties, in particular the Hindu-nationalist BJP, which became the largest party in parliament in the 1990s. At the same time, the political organs have lost their capacity to govern. Political actors try to mobilize, by means of populism and polarization, and society gets less done. As a result of political centralization and patronage politics, moreover, civic organizations have become the object of political incorporation and dominance.

Organizational development is still on a low level in India. Interest groups and other civic associations are normally weak. It is political parties that serve as the main linkage between people and government. For a long time, the Congress served as an accommodating umbrella party, able to uphold a broad political consensus and to integrate the politics and power structures at the localities into the national political system. But the decline of the Congress has brought with it a general downfall in these respects. Internal life in political parties is generally signified by elite domination. Many parties have scanty rank-and-file support and perform poorly in terms of policy coherence and parliamentary discipline. To an increasing extent, ordinary people turn to direct action of an anti-system nature. Political violence and various kinds of riots have

---

[26] In the Transparency International rating of 1998, India scores roughly 3. According to this estimate, then, the level of corruption is roughly at the same level as in sub-Saharan Africa and Latin America.

been on the rise (Rudolph and Rudolph 1987; Kohli 1987; 1994; Brown 1994; Chhibbar 1999).

Other tendencies, however, may be found as well: tendencies which can infuse Indian democracy with greater strength. The powers of the supreme court have been recently increased; this may help to improve control over the political and administrative machinery. In addition, the constitutional prerogative of the central government to dismiss, as an exceptional measure, State governments in favour of its own direct rule has been restricted; this right had been used very liberally at times. The new restrictions leave less room for a discretionary exercise of power at the central level, and may help to increase the autonomy of the states (Dasgupta 1997; Manor 1997). The local level has been strengthened too. According to a law passed in 1992, elected local organs—*Panchyati ray*—must be set up over the entire country. These units have been granted fairly extensive administrative powers. The impression is that these institutions have led to increased participation at the level of the base, and in general to a higher degree of inclusion and openness in political life. New groups are drawn into the democratic process and socialized by it. Participation in the local organs appears to be promoting integration and cooperation between different population groups. Popular confidence in local agencies is increasing as well (Mitra 1997). Perhaps this can enlarge the space for the exertion of influence from below within the political system. This would counteract the elitist and personalist patterns which have emerged over the course of the half-century that India has been free and democratic.[27]

How things will go in the future cannot of course been known. Indian democracy exhibits both promising and troubling tendencies. If, however, we compare conditions in that country with those in Africa, which is the natural reference point in terms of societal conditions, the prognosis for India looks distinctly favourable. With respect to indicators of socio-economic advancement, it bears recalling, the overall picture is not much better than in Africa. And where fragmentation is concerned the situation would seem, if anything, to be more troublesome in the case of India. In Africa, after all, there is no equivalent to the caste system. What gives India the democratic edge is the effect of institutions. Prevailing institutional structures tend, in India as

[27] Studies from Bengal, where strong local organs were established early on, indicate that such arenas for popular participation can also help improve governance capacity. The state acquires a partner on the local level, thus improving its implementation capacity (Mitra 1997).

opposed to in Africa, to counteract and to mitigate difficulties caused by societal conditions.

The institutional strength of Indian democracy arises mainly from its tradition of division of powers, involving a substantial degree of federalism and decentralization. This lays the ground for a high degree of political inclusiveness. At the same time it strengthens the capacity of political parties. The parliamentary form of executive selection stimulates such tendencies as well. The very fact, moreover, that India has managed to uphold a plural practice for such a long time has had favourable consequences. Over a period of a hundred years, a process of trial and error has been operating, leading to an unusually far-reaching—for third-world conditions—conciliatory capacity in political life.[28]

Corruption and a generally low performance level in the area of governance certainly prevail in India. Owing to the highly developed division of powers, however, the polarizing effects of the 'soft' governance appear to have been alleviated. It is the combination mainly of a lack of rule-governance and a high degree of political centralization that provides the impetus for an implacable, confrontational political culture. In a divided, decentralized structure, by contrast, the 'fruits of incumbency' can be more evenly distributed, which has the effect in turn of lowering the stakes in the game of politics; for with a broader access to political offices there can be something, potentially at least, to gain for everybody.

Yet such institutional structures are prone to breed weak forms of democratic involvement. Elitist modes of politics retain their ascendancy, either in a politically pacifying form—clientelism—or in an activating and polarizing form—populism. To the extent independent activity at the grass roots takes place, it tends to take the form of politically aversive popular movements, or is expressed through aggressive direct action of a mass character. It is the maintenance, and even intensification, of such political traits that the pessimists tend to emphasize when discussing the prospects of Indian democracy. The optimists, for their part, point to achievements in other realms. In a way, both sides are right. India has been remarkably successful in many respects. If the democratic project in that country is to be strengthened, however, further institutional reforms are called for.

---

[28] Of the entrepreneurs from all parties who keep the system running, James Manor (1997: 4) writes as follows: 'Indeed, this small army of political activists and fixers constitutes a major national resource which is unavailable to most countries in Asia, Africa and Latin America.'

Democratic development is a process in which a capacity for popular involvement in an active, and at the same time peaceful, way
is gradually developed. It is best if this process is started as early as
possible, and if, whenever it starts, it can be kept going. In the successful scenario a step-wise process tends to ensue. First, a recon-
ciliatory capacity is established, involving an atmosphere of mutual
trust and understanding, and a readiness among parties to dampen
conflicts by means of negotiations and compromises. Often, it is
interaction between elite actors that can accomplish this.
Institutions making for division of power, including an essential
degree of decentralization, makes the conciliatory process easier. At
a later stage a mobilization phase may follow, entailing broader
participation and a stronger bottom-up tendency in the political
system. This is encouraged by the existence of democratically functioning organs at the local level, which can nurture popular involvement and advance political skills among the citizenry. It is
furthered, moreover, by regulatory institutions operating in accordance with the rule of law. The existence of such institutions helps to
counteract the conflict-aggravating effects of political mobilization.
At the time of active mass politics, such help is even more needed,
since the political game then becomes more complex and conflict-
prone.

In Africa, this step-wise process is, one hopes, about to start.
Plural politics, albeit restrained and shaky, has been introduced in
many countries. The principal obstacle at this early stage is the
maintained concentration of powers. This bars the development of
more conciliatory relationships between political elites. In a zero-
sum game, in which the winner takes all and, moreover, the incumbent normally has a trump, there is little ground for the emergence
of the strategies of reciprocity that form a part of the consociational
package of conflict resolution. The countries of Latin America have
managed on the whole to move further along the 'route of democracy'. Plural politics is, in general, more firmly established in that
region. Furthermore, essential programmes of decentralization
have been launched in several countries. It remains to be seen,
however, to what extent this tendency can truly disrupt the long
tradition of political centralism.[29] As long as that tradition is maintained—and is combined, moreover, with low levels of rule-ordered
governance—the stage is set for continued elite dominance and,
especially under the auspices of populism, a conflict-ridden political

[29] Constitutional initiatives in countries like Peru and Venezuela have aimed at
strengthening the position of the executive branch of government. That can be seen
as a means of preserving the centralist trend.

culture. India's advantage rests mainly in its long experience with political pluralism and the separation of powers. Conciliatory modes of politics have accordingly been encouraged. To vitalize the system, however, additional improvements, particularly with respect to rule-ordered governance, appear to be needed.

Democracy, in short, is not the product of social and economic forces only. It is also, and to a yet greater extent, the consequence of prevailing institutional conditions.

II

Evolution of State Institutions

6

State Institutions

Hobbes is renowned for having emphasized the necessity of a state for protecting the well-being of society. Only through the cohesive power of the state, he argued, can such institutions as are essential for social life be upheld. But Hobbes was not the first, of course, to recognize the need for a state. Comments to that effect can be found already in the work of Aristotle. What is more, ordinary people have manifested this insight for several millennia through their practical undertakings. Hobbes's contribution lies mainly in the intellectual realm: in elaborating a theoretical rational for these endeavours. If the most fundamental public goods are to be upheld, stable rules of interaction must be in place. And to be effective, Hobbes taught us, these rules must be maintained by the state. Without a solid institutional framework setting the terms of interaction, people are condemned to a life of fear and insecurity. For want of an appropriate institutional structure, social interaction breeds hostility and strife; the end result is 'a war of all against all.' The state, accordingly, is a tool of social advancement. By reducing the costs of intercourse and transaction, it promotes collaboration between people. Hence, it enhances our collective potential.

The state, in other words, is a response to demands from society. It has been 'invented' as an instrument for improving society's collective capacity. This instrument has taken a variety of shapes at different places and times. Major changes in the economic, technological, and military realms have influenced the design of state structures. These structures tend to be enduring, however, and to leave a strong imprint on the organizational and cultural configuration of society. This affects democracy's prospects. Only certain institutional arrangements, tied to a certain mode of state, promote the evolution of the coordination capacities required for the practice of popular rule. I refer to the interactive state. A state of this type, I argue further, has the highest potential for governance, that is, for effectively carrying out its policies. It is also this kind of state that furnishes the best foundations in the long run for economic development. This mode of state, accordingly, is a key instrument of social progress. The problem is that it has proved difficult to put in place. Other modes of states have instead predominated over history: states related, more or less, to the autocratic model championed by Hobbes. As we know, however, the autocratic scenario has been broken. Other modes of states have evolved. Through a voyage back in time, we shall acquaint ourselves with the general traits of this development.

Before delving into the different forms of state, however, we should begin by identifying some of the general features of this institutional creation.

The State

According to Max Weber, who laid the basis for the administrative analysis of the state, the following traits characterize this institution:

1. The state is an organ for the governance of social activities within a delimited geographical zone.
2. Within its territory, the state can govern by means of coercion.
3. The state governs through fixed and clearly discernible institutions enjoying precedence over other societal institutions.

What Weber and his followers, such as Poggi (1990), have stressed as the foremost feature distinguishing the state from other organizations in society is its exercise of coercion—or, more generally, its role as the highest source of legitimacy for the exercise of coercion.[1] The capacity to rule through the exercise of coercion normally requires an ability to punish recalcitrants. This assumes in turn some sort of apparatus for the exercise of force. That the state is primarily characterized by its right to rule through the use of force *vis-à-vis* citizens would seem to be generally accepted. But coercion is not the only means of governance available to the state; it can also direct social behaviour in other ways. To clarify this, it may be fruitful to introduce a categorization proposed by Amitai Etzioni (1968: 96). This author distinguishes relations of three types: coercive, utilitarian, and normative. These involve the use of the following methods of governance (Table 6.1):

Norm enforcement based on coercion (1) finds expression in regulations, which enjoin certain kinds of action and prohibit others.

---

[1] Coercion exercised by actors other than the state—for example, parents or work supervisors—can be legitimized in a law-governed society only by the active or passive sanction of the state.

TABLE 6.1: *Three types of governance*

Relation	Method of enforcement
Coercive	Regulation
Utilitarian	Incentive
Normative	Information

Those breaking such rules are normally subjected to some sort of sanction. It is otherwise in the case of governance founded in a utilitarian relation (2). In this case, citizens are impelled to act in a certain manner by virtue of the benefits to be obtained thereby. Their actions, which in principle are voluntary, are affected by incentives of various kinds. Economic incentives are the most typical, as when citizens can acquire advantages through performing actions of a certain sort, or when they may incur costs if engaged in undesirable behaviour. When, finally, the relation is of a normative kind (3), governance is accomplished through a community of values among those involved, that is, the authorities and the citizens. In this case, citizens allow themselves to be governed because they approve, as a matter of principle, of the measures undertaken. To promote such a spirit in society, the state can undertake informational measures of various sorts (Vedung 1997).

Governance through incentive and governance through information do indeed have a certain advantage. When these methods are applied, citizens act in accordance with the will of the authorities, not because they are forced to, but rather because, out of self-interest or for normative reasons, they choose voluntarily to do so. Thus society is spared the extensive and often costly apparatus of sanction and control normally entailed by governance through regulation. There is also reason to suppose that such methods, generally speaking, are more effective in achieving their goals. When people are induced to act on the basis of their self-interest or normative conviction, the result is usually better. For, as Milton Friedman (1962) once pointed out, it is possible to force people to do many things, but not to do their best. At the same time, it is important to recall that regulation is the only possible alternative in the case of certain primary state functions. Certain basic tasks, like keeping the peace, enforcing a legal system to which all are subject, and so forth, cannot be carried out—in this Vale of Tears, at least—without the use of coercion. Similarly, redistributive policies of most kinds, whereby resources are transferred from one category of citizens to another, necessarily involve a substantial element of regulation. Such transfers can hardly be accomplished on a voluntary basis. Coercion is also normally required to finance long-range investments under the aegis of the state: for example, the building of infrastructure or the establishment of large-scale production and defence facilities. For such projects require broad financing, and they involve delayed returns, which may be of benefit only to future generations; usually, therefore, they cannot be accomplished unless the requisite resources are raised on a mandatory basis. If, furthermore, the government aims at radical changes in the institutional or socio-economic realms, this can normally be realized only by means of imposition. As has been said: 'when you want something very different done very quickly, you have to give people orders' (Dyker 1992: 6). In brief: the more the state engages in redistribution between groups or generations, the more it functions as a producer of basic collective goods, and the more radical its policy approach, the more dependent it becomes on the use of coercion *vis-à-vis* larger or smaller groups in the population.

Given these methods of governance at the disposal of the state, existing states have proved to possess highly variable degrees of 'statehood'. That is to say, their actual ability to direct social activities within their territories has varied greatly. Sometimes, in the case of weak states, it may be a largely juridical kind of statehood that obtains, inasmuch as the institutions which formally are the governing ones have very little governance capacity in practice (Jackson and Rosberg 1982). The weakness of state institutions may be founded in problems of an internal nature, such that the authority of the state is taken over by local power groups outside its sphere of influence (Migdal 1988). A sort of feudal relation thus prevails, inasmuch as real governance is 'enfeoffed' to actors outside the control of the state. But it can also—and sometimes at the same time—be a question of external weakness, that is, pronounced external dependence on the part of the state (Ake 1997; Bhagwati 1997).

When addressing the question of state capacity, it may be helpful to consider the work of Michael Mann (1986*b*). In the spirit of Hobbes and Weber, Mann stresses the necessity of the state: this institution is an answer to society's need for coordination, a need which cannot be met without an element of coercion. The establishment of such an institution has usually meant an increase in the collective capacity of the group or groups in question. Those peoples which have established states have fared better over the course of history than those which have not. Mann divides the power exercised by the state into two categories: the 'despotic' and the 'infrastructural'. The first-mentioned has to do with the power of norm-setting: to what degree is this power hedged in by various restrictions? Where such restrictions are wholly absent or very small, a high degree of despotic power is present.[2] In such cases, the setting of norms is conducted on a more or less discretionary basis. There are few if any restrictions on *what* the state may do or on *how* it may do it.

Turning now to the second form of power—what Mann calls infrastructural power—we see that it does not have to do with the norm-setting competence of the holders of public power, but rather with their ability to *implement* the norms which have been set. This is a question, in other words, of the state's actual steering capacity, its ability to carry out the policies promulgated. It is this infrastructural power—or what may be better termed *implementational* power—we are referring to when we speak of statehood: namely, 'the capacity of the state actually to penetrate civil society, and to implement logistically political decisions throughout the realm' (Mann 1986*b*: 113).

The degree to which the state possesses this capacity depends, according to Mann, on its ability to control certain strategic instruments of coordination, and to exploit them. He points to the quality of the communications system and to other largely technical capacities, which he calls 'logistical' and 'infrastructural techniques'. These concern, above all, the ability of the state to get its 'voice' heard in all parts of the realm—which prior to the era of mass communications, especially before the introduction of railroads and the telegraph, could pose great difficulties. Troublesome geographical conditions could at times put severe restrictions on statehood.[3] In addition to obstacles to communication, which historically have indeed been important, another factor heavily influences the state's ability to assert itself. I refer to the economic resources at its disposal. This capacity applies to all three of the governance methods. In the case of governance through regulation, a sizable apparatus of repression and control is needed, and this naturally incurs considerable costs. Governance through incentive also presupposes access to resources—the more the better—for it requires the ability to dispense benefits, often of a pecuniary kind, to various individuals and groups. Governance through information also requires resources to have its effect. More fundamentally

[2] It bears pointing out that I elaborate somewhat on Mann's conception here.

[3] See, for example, the difference in time required for sending a government dispatch a certain distance in Persia and Russia respectively, as reported by Richard Pipes (1995: 20–1): the messengers in Persia travelled almost four times as fast.

than anything else, access to economic resources circumscribes the actions of the state. The revenue of the state is the state, Edmund Burke remarked.

It is normally an advantage, moreover, to have access to the services of a skilled—that is, professional—apparatus of administration: what Weber called a rational bureaucracy. In addition, as Weber pointed out, governance in all its forms is accomplished more easily when it enjoys legitimacy, and thus some form of acceptance, among the subjects.[4]

The Emergence of States

The state, as we know, is not a modern creation. Yet it is a relatively recent phenomenon in the long wanderings of humanity. Archaeological finds give witness to the existence of states in the Middle East in the seventh millennium BC. These were city-states as a rule, the sway of which extended over a very limited geographical zone. States covering larger areas were subsequently formed. We know of such an early state formation in Mesopotamia in the early fourth millennium BC. Larger states emerged soon thereafter, among other places in Egypt and China (Tilly 1992).

Prior to this time, and in many places till long thereafter, human beings lived in associations of a looser sort. Among so-called hunter-gatherer peoples, such as the Indians in North America and various groups in Africa before colonialism, individuals were collected in small self-governing groups: tribes, clans, extended families, and the like. Often these units lacked distinct geographical boundaries. On account of weather, access to game, and so forth, they commonly moved across territories of considerable size. In organizational terms, they were characterized by a flat, non-hierarchical structure and a high degree of popular rule. The 'public power' was in large part a collective matter: it was exercised by all men capable of bearing arms. Chiefs and other leading persons owed their position largely to popular mandate. Governance was essentially founded in the consent of the group. In such simple communities there was little room for coercion; in case of dissension, members might leave the group or be excluded from it—an outcome which would, however, seriously reduce the strength of the group. In order to safeguard against such developments, adverse as they would be to the interests of the group, a strong

---

[4] Different bases of legitimacy are discussed in Chapter 9.

tradition of trying to reach consensus often developed in such communities. It was through such a spirit of compromise and conformity, coupled with a strong sense of identity within the group, that it was possible to hold the community together without resort to coercion. The group was kept together by a strong 'natural'—essentially ascriptive—affinity among its members. It was also on this strong foundation of kinship that collective governance rested. Governance was based on legitimacy, a strong normative unity within the collective.

The centralization of decision-making often required for the effective conduct of war tended to bring with it, even in these communities, an increased concentration of power in the hands of leaders. At the same time, however, such positions were limited in terms of time and strongly restricted in terms of competence. A 'circulation of elites' was typically practised, such that no one person occupied a superior position on a permanent basis. Moreover, the tendency was to return to the original flat organizational form once hostilities ceased.

In these stateless societies, in other words, a strong form of citizenship was practised. The body of citizens was the community of free men, who were both material producers and warriors. The functions most critical for a society's continued existence—the provision of sustenance and the maintenance of defence from external foes—were thus united in the same hands. There was no material basis, quite simply, for applying a division of labour to these tasks. Society was characterized by a high degree of equality. People were essentially propertyless, for the forms of production in use did not make the accumulation of a surplus possible. At the same time, a spirit of mutuality and reciprocity developed in these societies, which dictated that resources acquired by any given individual be distributed among all members of the group. This communalistic distributive principle, which acknowledged no real right of property, worked against the development of social and economic stratification.

The stateless hunter-gatherer societies were characterized by a high degree of equality in regard to the distribution of power resources. They were also static societies, with a low standard in both cultural and material terms. People were illiterate and often lived at close to subsistence (Mann 1986a; Johnson and Earle 1987; Davies, Davies, and Davies 1992; Bollen and Paxton 1997; van Crevald 999).

The appearance of the territorially extended state has often been associated with the emergence of agricultural society. This shift in the forms of production, which brought great social and economic changes in its wake, is known commonly as the Neolithic Revolution. It took place at different times in different parts of the world. When it occurred, it created a need for a new institutional framework. Economic resources were now available, moreover, which made such a framework possible. At the same time, people settled in one place and made investments in productive facilities. Fields were broken and buildings raised, and, at times, an extensive infrastructure was created, in the form of roads, canals, irrigation systems, and so forth. On account of these developments, together with the fact that products could now be saved and stored, the basis was laid for a palpable accumulation of wealth. With the onset of agricultural production, improved productivity and higher living standards usually followed. At the same time, an appreciably more stratified and unequal society came into being.

The investments made in fixed facilities and the production results thereby achieved increased the need for protection from external foes. For among nearby peoples, the incentive immediately arose to plunder the riches that had been accumulated; the ravages of the Vikings and the Mongols come to mind. A developed public apparatus was needed to mount the requisite defence. Such an agency was also required for building and maintaining infrastructure. It was necessary, then, to establish a state. Fixed public organs, accordingly, came into being which held sway within their territory by means of coercion, and which were able by such means to appropriate the resources needed for the performance of necessary collective tasks.

In the larger centralized units thereby created, better conditions also obtained for the economic 'risk management' which human associations of various sorts have often sought to achieve. This was usually, in primitive economies, a matter of gathering surpluses, primarily of foodstuffs, which could be used during periods when access to such goods was scarce: for example, in times of harvest failure. With the economies of scale yielded by the state, it became possible to do this in a manner which was safer and more efficient. The more numerous the persons comprising the foundation, and the larger the geographical area covered, normally the better was the guarantee against starvation and misfortune for the individual. Many of the early states functioned in large part as 'storage states', inasmuch as essential goods were collected in large storage centres administered by the state. These depots could be used in times of need for purposes of 'welfare', that is, to distribute food to a corner of the country afflicted by famine. First and foremost, however, these stores were for the state itself. It was these accumulated resources which sustained the leaders of the state, and the military and administrative personnel at their command (Johnson and Earle 1987: 208ff).

Agriculture is normally a highly stationary mode of production, and the same may be said of producers therein. In an agricultural society, people tend to live out their lives close to the 'turf' that sustains them. They are not, as hunter-gatherer peoples usually have been, constantly on the move in an effort to secure their subsistence. This means that an agricultural society is easier to control. It is a simpler matter to collect taxes and to require military service. The 'marshall' knows, as a rule, where he can find his taxpayer and his recruit: in the fields. In contrast to the freer life in hunter-gatherer communities, the conditions of existence in an agricultural society normally offer no simple exit to those seeking to elude various centrally laid-down decrees: a fact which facilitates, naturally enough, the exercise of coercion against citizens. When production is carried out on large plantations or *latifundia*, and where the producers are collected within a concentrated area, the prospects for control are especially good. Thus the opportunities for extracting a large surplus from the labour force improve as well. The same goes for agricultural production centred on large-scale facilities for irrigation or terracing. An autocratic state can emerge more easily in such societies. The opposite is true of societies in which production is carried out on small farms spread out over the countryside. As a generalization it may therefore be said, *ceteris paribus*, that economies based on the cultivation of sugar or rice facilitate a greater concentration of political power than do economies centred on the production of wool or wheat (Moore 1967: 419–20; Usher 1981: 35).

As a form of production, agriculture is at once more labour-intensive and more productive of wealth. Herein lies a tendency towards increased social stratification. A division of labour may take place, such that the tasks of producers and of warriors are separated. Worsening cleavages may furthermore arise among producers: between owners of land and of associated means of production and those bereft of property. One basis for such a development lies in the frequently restricted access to arable land. When the two cleavages mentioned coincide—as they have done many times in agrarian societies, such that those in leading military positions are also large-scale owners of land—an increasingly fixed social hierarchy takes shape. A permanent upper stratum in society emerges, in the form of an aristocracy of some kind: barons, big men, warlords, or the like.

It is not to be wondered at, against this background, that the appearance of agricultural society has been seen as the demise of the old, 'original' system of popular rule. It is often at the agrarian stage that the foundations for social hierarchy and a permanent division of power have been laid. Oppression came with the plough, averred the Arab philosopher Ibn Kaldun. And according to Karl Marx it is the division of property, the origins of which lay in agrarian society, that is the source of the social stratification and exploitation which has plagued the pathways of humanity through-out its history. The historical task of humanity, in Marx' view, is to resurrect the egalitarian stateless community it has lost (Gellner 1994).

The Hobbesian Scenario

The state formations which proved lasting often developed in such a manner that one among several existing barons or warlords rose to predominance, and was able to subordinate the others (Tilly 1992: 14–15; Olson 1993). That a strong man takes over in this way can be seen, in view of the circumstances that would otherwise prevail, as constituting a clear advantage. It means there is less room for internal struggles, and that society is better protected from external foes. Under the aegis of a single prince, moreover, the prospects are substantially better for establishing such legal arrangements as make productive economic activity possible. Enterprise is favoured by the prevalence of stable and predictable institutions (North 1990; Olson 1993). That prince capable of estab-lishing such an order has normally been able to reckon, Weber (1987) notes, with broad popular support.[5] The alternative has often been internal feuds, the absence of legal order, and an ensuing economic and cultural decline: a 'warlord-syndrome', as we in mod-ern times recognize from such countries as Liberia and Somalia, which cannot now be said to function as states (Reno 1998).

It was this threat of which Thomas Hobbes warned. Against the background not least of the protracted civil war that plagued his

[5] The following description of the time prior to the expansion of the Inca Empire in South America supports this argument: 'The constant state of war had high eco-nomic and psychological costs that made the regional organization and peace of the empire desirable. Warfare was over land; essentially each community fought to pro-tect the land necessary to its survival. The imperial superstructure imposed regional peace and a system of legal rights of land in return for labour obligations' (Johnson and Earle 1987: 257).

homeland, England, during the first half of the 1600s, Hobbes affirmed the strong princely power that had been established in several countries in Europe at the time. He was an adherent, in other words, of a system of unrestricted, absolutist rule. His argument was that absolutism was appreciably better than the likely alternative. Many would doubtless agree, faced with such a choice. Sooner a prince who maintains order and keeps the peace than anarchy, perpetual dissension, and the subversion of the state. Hobbes's solution to the well-known problem of collective action—the difficulty of achieving cooperation between self-interested actors—was to resort to 'third-party enforcement'. The purport hereof was that an actor—Leviathan—who stands free in relation to the citizens is entrusted with restraining their behaviour. Through coercion, citizens are made to cooperate.[6]

This may seem all well and good. Yet the Hobbesian objective is not easy to realize, experience shows. The monopolization of norm-giving power may be one thing. The capacity of the state actually to govern is another.

From the standpoint of governance it is advantageous, first of all, to be able to establish a rationally functioning administration. With access to a corps of competent, well-motivated administrators responsible for operative tasks, the leaders of the state can more effectively govern their territory. Those autocratic regimes which have succeeded in creating an apparatus which functions professionally have usually been appreciably more stable and long-lasting than others. As historical illustrations may be adduced the pharaonic empire of Egypt and the empires of China and Rome; in large part these were, at the height of their strength, bureaucratically organized regimes (Weber 1987: 65; van Crevald 1999: 128).

However, the servants of the state should not merely possess professional skills. They should also be faithful and loyal towards the leaders of the state. If the system of governance is to be well-suited to its task, the 'agents' of the state should not just be induced to do

[6] It bears mentioning that the governing unit in Hobbes may be either an individual or a collective actor: the Soveraigne Instituted is exercised by a 'Man, or Assembly of Men' (1982: 228). It should further be noted that sovereignty, according to Hobbes, has certain limits. The object is to protect citizens from the anarchy and violence which they would otherwise visit upon each other: 'the End of this Institution, is the Peace and Defence of them all', he declares (1982: 232). The consequence of this is that citizens may not be subjected to such coercion on the part of the sovereign as entails a comparable threat to their lives: 'Subjects have Liberty to defend their own bodies, even against them that lawfully invade them' (1982: 268). Regimes that inflict terror on their citizens—of which there have been many, in modern times not least—do not have, in other words, the benediction of Hobbes.

things in the right way—which is the administrative perspective; they should also be impelled to do the right things, that is, those things the state leaders want them to do—which is a question of political dominance. Not seldom have these two perspectives on governance come into conflict with each other. The risk is always present that the administrative apparatus, through the internal governance resources at its disposal, can acquire for itself a substantial measure of independence, and in this way counteract external control, that is, the political dominance of superiors. The example of the Prussian bureaucracy, which was unusually well-developed for its time, bears recalling here. It worked extremely well, technically and functionally speaking, and it constituted the operative backbone in the emerging German military state. But precisely on account of this—its standing as a guarantee for the efficient maintenance of the regime—it could attain for itself a considerable measure of autonomy. As a consequence, it could be hard to subject to political direction. A good many royal initiatives, including some reform attempts on the part of Frederick the Great, came to grief because the bureaucracy quite simply turned a deaf ear. From China, where the bureaucracy occupied a comparable standing for long periods, there have been similar reports. It was the existence of a professional bureaucratic apparatus, in large part, which stabilized the different regimes that governed China. It was this body which induced the vast administrative machinery to function. At the same time, the bureaucracy often functioned as a conservative institution blocking political reforms (Rosenberg 1958: 60ff; Weber 1987: 87ff; Theobald 1990: 20ff; van Crevald 1999: 136ff; see also Wuthnow 1986: 109–10). The advantages, in terms of the administrative capacity which a professionally organized administration can offer, must accordingly be weighed against the risks of losing political dominance. For the apparatus may not prove loyal to the 'lord' it is supposed to serve.

The problem becomes especially acute when subordination and loyalty are lacking within the armed forces. The military has a unique standing in terms of resources. First, it controls the primary means for the application of coercion. For a regime which bases its position first and foremost on such a form of governance, the capacity to command military units is of the utmost importance: should the regime's ability to command be undermined, its very existence is threatened. Military forces furthermore possess an organizational coordination and discipline which other groups in society often lack. This coordination capacity is not just a consequence of the hierarchical form of command. It is also founded on the *esprit de corps*—the strong sense of identity and internal solidarity—which frequently develops in military ranks. (Huntington 1968) The military apparatus holds, in brief, a vital governance resource in its hands, and its members often possess a substantial measure of social capital, both normative and organizational speaking. This makes it, potentially, an extremely important political factor. The examples hereof are innumerable. In modern history, Latin America in particular has many times witnessed how the 'men on horseback' have been able to dominate political life. Further back in time, too, this pattern was often pronounced. Under the empire in ancient Rome, it was to a high degree the military which determined who occupied the highest and 'all-powerful' office in the state. It was the Senate, in theory, which was charged with the naming of each new ruler. But this was often mainly a fiction. In practice, it was necessary that the chosen candidate enjoy the confidence of the army. It was frequently the praetorian guard—the military unit the supposed charge of which was to protect the person of the ruler— that functioned as the emperor-maker. It also happened that the guard interfered to strike the ruler down (Grant 1990: 28–9). Conditions in the Ottoman Empire were periodically similar. Here it was above all elite troops within the army—the Janissanary corps—who were able to exercise a decisive influence: 'Since they possessed a virtual monopoly of physical force at the centre of government, the Janissanites were able to establish a sort of unstable corporate military dictatorship during the late sixteenth and early seventeenth centuries . . . Between 1618 and 1730, no less than six sultans were disposed by their own soldiers' (Hale 1994: 8). The Janissanites also came to function as a long-standing effective block on any thoroughgoing attempts to change the military and administrative order, which became more and more antiquated with the passage of time (Hale 1994: 13ff).

In order to check tendencies towards disobedience or even usurpation on the part of subordinates, aspirants to bureaucratic office in the Chinese empire were required to undergo a long period of training. Besides guaranteeing a high level of cultural and technical proficiency on the part of future servants of the state, this training, which resulted in special civil-servant degrees, aimed in large part at instilling aspirants with the spirit of subordination and duty expressed in the Confucian doctrine of the state. A developed system of rewards was furthermore applied, such that high positions in society could be reached only through positions in the state apparatus. In China, there was no aristocracy of birth or stratum of landlords in possession of large properties. Access to landed properties of a comparable sort could be had only through enfeoffments from the state that were limited in duration. Conditions were similar for long periods in the realm of the pharaohs. All essential property in Egyptian society was controlled by the state. It was position within the state, which was tied to loyalty to the ruler, that guaranteed position within society. A system of dominance similar in its essentials, characterized by the establishment of an elite stratum dependent on the leaders of the state, developed in Russia in tsarist times. Peter the Great introduced an arrangement whereby noble status and access to landed property—the foremost source of wealth and social prestige—was tied to the occupancy of state offices, which the tsar could control. Success in life, in an outward sense, was connected, in other words, to standing in the public apparatus, and to demonstrated political loyalty (Weber 1987: 131ff; Jones 1987: 210ff; Downing 1992: 38ff, 48ff). Such an arrangement was also applied by the regime that succeeded the empire of the tsars. As in all regime shifts, other political loyalties were now at a premium. But the general method, whereby political dominance was established by means of dependence, was the same. One difference, however, was that this logic penetrated much more deeply into the life of society than during earlier epochs, on account of the state's far greater control over societal resources in the Soviet period. This method of political hegemony, based on the control and allocation of privileges, was known as the *nomenklatura* system (Voslensky 1984).

The *nomenklatura* state would seem generally to offer, when it can be established, an opportunity for the most unrestrained absolutistic rule. Through its direct possession of vital societal resources, the regime can, with the help of a recruitment policy through which it dispenses economic and social privileges, control its apparatus effectively, and thereby its population as well.[7]

In addition, there has been, since time immemorial, a series of other standard measures for ensuring political subordination and

[7] Alongside the examples here considered of this type of governance may be mentioned the Ottoman empire (Hale 1994) and the Inca Empire of South America (Mann 1986a). A distinctive form of the politico-administrative logic of dependence could be observed in the pattern of recruitment obtaining in the in the Ottoman Empire and elsewhere in the Orient. It involved the appointment of serfs or slaves, often prisoners of war from subjugated nations, to important positions. These persons, who were often viewed with contempt by the population they governed, enjoyed their position of power solely through the protection of the ruler, to whom they could therefore be expected to nourish a keen loyalty (Weber 1987: 115; Wuthnow 1986: 110–11).

dominance; and they are diligently practised in many places today.[8] They include:

- assigning offices in large degree to relatives or close kindred—in respect of culture or opinion—on whose loyalty one can naturally depend;
- instituting brief periods in office and a constant transfer of officials, so that subordinates never have an opportunity to establish an autonomous power base through their position. Accordingly, continues reshuffles should take place; and

- establishing a system for supervising officials; subordinates may even be directly spied on. Together with severe penalties and uncertain legal procedures, measures of this sort can furnish a strong incentive to acquiesce in the wishes of the state leadership. Patterns of unpredictability and fear have in all times served as effective tools of political dominance.

It goes without saying that methods which promote political obedience and dominance do not always contribute to a manner of conducting operations which is most suitable and efficient from an administrative or military point of view. The relatives and faithful supporters appointed to certain functions may, as Napoleon's crew of siblings may be taken to illustrate, be little suited for, or even interested in, the tasks to which they are assigned. Followers of this sort are loyal but no more. Instituting brief periods in office and a constant rotation among positions scarcely contributes, moreover, to the development of knowledge and competence on the part of officials. Nor does it create a motivation to take on existing problems and difficulties within the agency in question—why exert oneself? One will shortly be elsewhere! The inspection and auditing of agencies and officials is a natural element in a functioning bureaucracy. If such activities assume a broad scope, however, and are marked by secretive and police-style methods, they can easily cast a paralysing shadow over the operations of the bureaucracy. This particularly applies if it is hard to know in advance what constitutes 'incorrect behaviour' at the same time that the consequences thereof are severe. Such an environment scarcely encourages independence and initiative on the part of officials. It contributes, rather, to passivity and fear. Briefly put, ensuring both efficiency and obedience within the apparatus at the disposal of state leaders is a difficult balancing act, and at times an impossible one.

---

[8] A detailed account of the methods reported here is provided by Migdal (1988: 202ff). See also Wintrobe (1998: 33ff).

A fundamental challenge for the autocratic model is ensuring the ability to rule without the acceptance and support of the people. Often this is a question of forcing through the will of state leaders in direct contravention of the desires of large population groups— even, perhaps, of an overwhelming majority. If it is to succeed in so doing, the regime must command extensive powers of coercion. It must possess, in other words, a substantial repressive capacity. At the end of the day it is fear, as Montesquieu pointed out, which rules under a system of this sort. It is the knowledge of a state's repressive capacity which induces citizens to submit. Concretely, this means the regime must be able to field large-scale military and police forces in its behalf. This requires that the state produce revenues of a sufficient size. This presupposes the existence of an adequate tax base, that is, a society possessed of sufficient economic strength as to be capable of sustaining the taxes that must be levied. The general problem, in the words of Charles Tilly, is this:

As rulers form and transform states, they and their agents consume large quantities of resources, especially resources that lend themselves to military applications: men, arms, transport, food. Those resources are, for the most part, already embedded in other organizations and social relations: households, manors, feudal obligations, connections among neighbors. The ruler's problem is to extract the essential resources from those organizations and social relations, while ensuring that someone will reproduce and yield similar resources in the future. (Tilly 1992: 131)

A useful means to this end is provided by geographical expansion. By subduing other peoples militarily, state leaders have been able to make the costs of the system's maintenance fall largely outside their borders of their own country or core region. The most abiding autocracies from history of which we know have all been successful in this respect. Through lengthy expansion they have moulded themselves into vast empires, which has meant that the regimes in question have gained access to colossal areas as a taxation base. As long as the expansion continues, and to the extent that the newly won territories are reasonably easily defended, this financing method can be a brilliant affair. The result is an increase in the power and splendour of the regime. At the same time, the regime can usually count on a considerable measure of support from the core population, which may also obtain a share of the tribute.[9] And if, due to the stresses of war, the regime's legitimacy among its own

[9] As noted by Pipes with regard to the imperial expansion of Russia: 'Every major conquest . . . was promptly followed by massive handouts of land to servitors and monasteries and the opening of the acquired territories to peasant colonization' (1995: 119).

citizens should waver, it can rely for its continued power on the large military resources it has been able to amass. For these can be put to work for domestic purposes too.

The problem is that the military expansion eventually reaches its limit, for geographical and logistical reasons, and/or as a result of tough resistance from the peoples to be subdued (Kennedy 1987). The 'imperialist standstill' thereby ensuing can become extremely trying. The difficulty is that the constant preparedness for war required to defend the territories that have been won entails the need for a permanent military capacity of great scope. This requires a continued burdensome collection of resources, which must be gathered in all essentials from within the state's own borders. When, on account of local attempts at revolt, or as a consequence of pressure from surrounding states, the military demands intensify, the need for revenue can become so great as to weigh heavily even on the core population sustaining the regime. In its fiscal ardour, the regime may levy such tributes on society as make it difficult, on account of their scope and/or the heavy-handed and arbitrary manner of their collection, to maintain the vitality and health of the economy. Such a policy, which may become highly burdensome for citizens, can be upheld over the long run because the citizens—the subjects of taxation—are without a voice in the matter. This is the consequence of the autonomy of the autocratic state. The result is economic retardation, which means that society's ability to satisfy the fiscal demands of the state diminishes. The regime tends in this way to erode its own tax base. That in fact has been the fate of many once-impressive imperial states. The Roman and the Ottoman empires can be mentioned as historical examples; the Soviet Union is a recent case in point.[10]

---

[10] Michael Grant (1990: 57) gives the following accounts from the late Roman Empire: 'A terrible dilemma had arisen. There were no doubt whatever that the state had to have the revenue if it was to survive; and indeed the insufficiency of such revenue was one of the reasons why Rome fell—because the Romans could no longer maintain their army. Yet the collection of this utterly necessary national income imposed frightful miseries'. A fundamental weakness of the Roman state lay in the fact that, in its brutal efforts to equip and arm itself, it ended up undermining its fiscal and social base: 'one of the main reasons why the collapse occurred was because the "free" population, which had to provide most of the Imperial revenue, was so severely ravaged by these tax demands that it could not pay up any longer and, in consequence, ceased to be free at all, so that scarcely a trace of any viable commonwealth survived, and the empty husk of a community which alone remained could no longer resist the invaders' (Grant 1990: 68; see also Finer 1997 I: 586ff). In the Ottoman Empire, when the expansion phase came to an end, an inordinate intensification of internal fiscal exploitation ensued. As a result, large parts of the realm were practically ruined (Jones 1987: 175ff; Hale 1994: 7ff). As for

An autocratic regime without access to necessary economic resources is a regime in deterioration. While in its heyday such a regime tends to exhibit a markedly centralized structure, which entails a firm grasp on the vital parts of the state apparatus, the trend in its days of decline is usually in the direction of fragmentation. The apparatus now gradually breaks up, so that office-holders in different sectors assume for themselves an increasing autonomy. The enfeoffments and privileges, which had earlier contributed to a strict political domination, can be controlled by the central power no longer. These 'prebends' are 'appropriated' by their occupants, as Weber (1987) puts it, the typical result being the establishment of local elites which are free-standing and refractory *vis-à-vis* the state (Tilly 1992: 142).[11]

In this way autocratic regimes have broken down. The process often follows a general pattern. To begin with, the central power starts to lose its grip on the resource aggregation required to sustain its governance capacity. In the area of recruitment, moreover, local officials are able to acquire substantial autonomy, on account of their increased autonomy in terms of control over resources 'in the field'. Through their control over resources within their domains, they can direct internal recruitment and gain a more stable position *vis-à-vis* the central power. A central right of command remains, but it becomes ever more restricted in practice, for the central authorities lack the power to back up their words with force. When, in the end, subordination in regard to norm-setting dissolves

the Soviet Union, it has been estimated that defence costs during the 1980s came to 23% of the country's GNP. By way of comparison, the US spent 7% and the European Union countries 3% on average. The enormous military burden in combination with an economy that had completely halted was a root cause of the collapse of the Soviet Empire (Linz and Stepan 1996: 240–1; Nove 1989; Dyker 1992; Lane 1996).

[11] The Roman and Ottoman Empires ended up in a long process of disintegration; to an increasing degree the realm was governed by autonomous local strongmen. The same happened in China. At the end of the empire the trustworthy 'revenue pump' which used to serve the regime had run almost dry. The lion's share of the funds was kept by governors and other local figures, who functioned in large part as independent rulers of their domains (Skocpol 1979; Jones 1987; Fairbank 1992). A process of distinctive disintegration was notable in the Soviet Union too. Pure 'baronies' were established in the different parts of the system. Usually these autonomous groupings were regionally rooted. These coalitions of influential people, referred to as 'family groups', were maintained through the use of patronage. To a great extent, the resources distributed were locally extracted, through control—sometimes on a purely illegal basis—of the surpluses generated by economic activities within each region. This development culminated during Brezhnev's time as party leader (Gill 1994; Keep 1995).

as well—whereupon a local policy autonomy has in practice been established—the feudal structure is a fact. Titular and symbolic remnants of the old hierarchy may be maintained, to be sure, as was the case late in the day in the Roman and Ottoman empires. But it is only a matter of time before that shell too is broken.

The period following the fall of an autocratic regime has often seen the appearance of a similar regime in the place of the old. The prevalent trajectory—the rise and fall of state capacity—has thus tended, albeit at varying speeds, to be repeated. This process has been most abiding and recurrent in China: 'The Chinese statehood existed more than two thousand years. Over this period over twenty dynasties succeeded each other. Each of them started with the dictatorship of a military ruler and ended up as a decaying bureaucracy, with a puppet emperor at the top of a pyramid of power' (Korchak 1994: 52). It has also happened that the fall of a regime has brought with it a descent into that anarchical and stateless condition of which Hobbes warned. In large part this was China's fate, for example, after the fall of the empire.

We also know, however, that a third 'scenario' has been possible. In this scenario, elaborate forms of civil coordination have been possible without third-party enforcement. Civil order, which was the main objective in Hobbes, can here be upheld in association with political pluralism and freedom. It is the presence within society itself of a far-reaching coordination capacity which makes this possible. Such a capacity is hard to develop, clearly, under autocratic rule, for the latter tends to paralyze society. The potential for coordination, which is a matter of strong citizenship, develops most favourably within the context of a different mode of state. In what follows, we shall acquaint ourselves with the historical evolution of this institutional setting.

7

A New Mode of State

The state is the fixed form for coordination which human beings have created for the maintenance of social peace and the development of production and welfare. The state has proved to be a necessary, albeit not sufficient, organizational precondition for such progress. In their large-scale territorial form, states have often, as described earlier, come into being through coordination from above. A 'public entrepreneur' has been able, primarily through repressive means, to subdue various territories and peoples, and to lay the groundwork for a lasting state. The state power—or the prince—has built up an administrative apparatus making possible the appropriation of a considerable proportion of society's resources. The more efficient and penetrating this collection of resources has been, the more autonomous and detached the state has been able to make itself from society. This coordination from above—governance through imposition—has been possible to maintain for as long as the requisite infusion of resources has been assured. Where this infusion has diminished, the typical result has been disintegration, and sometime pure chaos. The latter alternative has generally been, from the standpoint of citizens, clearly worse than the former.

But aside from strict governance through imposition on the one hand, and the dissolution of social order brought on by state disintegration on the other, there is a further option. This is a state which manages to establish regular forms for combined action with society. It is an interactive state, one that is open for intercourse in regulated ways with its citizens. It is the emergence of this type of state which has laid the institutional basis for developments in the direction of broader popular rule.

In the Middle Ages a process of such nature started in Europe. In a manner that was historically unique, a form of state was there created which came to constitute the institutional foundation of that democratic form of government which was later to spread across the world. We shall now examine the main elements in this development.

The European Miracle

In the latter years of the Roman Empire, an advancing disintegration and administrative decline took place in Europe. This process, which was manifested in declining communications and a palpable economic retrogression, continued after the empire had been abolished in the fifth century and the new Germanic principalities been established. These princely houses were generally fragile. They enjoyed but weak legitimacy among the largely Latin population they ruled, and the administrative and financial resources at their disposal were inferior. A concentration of forces could be observed, certainly, under the Merovingians in France in the 700s. Upon having thwarted a large-scale Muslim attempt at invading the heartland of Europe, the Frankish kings succeeded, by means of militarist expansion, in subduing the larger part of western and central Europe. The ambition was to recreate the unity and splendour of the Roman Empire. As a token thereof, King Charlemagne had himself crowned emperor in Rome in 800. What was created, however, was not the Roman Empire as once it had been. Limited by deficient communications and bereft of a developed bureaucracy, the Frankish realm lacked the fiscal and administrative capacity needed to support its territorial claims. It lacked, for example, the capacity to maintain a standing army in peacetime. 'Such empire', it has been said, 'had more pulling it apart than holding it together' (Downing 1992: 19).[1] The consequence was a speedy disintegration. The realm was divided, and it decayed into a highly decentralized warlord system. In many areas, a full-scale system of local self-government emerged. During several subsequent centuries, the peoples of Europe were plagued by ceaseless struggles among competing warlords, and by the recurrent ravagings of plundering hordes from without.

In the course of the period here considered, the Catholic Church established itself as a significant power factor in Europe. The foundations of its position had already been laid during the Roman Empire. As a guarantor of the spiritual unity of the empire, the church had already enjoyed a strong standing at the time of Christianity's establishment in the 300s. It also gradually assumed

[1] Basically, the Carolingian Empire was a machine of plunder, of great proportions. Its coherence could be maintained only as long as geographical expansion, to the benefit of both warrior aristocracy and sovereign, was still possible. When that phase came to an end, the Carolingian aristocrats turned to domestic competition for increasing their power and wealth (Ertman 1997: 45–6).

an important administrative role. As a consequence of the regime's diminishing power of governance, the performance of general duties on the local and regional levels had to be assigned to the wide-ranging organization—that is, of bishops and subordinate priests—which the church was able to supply. In return, the church was granted substantial immunities and privileges. The clergy were exempted from taxes and granted the right to establish their own courts. In this way, the church came to develop its own legal tradition: that of canon law.

In the weak principalities established after the collapse of the empire, the supportive capacity of the church was still ardently sought. The Carolingians, for instance, relied in large measure on the legitimacy of the church, and on the administrative network at its disposal: not for nothing had Charlemagne had himself crowned emperor by the pope. Also, the emperors of German lineage, who sought with increasing success in the early eleventh century to restore the now-divided empire, used the capacity offered by the church to a high degree. The church contributed through its missionary activities to spiritual integration and sentiments of affinity within the population. It had also come upon extensive properties, among other things as a result of plentiful donations. Indeed, it became the largest landowner in Europe. It had a significant capacity, moreover, to collect taxes from its parishes. Its economic foundations were very solid on account of this. The church was also the primary trustee of writing and of bookish learning, which the emerging state could use to advantage.

Since its beginnings, the Catholic Church had stood at the disposal of the state. But it had done this in exchange for various rights and privileges, and its internal self-government had been confirmed. Since its early years, moreover, the church had proclaimed the limitation of the princely power. Even the prince was subject to divine law, and it was the role of the religious profession, in particular the pope, to interpret this law. There was also a well-developed legal tradition within the church—manifested in canon law—which could be wielded as a 'weapon' against a despotic worldly rule.

In practice, however, the autonomy of the church had been sharply restricted. In the collaboration between church and state, the latter had often acquired, due to the former's lack of military capacity, a decisive influence over the appointment of church officials. This had long been the case at the local level, in the choice of bishops and lesser officials. With the emergence of the German emperors, the worldly power came to prevail on the highest level also: a number of popes were in practice appointed by the emperor. This then changed in the late eleventh century, from which point a number of forceful popes, supported from below by a reform movement promoting spiritual purity among the clergy, successfully prosecuted the fight for autonomy from the emperor. This was the so-called Investiture struggle. In his defence, the pope could mobilize the support of the many nobles and princes opposed to the establishment of a strong imperial power. After many twists and turns, including the emperor's famous journey to Canossa, the result was a kind of compromise. Church officials would be appointed by the pope, but confirmed by the emperor as well. Compared with the conditions previously obtaining, this was undeniably a success for the church. Thereby strengthened, the pope could adopt a strictly hierarchical order for the church, with a large administrative apparatus at the centre. Through his control over this organization, which covered a large geographical area and commanded great resources, the pope became a power of rank in European affairs. The church had no army of its own, of course. Yet, through alliances with various princes and, in Italy, with the powerful cities, an effective front against the emperor could be maintained. In this way, the imperial power was weakened once more. The formal confirmation of the empire's effective dissolution came with the so-called Golden Bull of 1356, which stipulated that the emperor would be chosen by the German princes; the latter, moreover, were guaranteed a far-reaching autonomy within their territories (Hintze 1975: 314ff; Bendix 1978: 27ff, 130ff; Downing 1992: 19ff; Spruyt 1994: 43ff; Ertman 1997: 53ff).

An empire embracing all of Europe could not, accordingly, be brought into being. Nor has it proved possible at any later time to establish such a state, on any abiding basis, at least. Rather, a multiplicity of independent states emerged, which were able, on account of their increasing fiscal and administrative capacity, to attain a dominant position within their territories. Nevertheless, the powers of the princely houses thus established throughout Europe were usually sharply limited. The church and its claims remained. Other groups too, in time, demanded similar privileges and rights. Foremost among these was the powerful feudal aristocracy.

The feudal system that developed in Europe was primarily military in form. The pattern had been set by the Carolingian regime, which portioned out confiscated lands as a source of provision to its cavalry, the most important military unit. As the short-lived empire disintegrated, these relocated soldiers became largely autonomous

within their areas. Both the conduct of defence and the maintenance of civil order were undertaken increasingly in decentralized
forms. The local lord, who had been enfeoffed large properties for
his maintenance, came in this way to perform both military and
other public functions. He maintained preparedness through the
retention of a military force, and on his estate he presided over a
court responsible for juridical and administrative questions within
his fief. Entrenched behind their fortifications—castles of ever
greater dimensions were being built—these local captains were a
powerful counter-weight to the central power emerging in many of
the states of Europe beginning in the 1100s.

This powerful stratum—the feudal aristocracy—often took the
side of the church against the princely power. In general the aristocracy called, as did the church, for an electoral kingship, together
with clear restrictions on the decisional competence of the sovereign. For its own part it demanded, as did the church, the confirmation of its immunities and independent status through a declaration
of privileges and rights. In many cases these demands were
granted; the princes could do little else, on account of their weak
position. With the English Magna Carta (1215) as the prototype,
such guarantees were extended in many European countries.
Another item on the aristocracy's list, and on the church's, was the
demand for participation in state governance through representation. This demand too was met in many cases. The late Middle
Ages—from 1200 on—was the dawn—and a very lively one, at
times—of parliamentary assemblies.

In its internal structure, the feudal order was a hierarchical system of contracts among the participating parties. A lord concluded
a contract with a vassal, and the latter in turn entered into a similar agreement with a vassal of his own. According to the terms of
the contract, the vassal was to be granted a fief in exchange for a
commitment to place soldiers at the disposal of his lord. This pyramidal structure notwithstanding, the European feudal system contained several features serving to strengthen the position of the
subordinate party. It was a question, to begin with, of a contract:
thus, a voluntary agreement that could be cancelled. In this contract there was, furthermore, a critical element of mutuality: both
parties committed themselves to extending protection and aid to
the other in case of need. The vassal's standing was further reinforced by the fact that the contract was the object of legal regulation. Thus the vassal enjoyed a legally recognized autonomy, and in
case of conflict could see his case adjudicated. He had the right of an
open trial under the aegis of persons other than his lord. Also of

importance was the fact that a person could, through his fiefs, be the vassal of several lords. As a rule this reinforced his independence, since the different lords could be played off against each other. The European feudal system had been founded at a time when lords in the lower—that is, local—levels of the military hierarchy enjoyed a strong position. And when, in the late Middle Ages, fiefs were in most cases made hereditary, the pluralist and decentralized character of the system was strengthened (Hintze 1975: 33–4; Poggi 1978: 20ff, 30; Downing 1992: 23ff; Spruyt 1994: 38–9; Pipes 1995: 49ff; Ertman 1997: 48ff; Finer 1997 II: 855ff).

In order to illustrate the very special nature of the arrangements established in Europe, it may be instructive to consider the standing of the church and the aristocracy on other continents, including the south-eastern reaches of Europe. In the Byzantine Empire, the hold of the emperor over the Orthodox Church had been firm since the beginning. According to official doctrine, the emperor was the deputy of God on earth, with the right to govern both state and church autocratically. The emperor filled the leading posts within the church as he saw fit. There could be no talk on the church's part of any holy law standing over the worldly prince, and limiting his actions. Instead the church became the obedient instrument of the autocratic imperial power. In the Islamic world, for its part, there had of tradition been no separation between worldly and spiritual powers. The two spheres were seen as an organic unity; the deeds of Mohammed himself were a clear sign of this. It was in the Ottoman Empire, which became the dominant state in the Islamic world during the Middle Ages, that an organizational division first took place between the military-bureaucratic side of the state and its spiritual administration. Thus, a free-standing church organization was created. Its foremost dignitary, the mufti of Istanbul, had the highest authority where interpreting the holy law was concerned—a law which also embraced secular life. The mufti had the right, formally speaking, to cancel, or any rate postpone, the decisions of the sultan. In practical terms, however, this prerogative was without force. The powers of the sultan were unrestrained. The church organization was in reality subordinate to the central power, in whose hands all resources were concentrated. In China as well, religious forces were unable to threaten those wielding worldly power. The occupant of the imperial throne was regarded, like the pharaohs of Egypt, as a holy man: the Son of Heaven. No churchly body, as such things are understood in the West, existed in China. The dominant 'religion', Confucianism, was essentially a secular doctrine—and one strongly affirming authority—and it had no proper clergy.

'Confucianism became a state-sponsored doctrine of the empire, while ambitious officials assisted autocratic rule' (Bendix 1978: 57). In other parts of the world, in short, the centre for counter-power successfully established in Europe by the Catholic Church was lacking (Anderson 1978: 393–4; Bendix 1978: 35ff, 49ff, 95; Bendix 1986: 31–2; Finer 1997 II: 613ff; van Crevald 1999: 38ff).

As regards the position of the aristocracy on other continents, dependence on the central power—and a corresponding absence of autonomy—was the usual state of affairs. Conditions in China were described earlier.[2] Despite the entirely different state structure that emerged in India, where a splintered state system obtained, the position of the aristocracy was in one essential respect like that in China. Aristocrats were completely dependent on the state for their position and their livelihood. One difference, however, was that positions in India were allocated on a discretionary basis; it was the favour of the prince that counted. In China, by contrast, a much more rational and bureaucratic method of recruitment to privileged offices was used. In the Ottoman Empire, the dominance of the central power over officials was marked. Here the state was the owner of almost all arable land. Persons, often slaves, who had been recruited to the bureaucracy and to elite military units were rewarded with landed estates, which they could utilize for a specific period. There was, strictly speaking, no aristocratic stratum in the Ottoman Empire, for there were no hereditary privileges. Enfeoffments in the form of landed property were temporary, and holdings were rotated. In addition, the holders of such lands lacked juridical and administrative authority over their peasants. Nor could they determine the land rent, which was carefully regulated by the state. This arrangement was undeniably advantageous to the peasants—in India, by contrast, aristocrats could run things as they liked at the local level; conditions in Russia came to be similar. But this applied only in the heyday of the empire. When the geographical expansion of the empire came to an end, a lengthy period of degeneration ensued. With fiscal decline came administrative decay of a thoroughgoing character. The state's capacity to govern and to restrain its local potentates now became far less. The sultans developed a system of rule whereby, in return for the requisite tributes, the governors of the various territories were actually given a free hand *vis-à-vis* their subjects. In order to hold the system together, the leaders of the regime constantly appointed, dismissed, and transferred the incumbents of these offices. Widespread executions

---

[2] See pp. 143–4 above

and other heavy-handed punishments, under forms that were anything but ordered and predictable, were commonplace besides.
Through fear and discretionary favours, political dominance could
be meagrely maintained.

In the case of Japan, we encounter a striking exception to the general picture outside Europe. For in that country, a well-developed
feudal order was established. It came into being at much the same
time as its European counterpart, and the background was the
same. The feudal structure emerged as a local military system in
answer to the breakdown of central authority. As in Europe, moreover, this splintered warlord system gave rise to a civil strife which
at times was virtually unceasing. In its internal structure, however,
the Japanese feudal system was different. It lacked the contractual
form and surrounding regulatory complex that developed in
Europe. Nor did it exhibit a corresponding pattern of reciprocity in
respect of mutual obligations between lord and vassal. Japanese
feudalism was essentially structured according to a clientelist pattern. Organized on the basis of old clan identities, it was pronouncedly patriarchal and discretionary. In Europe, S. A. Finer
remarks, 'authority was based on law, whereas in Japan it was
based on a social pattern which simply reproduced the family pattern' (1997 III: 1092). It was not possible in Japan, unlike in Europe,
for a vassal to have several lords. The vassal enjoyed no free and
autonomous standing; in most cases, rather, he was highly dependent on his—single—lord. To be taken as a vassal was an honour and
sign of favour; it was to be answered with strict loyalty and subordination. Feudalism in Japan was less pluralistic, in other words,
than was feudalism in Europe. It was also more hierarchical and
discretionary in its internal structure. In military, fiscal, and juridical terms, the top feudal stratum—the *daimayo*—enjoyed considerable independence for long periods within the territories under its
control. However, its position was never regulated, as in Europe, by
a declaration of rights and privileges. A strict balance of power
undeniably prevailed, both between the different feudal clans and
between these and the central power established at the end of the
sixteenth century—the Tokugawa shogunate. But this pluralism
was never regulated and restrained. No institutionalized forms for
the resolution of conflict were created. 'The relationship between
the shogun and daimayo resembled more that of antagonistic states
in which there is stability, even peace, but little in the way of coming to terms, mutual trust and cooperation' (Downing 1992: 44).
Society, as represented by the feudal elite, clearly commanded great
resources in its dealings with the state. But no interactive relation,

in the form of a fruitful collaboration between state and society, came into being for that. In consequence, the Japanese state developed little in the way of vigour or effectiveness, as became embarrassingly clear when the country was visited by foreign military forces a few centuries later (Hintze 1975: 332–3; Anderson 1978: 388ff; Bendix 1978: 61ff; Downing 1992: 44ff; Finer 1997 III: 1086ff; Keyder 1997; Mardin 1997).

Now back to Europe. The distinctiveness of that continent's development did not just have to do with the church and the feudal aristocracy. Other actors too, representing lower social strata, played an important role in the political development of many countries. Of particular importance here were developments in the cities.

Beginning around 1000, a growing number of cities were established in Europe. They were found mainly in a belt stretching from northern Italy and Dalmatia in the south to Flanders, Germany, and parts of the Baltic in the north. The cities were able to take advantage of the power struggle among the crown, the church, and the nobles. Often they joined forces with the princes. They wished, as a rule, to be freed of dependence on local feudal lords—an outcome to which the central power was usually happy to contribute. The princes, for their part, needed support, especially of a financial nature. They were therefore prepared to offer the cities far-reaching immunities and privileges; often, moreover, these were stipulated in written charters. Thus the cities were typically able to establish a system of law clearly distinct from that of the surrounding society:

... the settlement of legal disputes through juridical duels was prohibited; courts operating outside the town were forbidden to claim jurisdiction over townsmen; town dwellings were proclaimed inviolable; and above all the juridical status of free men was granted to all townsmen, and often extended to all who were resided in the town for a year and a day (*Stadtsluft macht frei*). (Poggi 1978: 40)

In addition, the cities often acquired financial and administrative autonomy. They collected their own taxes and appointed their own officials. Often they were more or less autonomous in military matters. They surrounded themselves with high walls, and their citizens usually formed militias. It could also happen that they hired mercenaries for their defence. Their independence was founded on their strong financial standing. As centres of handicrafts and commerce, they were the scene of substantial economic growth and generation of wealth. It is here that we see the beginnings of the capitalism and industrialism that subsequently developed in Europe.

In some areas, the autonomy of the cities proceeded so far that they were able to cut themselves free of their overlords and form their own states. Around the year 1200, there were between 200 and 300 independent city-states in northern Italy. Over 50 such urban state formations existed in Germany at the same time, and in the Low Countries there were approximately 20. Although divided internally and often in conflict with one another, especially in Italy, they were capable of combining forces and collaborating in common leagues of defence. The Hanseatic League, the Lombard League, and the union of Dutch cities bear mentioning as important examples. By such means, and as a result of their economic strength, the cities were an important obstacle to the emergence of an imperial state in Europe.

The cities offered freedom and autonomy to their inhabitants, who were often of low status originally. The city was a melting pot, a gathering place for strangers. Even so, the population usually developed a strong corporative unity. The cities had often been founded as societies of oath-takers, underlining the commitment to mutual protection and support involved. Such newly created units have accordingly been described as 'centres of solidarity by single powerless people' (Poggi 1978: 37). Far-reaching organizational networks tended subsequently to emerge, in the form of guilds, fraternities, and societies. These lent collective strength to the various population groups, which were commonly defined by occupation.

The system of self-government within city walls was rather varied as far as the degree of popular involvement is concerned. At times there was very broad participation: decisions were taken in general meetings in which all citizens took part. Representative assemblies based on a wide suffrage also existed. Another practice sometimes found involved the allocation of executive commissions among citizens by lot. This was done so that as many persons as possible—potentially everyone—would be able to assume public tasks and to acquire the experience conferred by participation in public affairs.

However, the community spirit which thus stamped the internal life of the cities, and which has been celebrated by many a republican thinker, contrasted with other tendencies less favourable to popular influence. A pronounced stratification between different popular groups developed, making for serious tensions. This stratification sometimes emerged along class lines, sometimes—especially in Italy—along clan lines. In the same way, frictions often arose between groups involved in different economic branches, handicrafts and commerce especially. As a consequence, the cities were periodically plagued by unrelenting internal struggles. The tendency which predominated over time was an oligarchical one. Participation in city government came to be concentrated in the hands of an economic elite. The critical posts were monopolized by a thin stratum of patrician families. In many cases—for example, Milan, Florence, and the Geneva praised by Rousseau—the standing of the dominant families came to be formally regulated in law, so that an aristocratic form of government was established. In other cases, mainly in Italy, power was seized in the cities by military leaders (*condottieri*). Supported by mercenaries, these leaders proclaimed themselves princes with hereditary claims. The most brilliant of these were the Medici, who ruled Florence in the sixteenth century (Finer 1997 II: 950ff).

Of course, independent cities under more or less popular rule were not unique to the European Middle Ages. We know of the existence in Antiquity of such cities in Mesopotamia, as well as in Mediterranean countries, particularly Greece. In a comparative historical perspective, however, such cities are an unusual phenomenon. In China, the cities were strictly subordinate to the imperial administration. Of immunities and privileges there were none. The primary function of the cities was to serve as garrisons for imperial troops. The governing stratum had no wish to encourage commerce and trade: 'Challenges to state or mandarinate power from emerging commercial enterprises were met by stifling taxation, price controls, or demands for bribes, all of which combined to thwart rivals to official power' (Downing 1992: 49). In Japan it did happen, when the central power was established, that privileges and rights were awarded to the cities. The urban economic elite was granted self-government in collegial forms. It was more common, however, that the cities were either subject to strong central control, in accordance with the Chinese pattern, or were dominated by local warlords, as during long periods of feudal anarchy. In the Near East, meanwhile, under both Byzantine and Ottoman rule, the cities were subject to the central power and bereft of self-governing organs. The same state of affairs prevailed in India. It was the princes who controlled the government of the cities. Existing merchant and handicraft castes in India enjoyed, in occupational matters, a considerable measure of autonomy; they had, for example, their own legislation and system of justice. As Weber (1986: 297ff) stressed, however, cohesion and common organization never developed within the urban population. Inherited and ritually founded divisions of caste stood in the way of that. The fraternization and coordination between citizens which constitutes a *polis* or commune was something unique to the cities of Europe.

Not to be forgotten, finally, are the conditions faced by the peasants, who at this time made up the overwhelming majority of the population. A feature distinctive to Europe was the strong right of land tenure which the peasants came to enjoy. With the introduction of the feudal system, the peasants were commonly assigned the status of serfs, bound to the land and to their lord. Despite their formal subordination, however, they often were able to use their land as allodial property. With the passage of time, the rights and obligations of the parties evolved into a contractual relationship, based on customary law, marked by mutual obligations. These legal norms were but weakly developed, however; in practice, a lord could often break with prevailing customs and agreements and handle his vassals with great ruthlessness. Peasant uprisings might then result. But other counter-measures, of a more institutionalized kind, were available too. The peasants' right of land tenure, and their otherwise relatively free standing, put them in a position to exert collective pressure on the aristocrats above them. In many cases it happened, for instance, that peasants forced their lord to form a manorial court. In such courts, the peasants made decisions together with their lord, or his representative, on matters that affected them. In this way, the lord was deprived of his authority to lay down the rights and obligations of his subordinates unilaterally.

The great fall in the population of Europe resulting from the Black Death contributed, on account of the labour shortage to which it gave rise, to strengthening the position of the peasants. Peasants could now obtain better conditions, and in many cases these were codified and made permanent. The result was the abolition of serfdom. Moreover, instead of having to pay their landlord in the form of direct labour, peasants' duties were now fixed in pecuniary terms, which furthermore were presumed to apply for long periods. Thus the serf had become a tenant. Moreover, the increased penetration of the state on the local level, as seen in the replacement of feudally controlled judicial systems with courts subject to the monarch, helped to strengthen the legal standing of the peasants *vis-à-vis* the lords.

Special conditions tended to obtain in those parts of Europe which had been affected only in small measure, or not at all, by feudalism. These were usually areas covered by forests and mountains, natural features making such territories easier to defend against armies composed of mounted knights, which formed the backbone of the feudal system. This was the case in parts of Scandinavia, in the Swiss Alps, and in certain areas of the Netherlands[3] and the British

---

[3] The large-scale system of dykes in the Netherlands gave the peasants an advantage from a defence point of view. Heavily armed knights found it difficult to cross such terrain.

Isles. A far-reaching local self-rule, based on old Germanic traditions, was practised in these regions. Local administration was provided by village governments based on broad popular participation.
Local peasant militias for military defence were organized under
the leadership of the village community.

Like the cities, these communes, as they were often called, were
able to take advantage of strife between the aristocracy and the
crown, and to obtain immunities and charters confirming their
rights. Such charters typically included the right to establish juridical organs under village control and to form popular assemblies for
the running of local affairs. And just as the cities often joined
together in common defence, so did the villages combine when aristocratic forces tried to invade their territories. These peasant communities were able to establish various forms of collaboration with
the central power, particularly on military and fiscal matters. These
two parties often shared, after all, an interest in undermining the
position of the aristocracy. However, conflicts could also arise
between them, whereupon it happened that the peasants were able
to mobilize powerful resistance, and even to force princes from their
thrones; this applied in Scandinavia particularly, where the peasants were represented as an estate in parliament.

Special conditions also tended to obtain in settler communities, of
which there were a considerable number, particularly in eastern
Europe. In these frontier communities, where new land was being
put under the plough, peasants often enjoyed a favourable legal
standing, as well as the opportunity to practise a far-reaching local
self-government. Princes and local aristocrats alike often supported
such expansion: it widened their domains. They were therefore willing to grant particularly favourable terms to the population in question.

Outside Europe we find instead a pronounced exploitation and
lack of rights to be the typical lot of the peasants. Such were the conditions generally, for example, in large parts of the Near East. The
same can be said of India. Here there were certainly lively village
communities, but as a rule they were at the mercy of the local aristocracy, which was highly dependent in turn on the princely power.
Indian aristocrats had no hereditary right of property. An aristocrat
was allocated a collection of villages for his maintenance; in return,
he was to collect taxes and recruit soldiers for his prince. He could
be transferred from one area to another. A highly parasitic form of
government was commonly practised. The peasants were harshly
exploited, and consigned to an isolated village life. Their only contact with the state was in the form of the taxes they were forced to

pay. In China, meanwhile, there was a tradition of self-government in the villages, the inhabitants of which elected various local officials. This primitive peasant democracy was overshadowed, however, by the bureaucracy's strong hold on the villages from above. The villages collected taxes and organized public works of various kinds; everything, however, was done under the strict supervision of imperial functionaries. There was no real autonomy. The village administration functioned as the proxy of the central power, which the peasants had little or no capacity to influence. Far-reaching peasant rebellions periodically broke out, which were usually put down with great brutality. In Japan too, locally appointed organs existed, which the central power exploited as an instrument—during such times, that is, as a central power prevailed; otherwise the organs were dominated by local warlords. The peasants were usually bound to the land, but they also had certain rights against their lords, both through public decree and according to customary law. As a consequence, however, of the institutional dissolution that characterized Japan during long periods, they were often left at the mercy of their *samurai* lords. Aside from eruptive and often unorganized uprisings, which as a rule were crushed, the peasants were without opportunities for political influence (Downing 1992: 24ff, 55ff; Jones 1987: 196ff; Mann 1986a: 394–5; Bendix 1978: 81).

The status of European peasants should not, of course, be glorified. They were economically and socially oppressed; and of course their living standards diverged markedly from those of the aristocratic class which they supported. Yet such cleavages in respect of status and material conditions were not less severe on other continents; quite the contrary. Most critical was the fact that, to a degree unmatched elsewhere, European peasants secured legal protection and rights of participation in local decision-making: in manorial courts or independent village communities.

What Made Europe Special?

A pluralist order marked by exceptional vitality evolved in Europe. Alongside the emerging central power, there were several other important centres—the church, the aristocracy, the cities, and in some countries also the peasants—which in varying combinations were able to counteract any actor trying to dominate the political scene. Yet the multiplicity of the actors, the variability of the coalition patterns, and the resulting balance of power do not provide a sufficient explanatory background to the emergence of the special type of state formed in Europe during the period here examined (cf. Mann 1986a: 397). A far-reaching pluralism and a ceaseless power struggle between different groups have usually resulted, historically, in anarchy and the dissolution of social order: the condition, in other words, of which Hobbes warned. Elements thereof were certainly present in Europe, the protracted civil wars during the Middle Ages in Hobbes's English homeland being an example. If this tendency had become dominant, as in large measure it did in Japan, the Middle Ages would have deserved the epithet 'the Dark Ages'.[4] A tendency unique to Europe, however, emerged as a counterweight. I refer to the legal and institutional regeneration which took place parallel with the pluralist development mentioned, and in interaction with it.

Let us first consider the distinctive legal system that emerged. Law is an indispensable means for coordinating human affairs. It is this institution which makes an extensive social interaction possible: it enables persons to take the risk of mixing with others from outside their narrow family sphere (North 1990). The knowledge that a reasonably fixed norm system is maintained within a certain territory, or among a certain circle of individuals, means that we can, with a considerable degree of assurance, predict the outcome of various social transactions. If we know the norms regulating people's actions, we can foresee their behaviour. Fixed norms for interaction create confidence and predictability in the intercourse with others, thus lowering transaction costs. It is accordingly possible to establish, with rules of coordination, peaceful forms for the resolution of conflict. This in turn facilitates cooperation. This natural understanding has lain behind the building of our societies.[5]

Since rules of this sort are created more easily in small groups, the first societies were composed of a small number of individuals bound together by a strong identity. Usually, such communities had the character of extended families, and were based in large part on kinship relations (Eisenstadt and Roninger 1984). With time, these groups might be incorporated into larger units, such as tribes and

---

[4] The expression 'the Dark Ages' was coined during the Renaissance; it referred to the cultural standstill that had obtained, so it was thought, since Antiquity. The accuracy of this judgement will not be examined here. From the standpoint of political development, however, it is clear that the European Middle Ages were marked by the most significant transition and change.

[5] Harry Eckstein (1996: 490) puts it this way: 'Societies are built around *expectations* that actors have to other actors. Only if such expectations are reliably complied with can orderly, regular social interaction occur. Reliably fixed expectations are the nervous system of societies that bond their parts and particles into a whole.'

clans. These latter units, in order to achieve coordination, developed a system of customary law often founded in religious and spiritual conceptions. Since, in the beginning, there was no coercive state power to guarantee that the rules were followed, the group was held together by a strong sense of normative affinity that demanded cooperation and mutual assistance between members. The rules were maintained largely through a strong code of honour. Nothing was worse than losing your reputation and your honour, and thereby your status, as a reliable member of the community, for it meant others would want nothing to do with you. Outside the group, you were defenceless and alone.

Thus the clan and the tribe constituted the social framework of customary law. It was still a question, however, of relatively small units. This meant local—or what today we would call regional—groupings, which were held together by a shared identity and an established system of norms. These fixed patterns of interaction facilitated effective cooperation within the group. Thus it was possible to build up valuable social capital. At the same time, however, such communities had strictly defined outer limits, in relation, that is, to neighbouring units. The drawback of organizational and legal particularism lies in the fact that such an order, on account of its role in strengthening identity, which is required for the maintenance of the group, can badly complicate interaction with other population groups. A distinguishing mark of clan and tribal societies has typically been a latent suspicion and enmity, periodically erupting into open hostilities, between different segments of the population.

The emergence of universal norm systems superseding clan-based customary law has the effect of facilitating more wide-ranging interaction. If you have faith in the legal institutions spanning different particularist identities, such that everyone, Jew as well as Greek, is subject to the same rules and is treated equally, then the risks of 'investing' in cooperation with people of another sort than your own are immediately reduced. A universal system of law provides an important intermediary structure for the creation of interaction and cooperation between different population segments.

The states that were established did not usually alter the legal arrangements of the clan and tribal societies; rather, princes attained their legitimacy through guaranteeing the maintenance of the legal systems already existing. The Germanic kingdoms established in Europe were most often structured in this manner. To be confirmed, the prince had to travel round the different local courts and testify that he would uphold the time-honoured system of law.

The advantage of the framework provided by the state was that rules could be institutionalized in a more fixed manner. Through his power of coercion, the prince could offer a more efficient implementation of applicable law; this contributed to better security and improved opportunities for coordination in society. As a rule, however, the new states stretched over wider territories than had the earlier units. In consequence, they encompassed a number of legal systems, which at times differed greatly among themselves. Although each of these legal systems became stronger through the offices of the prince, the state was still founded on particularistic legal norms and identities.

At the same time, however, an additional integrative force of importance existed in Europe. I refer to the Roman Catholic Church. Since its early years, the church had maintained an independent internal legal system, that of canon law. It was based on Roman law, and in technical terms it was far more advanced than the Germanic customary law which was applied, in a variety of local forms, in the rest of society. It had an explicit logical structure, and thus was clearer and more coherent than the Germanic systems. It was distinguished as well by its more orderly and rational rules of procedure. These differences were exacerbated by the fact that canon law was codified, while Germanic law was long transmitted only orally (Berman 1983: 49ff, 85ff; Anners 1990*a*: 11ff, 109ff; van Caenegem 1992: 18ff; Poggi 1978: 33; Downing 1992: 32–3).

In its missionary activities, the church tried actively to break down the clan and tribal identities to which earlier religious and associated legal norm systems had been tied. The Christian church proclaimed the principle of a single norm system under God: a system of law common to all peoples. It was also opposed, on the basis of the same universalist principle, to legal discrimination. It demanded equal rights for all before the law, and worked for the abolition of slavery. In these strivings the church had great success. By the beginning of the eleventh century, it had won hegemony over nearly all of western and central Europe. As a result, the old particularistic norm systems, both spiritual and social, were successively dissolved. Clan and tribal identities were largely eliminated from the map of Europe.

Owing to its wide extension and its growing organizational and financial strength, the church became a political factor of great importance in Europe. This was especially true after its successful prosecution of the Investiture struggle with the emperor at the end of the eleventh century and beginning of the twelfth. The legal and administrative structure of the church came to a high degree to serve as the model for the new institutional order being established. The attempts at recreating the empire had been stopped. The model for the future was independent princes, who gradually strengthened their position against the local feudal lords. An important instrument in this context was the increasing penetration on the part of the central power in the administration of justice. The king's officials took over the handling of civil cases—in which citizens stand against one another—on the local level. The involvement of the aristocracy in the administration of justice was thereby broken. Revenues for the crown were also generated hereby, since these legal services provided a tax base. The princes therefore sought as a rule to create codified and more uniform legal systems. In respect of their content, these were connected, quite naturally, with prevailing Germanic customary law. In respect of their structure and procedural order, however, they were often highly influenced by the traditions of Roman and of canon law. In pursuit of their power ambitions, then, the princes brought about a legal standardization and consequent social integration within their domains. Technically more advanced, and administered by professional jurists—who often defended the system as a corporation—the civil legal order thus established laid an institutional basis for the unique commercial and industrial development that was later to take place in Europe (Hintze 1975: 330ff; Berman 1983: 199ff; Anners 1990a: 140ff; van Caenegem 1992: 24ff; Bendix 1986: 308–9; Downing 1992: 33–4; Finer 1997 III: 1298ff).

Within Islam too, the principle of a uniform legal order under the one God is held in high regard. And like Christianity, Islam is unambiguously egalitarian: all are equal before God, and so are of equal worth as individuals. Islamic religious law, which included several elements of Roman law, was in technical terms relatively well-developed. On account of the weak standing of the ecclesiastical body, however, the norm system of the church did not come to permeate secular life to the degree that it did in Europe. In the Muslim world the state did not, as a rule, come to penetrate the legal order at the popular level. The old clan and tribal society was left largely undisturbed, together with the systems of customary law tied to such identities (Hintze 1975: 335; Bendix 1978: 35ff).

In many respects, China had a highly impressive legal tradition. Already by the time Christ was born, the Chinese had developed a codified and highly advanced legal system, which in subsequent centuries they developed further still. Yet its technical qualities notwithstanding, the legal order had clear limitations in its application: 'Chinese law was unevenly applied, and the vast majority of

common people were not treated 'equally under the law. The edu-
cated officials and gentry were subject to one set of laws, the
impressively codified ones, and the masses to another, disparate
and unsystematized set of local customs' (Chirot 1985: 187).
Isolated in their villages, the great majority of the population lived
a life governed by ancient and highly patriarchal clan and family
traditions. Similar conditions prevailed in Japan. In that country
too, at least when a central power was present, there was a
significant legal-administrative superstructure, albeit a less developed one than in China. Essentially, however, social life in Japan
was regulated in accordance with ancient, spiritually based patterns of clan life (Hintze 1975: 328–9; Bendix 1978: 61ff; Downing
1992: 52; Finer 1997 III: 1300–1). India, finally, is the country in
which particularistic norm systems have prevailed most clearly. For
thousands of years, individuals in that land have been arranged
into castes, which have the character of ascriptive, religiously
founded communities. The castes have devised their own legal
systems, and their members have usually been sharply demarcated
from each other. Until modern times, as good as no overarching civil
system of law, with the ability to bridge and to integrate, has existed
in India alongside this social mosaic (Hintze 1975: 327; Chirot 1985:
185; Jones 1987: 197).

In Europe, the institutionalization of forms of conflict resolution
entailed by the establishment of a legal order took place in the constitutional area as well—which has to do here with the rights of citizens *vis-à-vis* the state, and with the allocation of competences
among different state organs. The official stipulations of rights in
the form of charters and similar documents, which various citizen
groups were able to extract in many countries, have had exceed-
ingly few counterparts elsewhere in the world.[6] This tradition of
rights had been introduced by the Catholic Church, which early on
had obtained legally guaranteed immunities and privileges.
Similarly, the aristocracy, the cities, and to some extent also the
peasantry were able to obtain official guarantees of their rights.
These charters meant that the limits of state competence were formally regulated in law, and, conversely, that the autonomy of various citizen groups was confirmed. And these were not, it bears
recalling, merely words written on parchment or on leather. They

---

[6] A well-known example is the Chou dynasty in China, c. 1000 BC. A multitude of
written charters stipulating rights and obligations were issued during this feudal-
type period. When, after many centuries of disintegration, new dynasties came to
power, a break was made with this institutional order. At no point later have similar arrangements been established (Downing 1992: 48; Bendix 1978: 51).

had a most substantive impact in their era, and for subsequent generations they often assumed a very great normative import:

Agreements negotiated by kings and subjects in the not too distant past were endowed with a quasi-religious aura. Charters became concrete acknowledgements of natural rights: Magna Carta came to be revered as an almost sacred document, enshrined as a holy relic. (Downing 1992: 36)

Another important feature of the constitutional order was the system of representation. As a general phenomenon, of course, this was not new. Popular involvement in decision-making on matters of shared interest had been common in tribal societies throughout the world. In a more developed and institutionalized form, moreover, a lively democracy was practiced in Greece; and for a long time under the Roman Republic, the populace took part in government in a far-reaching manner. Nevertheless, the representative systems established in many European countries during the Middle Ages must be ascribed an especial importance for the continued materialization of the concept of popular government. In the Middle Ages in Europe, a development got going which has continued up to the present.

The medieval assemblies were sprung, as Otto Hintze has shown, of many different sources (see also Finer 1997 II: 1029ff) Among the Germanic peoples, there had long been a tradition of local community gatherings; councils of a more regional type were also convened, at which magnates and their retinues assembled. A tradition of making decisions at conferences, moreover, had been established within the Catholic Church at an early time. For decisions on central questions of faith, as well on as other topics in dispute, synods and councils were convened at which a large number of representatives from the church organization, principally bishops, were present. These two traditions were interwoven in a most palpable manner under the Frankish Carolingians. King Pepin, who reigned in the 700s, convened church synods coinciding in time and place with the conferences he held regularly with his military captains. From this developed a practice whereby the foremost representatives of the church and aristocracy were represented in the councils of the king: the baronial *curia regis*.

The emergence of parliaments, which took place several centuries later, represented a continuation and broadening of this practice. These assemblies were larger, and they incorporated a wider range of social groupings, inasmuch as the burghers—and in some cases the peasants too—were represented therein. As compared with the working procedures of earlier deliberative organs, moreover, those applied within the parliamentary assemblies were a good deal more

institutionalized. Detailed and codified rules were worked out stipulating how deliberations were to be conducted within each chamber, and how contrasting opinions were to be merged into joint
decisions. They also stated how communications with the sovereign
were to be handled (Hintze 1975: 318–19; Poggi 1978: 42ff; Downing
1992: 33; Finer 1997 II: 1024ff).

The organs thus established, variously denoted *Parliament*,
Cortes, Estates, Diet, Landtag, Riksdag, and so forth, often gained a
considerable influence. Their main task was to decide on questions
of taxation. It was usually to obtain approval for new or higher
taxes that princes convened the representative assemblies. In addition, however, the assemblies often held deliberations on how the
revenues thus raised were to be used. Hence they might address a
broad spectrum of questions bearing on both domestic and foreign
policy. In many instances, this arrangement continued with a fair
regularity for several centuries; in some cases, in fact, it has been
retained, albeit in modernized form, up to our own time. Thus a pattern of collaboration between state and society was developed under
fairly regulated forms (Myers 1975; Marongiu 1968; Poggi 1978:
46ff; Finer 1997 II: 1035ff). Thus were established some of the basic
elements of an interactive form of state.

The system of representation by estates applied in such assemblies was of course natural. It matched the collective identities prevailing within the portions of the population that were politically
most significant. It is important to note that these identities were
defined in horizontal and class-based terms. The bonds of affinity
between people characteristic of the clan and tribal society had been
broken down, mainly on account of the church. The form of feudalism created in Europe worked in the same direction. Unlike under
feudal systems elsewhere—in Japan in particular, but in Islamic
states too—the intercourse between lord and vassal under
European feudalism was not tied to ethnic or spiritual identities.
Nor did it take the familial, arbitrary, and highly patriarchal form
common elsewhere. In Europe, the relationship was built on contract, and the parties were often of differing ethnic origins (Hintze
1975: 334ff). The growing central power also made an important
contribution. The standardization of civil law facilitated the integration of the population, which is a precondition for the reformu-
lation of identities along horizontal lines of class.

The institutionalization of constitutional rights, in turn,
strengthened these tendencies. The charters issued were typically
addressed to the different corporations, which in this way became
the object of legal regulation. Rights were attached to groups,

reinforcing identity within the class-defined segments. The system of parliamentary representation, which was structured in the same corporative manner, had a similar impact. The estate-based assemblies functioned as arenas for contact and cooperation between persons hailing from different parts of the country, who in many cases would never otherwise have had occasion to meet; it bears recalling that, as a consequence of conditions obtaining within production and communications, a pronounced localism prevailed. Through regular interaction along lines of class, and through the support from below that had to be mobilized in protection of corporatively awarded rights, the horizontal identities attending the division into estates were reinforced. At the same time, the parliaments served as a forum for contact between the different groups. Gaining influence for one's own segmental interest demanded an ability to cooperate with the other estates, for a majority among the chambers was often needed for a decision to be made. Representative institutions came hereby to function as organs for the peaceful resolution of conflict, and as instruments for national integration (Hintze 1975: 325–6; Poggi 1978: 37–8, 42; Downing 1992: 31).

Why is the emergence of horizontal organization important? On the one hand, such units in which people of similar socio-economic standing join together often acquire an internal structure, which is more favourable from a democratic point of view. Since social status and economic standing generate power resources, organizations composed of social peers have a 'flatter' structure as a rule.[7] If we furthermore consider the organizations' external function—that is, how they interact among themselves, which political pluralism requires—we find that there are additional strong points in favour of class-based associations. The argument may be summarized in the following three points.

First, traditional identities based on kinship loyalties are geographically highly restricted as a rule. As seen on a map, the different areas lie like islands in an archipelago: close to each other, yet delimited and distinct. Horizontal organization breaks this closed localist pattern. It means that people with similar socio-economic interests form a unit, which in principle everyone with the same interest, irrespective of place of residence, can join. Through their frequently wide extension over space, horizontal associations serve as an instrument for a pattern of interaction across geographical zones.

Second, traditional identities are commonly of an ascriptive nature: they are associated with communities into which you are

---

[7] See Chapter 2, p. 37.

born and to which you belong your whole life—the Indian caste system is a clear example. Class organization builds on identities rooted primarily in the position of individuals in production. To be sure, such stratification can be highly stable and inflexible in certain societies, with the consequence that, where class is concerned, you become what you are born to; this applies particularly in the case of agricultural societies in which the ownership of land is highly concentrated. Yet, assuming a degree of dynamism in productive life, the prevailing socio-economic stratification has the potential to become looser and more flexible, so that the boundaries between the segments become vaguer, and a rise on the class ladder becomes possible and takes place more frequently. It is furthermore the case that class organization often builds on a broad category of people—burghers, peasants, and so on—within which interests may partly diverge. Within the estate of burghers, for example, practitioners of handicrafts may be threatened by competition from industrial enterprises, and both production interests may come into conflict with commercial interests. In the same way, peasants in forest areas may differ in their conditions of production from their counterparts on the plains. On account of the greater internal heterogeneity found within classes, and in view of the potential for mobility between different strata, organizational patterns based on class identity are less monolithic and closed than are those which are ascriptively based. Persons divided according to the former, class-based, type of segmentation therefore find it easier to interact with each other.

Third, ascriptive bonds between people are often based on inherited loyalties of a mystical and spiritual nature. In order to hold the unit together, fixed norm systems, related to honour and duty, are laid down regulating individual behaviour. The rigidity of the norms provides the cement holding the group together. Classes, by contrast, are more instrumental in nature. They exhibit a largely pragmatic orientation: their concerns are of a businesslike nature, that is, improving the economic and social conditions of their members. On such matters, it is easier to compromise and find solutions together with other groups. In this way too, horizontally structured organizations facilitate external interaction (Rustow 1970; Horowitz 1985: 223–4; Hadenius 1992*a*: 112–13; Kaufman 1996).

The problem is that such organizational patterns are also appreciably harder to create. It is not just that the horizontal community differs fundamentally from the original kinship bonds that held people together for millenia. It is also the case that it often runs directly athwart such traditional identities, and actively breaks them down. The existence of supportive institutional structures is therefore of great importance. In Europe, the Catholic Church offered such support, and in time the central power did as well. It was a question of introducing rule-systems of a universalist character—rules that transcended and in time replaced the parochial norms that had governed people's lives since time immemorial. The constitutional rights and representative systems that were established also contributed greatly to the emergence of horizontal identities.

Outside Europe, such institutional elements were conspicuous by their absence. In such countries as India and China, a form of occupational self-organization could certainly be found resembling the societies and guilds of Europe. These were permeated, however, by the prevailing ascriptive pattern of society. In India they formed part of the caste system; in China they were stamped, in the absence of legal regulation, by identities of kinship and of clan. In both cases, Hintze (1975: 329) says, in the spirit of Tönnies, it was a matter of *Gemeinschaft* and not of *Gesellschaft*. In Japan too, as in the Muslim world, clan communities supplied the primary form of identity. There was, as we know, a free-standing and highly self-conscious aristocratic stratum in Japan, which often was able, with great and sometimes devastating success, to hold the central power in check. Here, as in Europe, the prevailing balance of power often led to negotiations and agreements with the central government. Yet it did not lead to the establishment of fixed forms for the resolution of conflict: 'negotiations in various forms . . . were never institutionalized; even under favorable conditions conflicts had to be solved militarily' (Bendix 1986: 313).

Europe had a pluralist order without peer. A number of autonomous social groups, which could combine in different ways, made for a balance of power. These were groups held together essentially on the basis of class identity, which made intercourse between different popular segments easier. The institutional context, furthermore, was special. Different groups within civil society had obtained guarantees of autonomy from the state, in the form of declarations of rights. These groups were also granted access to the state, and thus to participation in political decision-making at the central level. Along the way, a regular interaction was established between the state and society, and this was done under conditions promoting the peaceful resolution of conflict. At the same time, the institutional order helped reconstruct prevailing social identities and patterns of association. In this way, society's coordination capacity was strengthened. Its ability to act as a counter-weight to the central power, and at times to enter into partnership with it, was enhanced.

In other words, some of the conditions which generally facilitate political power-sharing were present in Europe.[8] The political game involved several collective actors commanding fairly equal, or at least not terribly unequal, resources. These actors were able, furthermore, to apply strategies of reciprocity, thus making intercourse and cooperation possible. The nature of the segmentation, based on class identities, that had developed in Europe made this process easier. These outcomes in turn were promoted, both directly and indirectly, as we have seen, by advancements made in the institutional realm. I refer to the particular regulatory instruments in the area of civil and constitutional law that had arisen in Europe.

It bears emphasizing, however, that it was only an embryonic institutional order that had come into being. Despite the development towards greater uniformity that had taken place within civil law, the system still bore a good many of its old fragmented features. In the cities, for instance, different systems of law were often applied to different societies and guilds; this probably contributed to the dissension and inability to solve conflict that often marked the life of the cities. This was particularly true in Italy.[9] Furthermore, much of the regulation undertaken in the constitutional area was of an ad hoc character. The charters that had been issued left many questions unanswered, and they embraced certain groups more explicitly than others. And, notwithstanding the procedural regularity and orderliness that had come in many cases to characterize parliamentary affairs, the tasks of the different organs were unclear, as was their relation to the sovereign. As a rule, the assemblies convened at the initiative of the king, typically because the state treasury needed filling. The decision-making agenda was generally set by the matters taken up by the king. It should be added, moreover, that the administrative side of the state was scarcely made the object of regulation at all. The administrative apparatus, which now began slowly to expand, was left in all essentials in the hands of the sovereign, and was typically run in patrimonial fashion as part of his household (Poggi 1978: 52–3; Weber 1987: 95ff).

---

[8] See Chapter 2, pp. 45–6.

[9] Quentin Skinner (1992: 59) makes the following comment: 'The gloomy moral drawn by most political theorists of early modern Europe from the history of the Italian city-republics was that self-government is simply a recipe for chaos, and that some form of monarchial rule is indispensable if public order is to be maintained.' There can be scarcely any doubt as to which political theorist is first of all intended! On legal conditions in the cities, see H. Berman (1983: 339ff).

As for popular participation, it cannot be gainsaid that it was most limited. The nobles, the higher clergy, and the leading strata in the cities were represented in parliament. Even taken together, of course, these elements came to but a small proportion of the population. The degree of representativeness was naturally much higher in the few countries where peasants were represented in parliament too. On the local level there was, in certain periods, a broad-based participation in the governance of the cities. As a rule, however, power at this level was in the hands of a thin layer of patrician families. As for the countryside, old village assemblies were retained in many places. Where feudalism extended, moreover, there was often an opportunity for representation in the manorial courts. Even so, the feudal lords enjoyed an entirely dominant position on the local level. In protest at this situation, peasants resorted to large-scale rebellions on repeated occasions. These undertakings were generally hopeless, and were often met severely.

Political influence was essentially restricted to the elite, and the institutions established were in many ways poorly structured. Nor does the conflict-dampening effect of the institutions mentioned deserve to be praised to the skies. Civil wars took place intermittently on a considerable scale well into the late Middle Ages. The point is simply that the sword was far from being the only method available for the resolution of disputes. Judged by modern standards, the gains made can appear very modest. But modern standards do not, of course, supply the relevant basis for judgement. As I have sought to show, it is in comparison with other continents that we see the uniqueness of the political developments that took place in medieval Europe.

8

Breakdown and Continuity

Far-reaching changes in political life took place in Europe at the end of the Middle Ages. The balance of power that had previously obtained in large part disappeared, along with much of the institutional order that had been established. The 'New Era' proved to a high degree to be the epoch of the emerging and expanding princely power. An important background factor here was the change that had occurred in the area of military technology. The armies of armoured mounted knights that had formed the basis for the feudal system lost their dominance on the battlefield at the end of the Middle Ages. As several noteworthy battles made clear, well-organized foot soldiers equipped with pikes or powerful bows could more than hold their own against mounted troops. The introduction of firearms shifted the balance yet further to the knights' disadvantage. Mounted warriors could not offer much resistance to infantry equipped with muskets and cannons. Nor could they count any longer on safety within the walls of their castles, for these could be blown to bits by cannon balls and gunpowder.

From the new military technology followed a renaissance for the foot soldier: that is, for the infantry. These troops were fairly easily equipped, so the creation of large-scale military units became feasible. This required, however, economic resources on a large scale, necessitating a form of political organization capable of mobilizing such resources. This furnished the princely power with a trump card. By imposing taxes within their relatively far-flung domains, they were able to accumulate such resources as enabled them to form an army under their own control. An administrative apparatus standing at the disposal of the prince was usually established at the same time. Then, through a combination of military and administrative strength, the prince could free himself from dependence on the parliamentary organs. Taxes could now be collected without them.

There were two further circumstances which each, and in some cases together, helped to strengthen the central power in several countries. With the introduction of Protestantism, the state had a golden opportunity to seize the oft-considerable properties administered by the Catholic Church. This meant, for many princes of lesser means on Europe's northern and western edges, an increment of resources which greatly strengthened their position in both domestic policy and foreign policy.[1] Naval expansion was another factor of importance. The discovery of new trade routes to Asia and America, and the colonization thereafter commenced, created enormous riches. These revenues mainly filled the coffers of those countries, in Europe's western and southern portions, that were involved in such enterprises (Hintze 1975: 332ff; McNeill 1982: 65ff; Mann 1986a: 453ff; Kennedy 1987: 20–1; Downing 1992: 56ff; Spruyt 1994: 166).

The New Era brought a change in the balance of power. It was the two strong counter-poles to the princely power—the aristocracy and the church—that were affected most strongly. From the aforementioned changes in military technology followed an erosion in the military basis of the feudal system. The prince was no longer dependent, when prosecuting war, on the assistance of his barons and their vassals. Now he could establish armies under his own control. In addition, the feudal system had been weakened in an economic sense. The peasants forming the economic base of the system succeeded in many areas of Europe, especially its western portions, in achieving a freer position. Often this happened with the support of the royal power. For the improvement in the position of the peasants weakened the standing of the feudal lords; moreover, freeholding peasants provided a welcome tax base for the crown.

As we shall see, however, developments took another course for the peasants in eastern Europe, where they lost their free standing. This was not, however, a sign that the aristocracy had strengthened its position; rather the opposite. The aristocracy in eastern Europe was made dependent on the state to a higher degree. It retained a portion of its privileges, which became associated as a rule with the holding of office in the bureaucracy and military. However, its autonomy in the form of control over its own military, economic, and

---

[1] Reinhard Bendix (1978: 280–1) presents the following calculations from England regarding Henry VIII's confiscation of church properties in the 1530s: 'There were at least 825 religious houses in England and Wales with a total collective income of over £160,000 a year, derived from about 25 percent of the country's agricultural land. Royal revenue from land was about £40,000 a year; thus, the landed property taken from the monasteries brought the crown a fourfold increase in its annual income. Other valuables confiscated from the church added a further £1 million to the royal treasury.'

administrative resources, became weaker. Developments proceeded, in other words, in an 'Oriental' direction. With the aristocracy's decline and growing dependence on the state, a pattern was
established resembling that long obtaining in China, India, and the
Ottoman Empire. The aristocracy of western Europe also lost, for
the reasons earlier mentioned, its autonomous role in the military
area. Its juridical and administrative tasks were reduced as well, on
account of the state's penetration at the local level. It often retained,
however, a relatively independent economic position through its
large-scale possession of lands still producing a considerable yield.

The actor in the former balance of power which suffered the clearest decline in its strength was the church. Developments in this
direction had started already in the late Middle Ages, when an
internal opposition of increasing strength had made itself felt.
Criticism was aimed at the church's rigid hierarchical order, and at
the misrule and religious decay that had come to characterize its
internal life. At the height of his power, in the centuries following
the Investiture struggle, the Pope had stood at the head of a cohesive and integral religious community with a dense organizational
network spanning a large part of the European continent. The
church also commanded considerable economic resources. It was
the largest landowner in Europe by far, and it possessed an internal
taxing power scarcely second to that of any prince. What happened,
however, was that the internal cohesion of the church began to
decline. Its unity was thereby destroyed. In the 1500s, a Protestant
movement broke with papal supremacy and formed its own independent congregations. In countries where the new faith was
adopted, the church was incorporated into the state, and in the
process lost both its economic and its administrative autonomy. No
comparable incorporation took place in the Catholic states. Even
here, however, the church lost much of its former position as a
counter-power to the crown, instead being incorporated as a support
organization for the latter. During the bitter and protracted religious struggles that now followed in Europe, the Catholic Church
became more dependent, as did its Protestant counterparts, on the
princes who defended its position. As a power factor of major importance, the church had played out its role.

The cities in many cases found their autonomy sharply restricted
as well. Of the several hundred free city-states that had existed in
Europe during the high Middle Ages, only a handful remained in
the 1700s. Of these, the republic of Venice was able to survive
almost till the end of the century—falling to Napoleon's assault in
1797—while certain north German free cities, such as Hamburg

and Bremen, kept their independence until German unification in 1871. The number of free cities fell, first of all, because the larger fish ate the smaller ones. This was especially the case in Italy, where feuds between cities were virtually a permanent condition. In this way, city-states were able to develop into extended territorial states, Florence being an example. In some cases, the original city-states—Genoa and Venice in particular—even expanded into maritime empires. Usually, however, it was the princes of previously existing territorial states that absorbed the free cities.[2] Although in many areas they formed leagues of defence, the cities were unable as a rule to match the military strength that the princes could field. The outcome for the cities proved highly various, however. In some countries they were eliminated altogether, politically speaking, while in others they succeeded in keeping a large part of their autonomy. The first tendency prevailed in eastern Europe; conditions in the west were more varied (van Crevald 1999: 59ff).

In what follows, we shall look at some of the institutional changes that took place. We begin with four cases involving a clear break with medieval constitutionalism and pluralism. We proceed then to some cases in which, by contrast, the medieval institutions could in large part be retained and further developed.

Breakdown: Russia, Prussia, Spain, and France

During the Middle Ages, the western parts of what today is Russia formed a loosely composed state under the leadership of Kiev. This state amounted in fact to a confederation of local principalities under the nominal rule of the prince in Kiev. Many of these principalities were important trading cities along the Dnieper and Volga rivers. The peasants, for their part, were generally free, and enjoyed a strong economic position. Through local village councils, they were able in large measure to run their own affairs. There were also lively councils of notables in the cities, while in the countryside the nobles were represented in organs known as *Boyar Duma*, with which the prince cooperated. The church belonged to the Greek Orthodox branch of Christianity, and stood autonomous from the secular power; it was subject to the patriarch in Constantinople. This arrangement was thoroughly crushed, however, in the brutal

---

[2] This was also, as we know, the fate of the city-states of ancient Greece, which were incorporated into the kingdom of Macedonia.

Mongol invasion of the mid-1200s. Under the Mongols, whose rule lasted about 200 years, the principality in Moscow became the strongest of the vassal states under the Khan of the Golden Horde. It was one of the princes of Moscow, Tsar Ivan III, who succeeded in driving out the Mongols in the latter part of the 1400s, thus laying the basis for a new Russian realm. This basis was autocratic and militarist to a high degree. It was, it bears stressing, a tormented land that now raised itself up. In addition to the ravages of the Mongols, Russia had been subjected during this period to incessant invasions by its western neighbours. The antidote chosen was the strongly centralized 'gunpowder empire' established by the tsars, a state oriented to the achievement of military objectives.

The aristocracy, which had enjoyed considerable autonomy when Kiev was the leading principality, was made strictly subordinate to the state apparatus under the tsars. As their realm expanded, the Moscovite princes subdued large areas of land—often through brutal and lawless methods—of which they dealt out portions to a new stratum of nobles in the service of the state. These latter received land and tax privileges in exchange for military service. This arrangement developed into an elaborate *nomenklatura* system under Peter the Great. Ranks and their accompanying privileges were carefully specified. But substantial services in return were required from those thus favoured. Peter the Great decreed that every nobleman perform a certain service, often a lifelong one, for the state; otherwise the privileges in question were forfeited. Thus was the nobility pacified: 'Compelled by permanent service, shunted about by central commands from assignment to assignment and from region to region, the nobility became an aggregate completely dependent upon the state' (Skocpol 1979: 86). These service requirements were later loosened up somewhat, under Catherine the Great especially, and the nobility gained greater opportunities to own the lands that they administered. As a result of the low productivity of Russian agriculture, however, the economic yield from these properties was often very limited. A post within the state was usually required to achieve a manner of living consistent with aristocratic status, and the competition for such posts was hard. Submission and rigid obedience to the tsar and his representatives were demanded of those seeking advancement. The competition for such offices scarcely contributed to unity and solidarity within the aristocracy. The nobles also lacked firm local roots which might have helped cement a common identity, since their properties were usually spread out across the realm. Nor did they dispose of institutions supportive of class formation. Such aristocratic assemblies as existed—the *Duma* and the *Sobor*—were controlled in all essentials by the state. They were organs of consultation between the government and its dependent subordinates. Hence they furnished no counter-weight to royal authority. By the early 1700s, they had gone out of existence.

The members of the aristocracy lived on privileges conferred by the state; as a collective, they possessed no political capacity. The special organs for the nobility—*Assemblies of Divoriane*—created by Catherine in 1785 did not change this state of affairs. These assemblies were virtually devoid of competence; nor were they combined with any corporate rights and immunities. Lacking coherence and identity as a group, and bereft of any local or regional footing, the nobility was unable to balance the power of the monarchy.

Under the Mongols, the Greek Orthodox Church had still enjoyed an independent standing. After the rule of the tsars was established, however, the autonomy of the church was successively curtailed. It was made into a kind of department of the state in the early 1700s, and one strictly subordinate to the ruler of Russia. Moreover, of the once prosperous trading cities that had existed at the beginning of the 1500s, only Novgorod remained free: an oligarchical rule of burghers prevailed there, in accordance with the pattern of city-states in western Europe. The crushing of Novgorod in 1570 by Ivan IV—otherwise known as Ivan the Terrible—marked the end of the free cities. This was also the beginning of the end for the burghers as an economic and political power factor in Russia. In the mid-1600s, the inhabitants of some of the larger cities—Moscow and Novgorod among others—revolted against the heavy taxation to which they were subject, and the revolt spread to some agricultural provinces. Once the uprising had been crushed, the cities were placed under strict supervision. Their administration was incorporated into that of the central power, and crafts and trade within their bounds were strictly regulated. A significant proportion of the town dwellers— traders and artisans, that is—was even declared to be serfs: a circumstance unique in Europe. Sharp restrictions were placed on migration to and from the cities, isolating them from the surrounding society. As a result of this policy, the cities lost their economic importance, and they were assigned mainly military and administrative tasks instead. They came under the administration of subalterns of the tsar, and service personnel accounted for a growing share of their inhabitants. Stripped of all autonomy, the cities were made into outposts of royal authority in the vast Russian realm.

The population of the countryside scarcely fared better. The peasants, who formed the productive base of the prevailing system of privilege, were declared to be serfs. Isolated in their villages, they were left to the tender mercies of the aristocrats charged with their governance. 'Prohibited from lodging complaints against landlords and indeed forbidden to appear in court, the peasant was completely defenceless *vis-à-vis* anyone in authority' (Pipes 1995: 154). Completely without legal and political rights, and pressed by the state and its privileged stratum of servitors, who took with both hands and gave nothing in return, the peasantry viewed all authorities with hostility. A leftover from earlier times was seen in the village councils—*mir*—which continued to operate. These were responsible for the collection of taxes, the conscription of soldiers, and the performance of various labour services. Otherwise, however, they were powerless. This system was greatly valued by the regime, for it imposed a collective responsibility for the payment of taxes and the performance of other duties: if a subject escaped from the village, which was strictly forbidden but took place constantly, the others had to carry out the duty instead. Under conditions much like those prevailing in China, the pattern of an atomized hourglass society was established. People lived in dense and closed communities at the local level. In the absence of any kind of intermediate structure, however, they were cut off from all contact with each other; nor did they have any upward links with the elite ruling over them. Russia became, like China, a country of mighty peasant uprisings. These revolts were commonly led by the warlike Tartar tribes living on the shores of the Black Sea, and they were often very violent. They were driven by poverty, flagrant oppression, and land hunger. In the absence of organization and coordination, however, such popular mobilizations could not contend over the long run with the well-armed and disciplined troops of the regime. Yet on the day any of these conditions strengthening the regime and weakening the peasants changed, Russia would be shaken by a great political convulsion (Anderson 1978: 349ff; Bendix 1978: 88ff; Skocpol 1979: 81ff; Downing 1992: 38ff; Finer 1997 III: 1405ff; Pipes 1995).

During a critical phase at the end of the Middle Ages, then, Russia was transformed into one of the great strongholds of autocracy in Europe. All pluralist tendencies as had once existed had been systematically done away with. Organs of representation were dismantled. Rights and immunities for various social strata were conspicuous by their absence. The Russian state was heavily centralized; affairs out in the regions and localities were run by servitors of the tsar; they were given a broad competence but entrusted with a very short tenure, and thus they moved constantly across the realm. In no respect were the tsar or his servitors affected by legal restrictions. To the extent any legal system of a universal character can be said to have existed in Russia before the mid-1800s, its function was to codify the rights of the state as against its subjects (Anners 1990*b*: 176ff).

A similar development, if not fully so pronounced in a despotic direction, took place somewhat later in the nearby state of Brandenburg-Prussia. Conditions at the start here were also, interestingly enough, altogether different from what they later became. Brandenburg-Prussia possessed at the dawn of the New Era a form of government which by the standards of the day was free, pluralistic, and constitutional to the highest degree. The area had been settled in the Middle Ages by German peasants. The result was in large part a frontier society, and one with a lively system of local self-government. The peasants had a strong economic position, and were guaranteed far-reaching civil and constitutional rights in law. There were also a number of significant trading cities, such as Königsberg and Danzig. The cities had combined into associations, and many were members of the Hanseatic League. The nobles were in many cases large landowners, but they had no juridical or administrative privileges. Decisions made at the village court—the *Landding*, which was dominated by peasants—governed nobles in the district as well. On account of their legal status and guaranteed rights, the peasants of Brandenburg-Prussia were among the freest in all of Europe.

To a high degree, moreover, Brandenburg-Prussia was a decentralized state formation; the population out in the provinces in large part governed itself. The central power, represented by the Elector in Berlin, had for its part a rather circumscribed role. One factor contributing to this was the unusually lively parliamentary tradition that had developed: 'By the early seventeenth century the estates had developed into able representative bodies that shaped foreign policy, supervised and audited the crown's undertakings, influenced the appointment of ministers and local administrators, and handled the collection of taxes and tolls they had approved' (Downing 1992: 85).

Like Russia, however, Brandenburg-Prussia was subjected to far-reaching assaults from surrounding states, with plunder, ruin, and death the result thereof. Worst of all was the devastation in the Thirty Years' War of 1618–48, when large land areas were laid waste, above all by the ravages of the Swedes. The difficulties were in large measure caused, as in Russia's case, by geography. A country of open plains is easy to invade. But it was also a consequence of

the form of political organization. In order to field the large armies
now needed for a successful military defence, it was necessary to
mobilize the forces of the nation in a manner which the decentralized and pluralistic state of Brandenburg-Prussia found most
difficult. During the latter part of the 1600s, therefore, the
Hohenzollern princes ruling the country undertook to alter this
state of affairs. Through an agreement in 1653 with the *Landtag* of
Brandenburg, Frederick William I succeeded in obtaining revenues
for the maintenance of a standing army of limited size. With this
force at his disposal, he could subsequently decree tax increases on
his own, making possible a continuous growth in military strength.
Parliamentary organs opposed to such decrees were brushed aside.
This strategy was successful because of an alliance with the nobility, which had been badly knocked about during the preceding wars.
In the new type of state now established, the aristocracy was
accorded a highly privileged position. The victims of this settlement
were in the first case the peasants; they were bound to the soil
and deprived of their former right of local self-government.
Administration in the countryside was subsequently conducted by
the crown, in cooperation with local landowners, the *Junkers*.
Several cities, with Königsberg at their head, protested against the
levies imposed. After 1674, however, when Königsberg was subdued
and its municipal independence abolished, the opposition of the
burghers was ended for a long time to come.

The Hohenzollern princes rapidly built up a formidable military
machine, and by the mid-1700s Prussia was one of Europe's foremost military powers. This was accomplished by means of a far-
reaching centralization, together with a strict focus on military
objectives. As the Sparta of the modern age, Prussia became the
very emblem of the military state. The price for this was paid by the
previously free peasants, who had now become serfs, and by the
town dwellers, who had seen their cities transformed from free trading centres into garrison towns under the control of the central government. There could be no doubt that, from the standpoint of
power, it was the Elector, later the king, who had emerged from the
contest victorious. Decentralization and pluralism disappeared, as
did the representative assemblies: the last *Landtag* was held in
1704. Among the other actors, the nobility had clearly met with success.[3] The *Junkers* were guaranteed exemption from taxation. It
was also they who came to administer the growing state apparatus.

---

[3] Since Prussia was a Protestant country, its church had been subordinate to the
state since the 1500s.

It was, however, above all in the officer corps that aristocrats became, through explicit privilege, the dominant social force. They also gradually acquired a strong position in the bureaucracy. In addition, the *Junkers* carried out administrative tasks in the countryside, where their landed properties supplied them with an independent economic base. But this base was generally insufficient. The nobles depended on their positions in the military and administrative apparatuses to maintain their economic status.

Dominated as it was by extensive agriculture, Prussia was not a rich country; nor was its population a large one. What made its militarist build-up possible was a highly efficient state machinery, the administrative backbone of which consisted of the *Generalkriegskommisariat*, a body responsible for both military and fiscal tasks. Administration on the local level was handled by aristocratic councils: *Landräte*. Both individually and collectively, in other words, the *Junkers* were inserted into the Prussian military state. At the same time, they were the object of extensive control. Noblemen were forbidden to carry on trade or to enter a profession, and their social life—patterns of marriage, journeys abroad, and so forth—was strictly regulated too. It was a service nobility that had been created, with privileges granted by the state, and with duties of a far-reaching character also (Bendix 1978: 145ff; Anderson 1978: 251ff; Poggi 1978: 71ff; Downing 1992: 84ff; Ertman 1997: 224ff; Finer 1997 III: 1358ff).

Due to the administrative skill of its bureaucrats, in combination with the fiscal prudence of its rulers—the Hohenzollerns were renowned for their austere manners—Prussia was capable of fielding a standing army of an amazing size. Continuing military victories during the 1700s helped extend the territory and tax base. Nevertheless, Prussia remained a small state in demographic terms, and it was based on an undeveloped agrarian economy. When, after the French Revolution, Prussia was faced with a rival commanding greater resources, it proved incapable of catching up. The state went bankrupt in 1795. When the country was attacked by Napoleon some ten years later, the Prussian army was completely crushed. Several years of occupation by the French army followed. For over a century, then, resources had been successfully mobilized for military purposes, but now both the state and society were exhausted. The garrison state of Prussia had become overextended (Ertman 1997: 252ff).

In Spain, too, there had been a long tradition of parliamentary representation since the Middle Ages. Estate-based assemblies—*Cortes*—had been convened as early as in the thirteenth century, and these organs had achieved a constitutional standing of particular importance in that part of the country which, until Spain's unification at the end of the 1400s, had constituted the kingdom of Aragon. In the realm's other portion, Castile, representative arrangements had attained a substantially lesser degree of institutionalization: the *Cortes* was convened on a more ad hoc basis than in Aragon, and with prerogatives of a more restricted nature. Once the country had been unified and the Moors expelled,[4] the royal power increasingly disregarded the *Cortes* in Castile. In this, the most populous part of the realm, the king could in practice push through, on his strength of his own authority, the progressively heavier taxes needed for his growing military apparatus. The church and the nobility, for their part, were pacified by grants of exemption from taxation. For the aristocracy, moreover, profitable careers opened up in the bureaucracy and the military. The nobles were also able to appropriate large landed properties in the areas recently controlled by the Moors. The tax burden fell on the peasants and on the burghers of the cities. The latter group sought in the 1520s to defend itself through a large-scale uprising. Demands were raised for a strengthening of the *Cortes*. The authorities were able, however, to crush the revolt. The political subordination of the cities to the crown was thereby a fact. This would be followed in time by a palpable retardation, in economic terms too, for the once flourishing trade centres of Castile.

The peasants, be it noted, gave the burghers no assistance in this struggle. The former population group, which naturally overshadowed all others in size, had a very weak standing in Castile. The countryside was dominated by large aristocratic estates. The peasants were usually either tenants, in highly straitened circumstances, or day labourers on the estates. The latter arrangement—the *latifundia* model—became the more common in the course of time. Strongly dependent as they were on their lords, the peasants were politically marginalized. As in Russia and Prussia, they bore the swollen garrison state largely upon their own shoulders, through the taxes they paid to it, yet they lacked all influence over it. In contrast with their counterparts in Europe's eastern regions, however, the peasants of Spain were not bound to the soil. This may be explained by the fact that, unlike in eastern Europe, there was a large surplus of labour in the Spanish countryside.

An extremely important supplement to the Spanish treasury from the mid-1500s on was provided by revenues in the form of

---

[4] The Arab Mores invaded Spain in the early 700s, and were finally driven out at the end of the 1400s.

large cargoes of silver shipped over from South America. Backed by this ample influx of resources, the Spanish crown built up a large and well-equipped army, the peer of which was not to be found in Europe. The navy too was greatly expanded. Half a century and more of expansionary militarism would now follow, sustained by an administrative structure of a highly centralized kind. Already under Ferdinand and Isabel—the rulers who had united the two kingdoms—the basis for the hegemony of the central power in Castile had been laid. The castles of the nobles had been torn down, and the governance of the cities was taken over by administrators obedient to the crown. Subsequent rulers—now of the Habsburg dynasty, Charles V and Phillip II—pursued the same policy with a firm hand. A far-reaching and, for its time, remarkably well-ordered central administration, under the command of the king, was established.

But this applied only in Castile. Conditions elsewhere in the realm were otherwise. The mighty kingdom of Spain, which at the close of the 1500s extended to Portugal, the Low Countries and large parts of Italy, was in administrative terms a strongly divided state. Each part had its own special privileges and legislation. In Aragon, with its more vibrant *Cortes*, the influence of the king in Madrid was sharply limited. Attempts were made to apply a Castilian form of government in Aragon also. This led to a serious rebellion in the 1600s, and France intervened on the side of Aragon. The central government was forced to yield and to abandon its earlier claims.

In other parts of the kingdom too, rights of various sorts had been instituted which curtailed the penetration of the central power. This was reflected above all in the fiscal area. Notwithstanding the vast geographical extent of the empire, it was in reality only Castile, with its hard-pressed peasant population, which yielded substantial revenues to the treasury. Then there was the flow of silver from America. At the most this accounted, in the late 1500s, for 20–25 per cent of state revenue. But given the enormous expenditures required for the numerous and protracted wars, this was insufficient. The influx of coin from without also undermined Spain's economy over the long run, through the price increases it occasioned, which harmed the competitiveness of agriculture, crafts, and the budding industrial sector. The internal tax base was thereby undermined. As a result, the state was unable to repay the large-scale loans it had incurred to foreign bankers. On repeated occasions, therefore, the crown had to declare bankruptcy. The situation got no better when, in the 1600s, the revenues from America successively declined. This was a result of the silver mines' exhaustion, but also of the fact that the English and Dutch fleets were now seizing ever more of the floating treasure.

It was precisely the encounter with England and the Netherlands which largely settled the fate of Spain. Phillip II sent a great armada to subjugate England, with a thoroughly dismal result. At about the same time—towards the close of the 1500s—the Dutch rose in protest at the attempts of the king to curtail their autonomy and to increase taxes. Hereupon followed a war that lasted almost 80 years and drained the Spanish treasury completely. In the end, the Netherlands won its freedom. Portugal broke loose at the same time. The possessions in Italy were also lost. At the end of the 1600s, Spain was a power at the end of its tether.

Parallel with this decline internationally, a softening-up of the state took place internally. The Castilian royal power retained, to be sure, much of its closed and despotic character. But the central bureaucracy decayed, and on the local level it was increasingly the landowning aristocracy and the church that carried out administration. The root of the problem was the worsening lack of revenue. The regime therefore turned to the sale of offices and appointments on a large scale: a strategy which tended to erode the political and administrative control exercised by the state. A turn for the better took place, however, with the accession of the Bourbon dynasty, which was installed in the early 1700s through the intervention of foreign powers. Reinforced by new mineral finds in America, and sensibly refraining from foreign adventures, the regime was able to recover and to increase its internal strength. What followed was a renaissance for the centralist order. The means was the reconstruction of a professional and well-functioning administration. A more unitary state could now be created on the Iberian peninsula. This entailed the abolition of representative organs, which had placed a limit, especially in Aragon, on the power of the kings. The population—uncoordinated, splintered, held down by the state—could offer little in the way of resistance. Spain entered the nineteenth century as one of Europe's most autocratic states, its competitors in this respect being Russia and Prussia. In none of these countries were there representative organs of any significance; nor was the royal power hemmed in by constitutional restrictions of another kind. Thus had it been in Russia for many centuries. In Prussia and in Spain outside of Castile, the autocratic structure was completed at a later date, but seemed now to be firmly established (Myers 1975: 59ff, 97ff; Andersson 1978: 62ff; Kennedy 1987: 41ff; Burkholder and Johnson 1994: 70ff, 234ff; Ertman 1997: 57ff; Finer 1997 III: 1286ff, 1383ff).

Autocracy reigned in France too at the start of the 1800s: Napoleon Bonaparte had usurped power and proclaimed himself emperor. A short time before, dramatic upheavals had taken place in France. The old royal regime had been thrown out by a popular revolution. A new constitutional order had seen the light of day, and for a brief time had functioned.

Let us first, however, go back in time. The state established by the French kings in the Middle Ages was a rather loose unit. It had been created through agreements with various regional and local power groupings; in legal and administrative terms, consequently, it was highly splintered. Each of the many provinces, and sometimes units within them as well, possessed special privileges and rights which the central power had undertaken to respect. A plethora of rules applied regarding taxation and the administration of justice. A wide variety of measurements, weights, and currencies was in use. These conditions largely persisted right up to the French Revolution.

As in many other countries of Europe, a parliamentary tradition had developed in France during the Middle Ages. Especially during the Hundred Years' War with England, the representative assemblies—Estates—had succeeded in strengthening their position; their approval was needed, after all, to gather the heavy taxes required. The provincial assemblies, however, were the important organs; it was with them that the royal power had to negotiate on a more regular basis. At particular times, and often at long intervals, an Estates-General was convened, with the charge of representing the entire realm. This was an unwieldy assembly, for the representatives composing it, who were appointed by the provincial estates, had usually been granted but a limited mandate. The centre of gravity in the interchange between people and king lay at the provincial level. For this reason, no national arena capable of binding together the different regions and population groups had ever really been created in France.

In France, the nobility had been society's dominant political group to a high degree. True, its military hegemony had been lost, like that of its counterparts in other countries, on account of developments in military technology. Moreover, with the liberation of the peasants and the strengthening of their economic position, the juridical and administrative standing of the aristocracy had been weakened at the local level. The extension and local penetration of the state administration had had the same effect. Noblemen were gradually 'released' from many of the tasks they had performed as governors of their home districts. Yet the aristocracy was very well-off in economic terms. France was a rich agricultural country, and the nobles held large estates. They were exempt from taxation besides. Through their strong position in the organs controlling legislation, moreover, they exercised strong political influence. It was the nobles who played the leading role in the provincial estates. They also controlled the juridical organs known as *parlements*. These operated in all reaches of the realm, and functioned as the highest court of appeal; they also wielded a portion of the legislative power. For royal decrees to gain legal force, they had to be confirmed by the *parlements*. The striking thing about these organs was that they were staffed by officials who disposed over their post as a personal property: these offices were bought, and they could be inherited or sold. Staffed by unremovable persons of high economic standing, noblemen as a rule, the *parlements* had acquired great autonomy *vis-à-vis* the royal power they were charged with supervising. Many other state offices stood at aristocratic disposal as well, for in these cases, too, vacancies were filled through sale. Such sales were a way for the state to gather revenue. The French aristocracy did become a service nobility of sorts. But not on Prussian or Russian terms. Aristocrats in France enjoyed an independence *vis-à-vis* the central power lacked by their counterparts in the east. The services they rendered, furthermore, were commonly of a much less demanding sort. Often it was a question quite simply of sinecures, created to glorify their occupants and to enable them to strengthen their economic standing at the expense of the treasury. Many French nobles lived a life of frivolity and ease far from the frugal conditions faced by their counterparts under Tsar Peter and the Hohenzollerns.

Through an agreement with the Pope in connection with the Reformation, the king of France had acquired the right to appoint bishops, as had the king in Spain. As an institution, therefore, the church was not independent from the state. It retained its large properties, which were exempt from taxation, and priests formed an estate of their own in the representative assemblies. There the priests usually made common cause with the nobles, for the dignitaries who represented them were usually of aristocratic birth.

France formed part of Europe's urban belt. Here, however, the superiority of the territorial power showed itself rather early. The cities were placed under royal rule. Yet this was often done in a manner retaining much of the older forms. The cities were usually allowed to keep their system of internal self-government. They could also acquire various privileges and special conditions in the area of taxation. In the estates, the cities—or their oligarchical elite, more precisely—constituted the Third Estate.

In the late Middle Ages the peasants of France had been able to improve their lot in several ways. No longer were they serfs bound to land and lord. They were free, and they enjoyed—in reality, though not yet formally—property rights over the land they worked. Over large portions of the country, moreover, they had established vibrant village communities. These popularly governed bodies attended to various public matters. They regulated farming, and they administered common property like the village pasture. They saw to the maintenance of roads, bridges, and so forth, and they appointed local officials, such as those responsible for collecting taxes. Here we find parallels with conditions in Russia. The French peasants were certainly much freer and more prosperous than their brethren to the east. Yet their forms of local government were remarkably similar. There was also a long tradition in both cases of rebellious behaviour on the part of the peasants; and, notwithstanding the difference in living conditions, this was a similarity destined to persist. What they had in common was the existence of a local social capital which, in the absence of any institutionalized connection with the organs of state power, got channelled into violent, uncoordinated outbreaks of popular protest. Such is the nature of an hour-glass society:[5] a local collective capacity is at hand, but it is restricted and curtailed. Due to the lack of intermediary structures, it cannot get any outward expression in orderly manners.

The contrast with Prussia is striking in this regard. Peasants in the latter country were scarcely freer than those in Russia, and economically they were usually worse off than their counterparts in France. Yet no peasant uprisings took place in Prussia.[6] The reason for this, most likely, is that Prussian peasants had been deprived of a crucial form of social capital they once had possessed: access, that is, to local arenas of action under their own control. The situation was the same for the hard-pressed peasants of Castile, who could not rise up against their oppressors either. In these countries a collective capacity at the bottom of society was conspicuous by its absence. This observation seems to modify William Kornhauser's notion of the passive-cum-eruptive character of mass society.[7] The most eruptive conditions, involving the greatest risk for the powers that be, tend generally to exist in those societies that contain a vital degree of encapsulated social capital at the bottom of society. When,

---

[5] See Chapter 2, p. 34.

[6] This did not happen even when other groups took up the cudgels, as in 1848.

[7] See Chapter 1, pp. 9–10.

on the other hand, people at the grass roots are completely atomized, conditions for the ruling elite tend to be much safer.

Now back to France. The French crown had emerged strengthened from the Hundred Years' War. In order to be able to drive out
the English, who for a long time had enjoyed great success, the king
had been furnished with a small standing army, for which he had
the right to collect taxes on a running basis. This arrangement persisted in peacetime as well, so that the French kings had achieved
a relatively strong position by the onset of the New Era. But conditions soon changed. The wars of religion that broke out in Europe in
the 1500s struck the religiously splintered kingdom of France with
particular ferocity. The central power was markedly weakened
thereby. For long periods, in fact, virtual anarchy prevailed in the
country. Once the turbulence had subsided, however, with the victory of the Catholic side, a clear trend back to centralism got under
way in the first half of the seventeenth century. Under forceful royal
ministers—cardinals Richelieu and Mazarin—a central administration was built up, with efficient branches reaching down to the
local level. The links in this system were furnished by *intendants*.
These royal representatives had very far-reaching tasks. They
supervised tax collection and military conscription, and they
assumed many administrative duties previously carried out by
nobles, burghers, and peasants. The representative assemblies, for
their part, were assigned a more modest role. The national organ,
the Estates-General, was not convened after 1615, and the majority
of provincial assemblies soon became wholly inactive.

The *intendants* collected taxes by military means. In protest at
the increasing centralism, and in defence of old rights, an aristocratic uprising known as the *Fronde* broke out in the mid-1600s.
The uprising was violent, and in many areas it was supported by
peasants weary of heavy taxes. Several cities joined the revolt too.
In the absence, however, of any coordination between the various
actions, the movement was unable to hold off the royal army. The
latter's victory was the signal for a great militarist and autocratic
build-up under the forceful leadership of Louis XIV. It was now possible to field well-equipped armies on a gigantic scale. Following the
decline of Spain, France emerged as the outstanding power of
Europe. Taxes were collected by a hierarchically structured and
well-manned administration. Such peasant uprisings as flared here
and there were put down. Little space now existed for opposition in
traditional institutionalized forms. The provincial estates that still
met had but small influence, and through royal decree the *parlements* were deprived of their right to influence legislation. 'L'État

c'est moi', Louis XIV explained (Myers 1975: 101ff; Anderson 1978: 89ff; Bendix 1978: 327ff; Skocpol 1979: 118ff; Downing 1992: 114ff; Ertman 1997: 91ff, 125ff; Finer III: 1358ff).

Yet despite the splendour surrounding the 'Sun King' and his successors, this mighty new power suffered from the same problem that Spain had, and later also Prussia: it consumed far more, in the way of revenues, than it took in. This fiscal imbalance became increasingly acute during the 1700s. Enormous sums, for which no corresponding taxes were collected, were spent on recurrent martial undertakings. Nor was the situation improved by the fact that, increasingly, such military ventures turned out badly for France. It was England, once again, which was the 'villain of the piece'. In order to escape the fiscal trap in which it had been snared, the regime tried to make fundamental changes in its tax system in the 1760s. The ambition was to broaden the tax base so as also to include the great landholdings of the nobility and of the church. Royal decrees of such an import encountered, however, ferocious resistance. The *parlements* abolished by Louis XIV were reinstated following his death in 1715; with time, moreover, they re-assumed their role as a vigorous check on the royal power. It was these organs that led the resistance to the proposed new taxes. In addition to an intensive war of words, in which the decrees were branded an expression of despotism and banditry, certain *parlements* also staged acts of flagrant civil disobedience, arresting the state functionaries responsible for taxation in their province. In the *parlements*, it became clear, the nobles had a highly effective intermediate structure. These organs, which together consisted of about 1,000 magistrates, were closely connected with each other, and they were firmly anchored in the aristocracy of their respective areas. This gave the *parlements*, and the social group they represented, a capacity for forceful collective action lacked by other groups. As a consequence, the king retreated. But since, on account of continued foreign adventures, the fiscal crisis worsened with each new decade, the royal tax proposals re-appeared. The king also tried on several occasions to break the *parlements* by removing their political functions or replacing them with other organs under the crown's control. But all such strategies failed. This failure resulted first and foremost from aristocratic obstruction, but also from the fact that, in its struggle with the king, the nobility enjoyed strong support from an ever larger intelligentsia, which exerted a significant influence over opinion formation. Attacks on the royal autocracy, and on the decadent, luxurious life surrounding it, were legion in such quarters.

The critique launched by the *parlements* was often based on liberal legal principles. The demand was for taxation by consent. The *parlements* demanded that an Estates-General be convened. Its task would be to confront the fiscal problems of the realm and to adopt a constitution limiting royal power. In this, the *parlements* believed they spoke for the entire nation. And, notwithstanding the narrow social base of these organs, such a claim was not without merit. The church, the leading stratum of which was dominated by aristocrats, took the same position as the *parlements*, especially since its own exemption from taxation was in danger too. The burghers, whose commercial sector had often enjoyed prosperity under the absolute monarchy, long played a passive role politically; as a rule, however, they sympathized with the opposition to tax increases, which, after all, would strike them too. Opposition to the *ancien régime* was strongest, however, among the rapidly growing professional strata. These joined with the nobility in repudiating the prevailing 'despotism' and in demanding constitutional reforms. It was here that the opposition had its central power base.

Pressed by worsening debts, and unable on his own to devise a solution, Louis XVI agreed to convene an Estates-General. The date was set at May 1789.

The organ that was to convene had not met in 170 years. In important respects, in fact, it was a new representative body that had been established. First of all, it was an elected body. Previously, the representatives for the different estates had occupied their places by right of inheritance or, in the case of priests and the Third Estate, *ex officio*, so that the cities, for example, had been represented by their officials. This time, however, there were individual elections. Moreover, an extremely wide suffrage was applied. Almost the entire male population had the right to participate. Nothing of the kind had ever been seen before in the history of Europe. The way in which the voting was done, however, was of a traditional, highly particular sort. Elections took place in steps: citizens first gathered in local meetings, at which the members of each estate chose representatives to regional organs, where the final selection took place. Those assembled at local meetings were not just to choose representatives; they were also to choose the demands they wanted their representatives to make. This electoral procedure had a strongly mobilizing consequence. Suddenly, at about 40,000 meetings all around the country, arenas were made available for popular contact and deliberation. The application of this electoral system, which was designed for an ancient mode of representation,[8] in combination with broad-based suffrage, turned out to have strongly polarizing effects. What had been prepared was no less than a bomb.

Among the broad mass of the people, there was an aggressive discontent with the prevailing order, and especially with the nobility's remaining local rights: production monopolies, tithes—that is, land rents—from the peasants, rights to hunt on their land, and so forth. These sentiments could now be aired and shaped into distinct collective identities. And not just that. Due to its step-by-step structure, the electoral process provided an institutional link which had not previously existed between the countryside and the cities. An arena for cooperation between representatives of the different groups was created in the regional assemblies. This contributed to an increased collective capacity on the part of the lower strata. Given the prevailing discontent at the grass roots, which now could be 'tapped', and due to the deliberative nature of the proceedings, the electoral process tended at each step to further radicalize the political demands. A long-prevailing hour-glass structure was suddenly opened up, setting the stage for aggressive pressure from bellow.

Those sent to Versailles as representatives for the Third Estate were usually members of the urban professional stratum, and they had often won their mandate with a fierce criticism of the prevailing order. A selection by stages also took place in the other estates. This had the result, in the case of the priestly estate, that the dignitaries who had traditionally served as spokesmen were now weakly represented. The majority were priests from the grass roots level, with great sympathy for popular discontent. Within the nobility, on the other hand, a selection took place in the opposite direction. Those who departed for the royal palace were those wishing most ardently to preserve the traditional social order—but combined, as in former times, with representation.

Those who met in Versailles were representatives for a society splintered along the lines of class. The privileges of the aristocracy had not diminished with the years; if anything, they had been

[8] It derived from the practice applied in the old Estates-General, which had had a very restricted decision-making capacity. The idea was that the persons chosen from the various constituencies were not representatives with a free mandate. They were delegates, rather, and their task was to convey their constituent's wishes to the king. Each electoral assembly had to write up a document—or *cahier*—summarising its deliberations and furnishing its representative with instructions (Aminzade 1995; 48: Furet 1996; 51ff).

reinforced during recent decades.[9] Aristocratic privileges at the local level remained; but now, they were not combined with any administrative duties. Indeed, the presence of the nobles in the locality was not even required. This made for sharp social tensions, which were now exposed to the light of day. Opposition to the royal power, which had united the nobility with parts of the bourgeoisie, no longer cemented the two groups together. Their positive programmes were too different. The nobility sought, in the spirit of Montesquieu, to return to the division of power that had obtained before the autocracy. The Third Estate wanted a new constitutional order based on individual representation, not on representation by estate. One important question, when representatives for different camps gather, is what kind of representatives these are. Things proceed most easily when all sides are represented by soft-liners—persons disposed to make deals and to compromise (Przeworski 1991; 1992). But of this spirit there was little in Versailles in May 1789. It was in reality a new organ that had been established, and within it there was little of that habituation to resolving conflicts that long-functioning parliamentary institutions are able to establish. Those present were all 'freshmen', without experience of wheeling and dealing and compromise, and in many cases they had been chosen for the sake of their uncompromising views. The assembled representatives were mostly hard-liners.

Confrontation came immediately. The Third Estate demanded an amalgamation into a single assembly, which it would be able to dominate. When the king, who now took the side of the nobles, tried to intervene, the Third Estate proclaimed itself the National Assembly. The revolution was now, in a constitutional sense, a fact. But the social upheavals, and the more fundamental political changes flowing from them, took place outside of parliament, in accordance with a largely self-generating logic.

Spontaneous popular revolts now broke out all over the country, in both city and countryside. The Bastille was stormed, and in Paris the electoral assembly which had preceded the election took power. The same thing happened in many other cities too. In the countryside, peasants attacked aristocratic estates. This was no question of ordinary plunder; what the peasants wanted was to tear down was the entire feudal system, socially and economically. These revolts had already started in connection with the elections in the spring,

---

[9] A clear sign of this was the fact that only nobles of the fourth generation, that is, the old aristocracy—the king could always make new nobles by raising bourgeois to noble rank—had been granted the right to serve as officers in the army.

and they were strongly influenced by the mobilization around common interests which had then taken place: 'Extraordinary as it may seem, every peasant community was invited by order of the king to ruminate collectively upon its troubles. The result surely was, on the whole, to heighten possibilities for peasants to rebel, especially against seigneurs and nonlocal recipients of the tithes' (Skocpol 1979: 123).

The assaults on the nobles' domains gradually became more widespread and violent. The major economic foundation of the aristocratic class was all at once threatened; and the royal power, which in other circumstances could have come to the aid of the nobles, now had no help to give. The king had been arrested by the rebelling popular masses, and he had acknowledged the authority of the sitting National Assembly. Soldiers in the army deserted, or attacked their aristocratic officers. *Intendants* and other representatives of the crown could be easily driven away, for they lacked military support (Zolberg 1986; Palmer 1964: 86ff, 448ff; Bendix 1978: 357ff; Skocpol 1979: 123ff, 178ff; Downing 1992: 130ff; Mann 1993: 168ff; Ertman 1997: 139ff; Finer 1997 III: 1519ff).

The nobility had been, economically speaking, society's leading group. Through the positions held by its members in the state apparatus, and due to institutional structures serving to promote cohesion and coordinated action, it had been able over the course of the preceding century to advance its position considerably. Its ambitions rose during this period. Its aim was to gain a constitutionally regulated influence over the state power. The process it initiated, however, provided power resources to groups which had been shut out from all influence earlier. These groups took central control and proclaimed the National Assembly, whereupon the nobility, as an estate, was politically excluded. On the local level, meanwhile, popular rebellions broke the aristocracy's economic base. Almost in a single blow, the group which had been central in driving the process forward became its primary victim. The groups into whose hands the aristocracy had placed political resources, in an effort to humble the royal power, turned their weapons on the nobles themselves.[10]

The turn of events was the outcome of the combined effect of two particular factors. Significant collective capacities, first of all, were at hand both at the top and at the bottom of society—which is

---

[10] The influential *parlement* in Paris, as well as that in Grenoble, had in fact demanded an even wider suffrage than that ultimately applied: that is to say, full universal male suffrage (Palmer 1964: 479).

unusual.[11] Through attempts to join these forces, which had both
been politically excluded, new institutional arrangements were set
up through initiative from the top. The specific nature of these institutions—that is the second factor—came to have dramatic, and
unintended, consequences. New arenas and channels for popular
interaction were created. The founding of these institutions gave
rise to an eruptive mobilization from below which their architects
were unable to stop.

The French Revolution is a milestone in the history of the
Western world. We regard the constitutional rights then proclaimed
as among the basic ethical principles of democracy. For the concrete
political life of France, however, the revolution was in many ways a
failure. The process soon deteriorated into terror, dictatorship, and
lawlessness. Scarcely more than a decade after the overthrow of the
absolute monarchy, moreover, a new autocracy, now under military
auspices, was established.

Due to certain conditions at hand in France, a strong capacity for
mobilization from below was made possible. This ability was not
paired, however, with a conflict-dampening, conciliatory capacity,
which might have mitigated the polarizing effects of political pluralism. No tradition of inter-segmental cooperation existed in
France. The revolution became a brutal winner-take-all game. The
scars of relentless conflict were to remain for many generations to
come.

In France, as opposed to Russia, Prussia, and Spain, autocracy
was done away with at an early point in time. But the pluralist project failed: autocracy was soon to be reborn in France. In certain
other countries, as we shall see, the pluralist venture turned out to
be more successful.

Continuity: England, Sweden, the Netherlands, and North America

The English state was the product of the military conquest carried
out by the Normans in the mid-eleventh century. In comparison
with other states of medieval Europe, therefore, it was unusually
centralized and cohesive. As we know from other examples,

---

[11] In Russia and China, as we saw, independent social capital existed at the bottom, but not at the top, since the aristocracy was firmly tied to the regime. In
Prussia and Spain, neither the elite nor the rank and file had any collective capacity independent of the regime.

however—Prussia and Russia in particular—the conditions prevailing during the Middle Ages could undergo palpable change at a later time. This happened in England too, but the change in question went in the opposite direction from that in Prussia and Russia. For in England, no basis was created at the outset of the New Era for the militarization of society, or for the establishment of an authoritarian political order. Several English monarchs attempted, certainly, to push developments in such a direction. But the forces of civil society were able to mount an effective resistance.

England developed a state with very limited autonomy *vis-à-vis* society. No decisions of any import could be made without negotiating with society's leading groups. Without such 'acceptance', there was little the state could accomplish. Yet this state, sharply curtailed though it was in its decisional capacity, would prove to possess an exceptional capacity for action. In the course of several centuries, starting in the late 1500s, England was to break the power of successive autocratic great powers on the Continent by turn. The party which was the weaker, in terms of concentrated decisional capacity, emerged the stronger in the course of several contests with European rivals. The English state developed a capacity for statecraft which its autocratic competitors could not match.

Let us return to the beginning: the Middle Ages. At this time, England had large possessions in France. This gave rise to perpetual conflicts with the French crown. One war between the rivals began in the mid-1300s and continued for 100 years. In the early period the English were successful, and France suffered severe treatment at their hands. England had a more cohesive administration, and it had adopted the new non-feudal techniques of warfare earlier. It was first when the French royal power had been greatly strengthened, above all through the acquisition of the right to tax on a continuing basis, that the fortunes of war shifted. As a result, England lost its possessions in France. Thus it was no longer a Continental power. Its domains were from now on restricted to the British Isles. This was a setback; but it paved the way for England's future success.

A tradition of representation had been established in England during the wars. For a long time, Parliament had been passive. It did not involve itself in executive duties, as did its counterparts elsewhere in Europe. It acquired, however, an established power of veto: taxes could be levied only with its consent. It consisted of two chambers: the upper for the higher nobility and the dignitaries of the church, the lower for the 'commons'. The leading strata of the cities were represented in the latter; however, the lower chamber was primarily an arena for the lower nobility, or gentry, who were based primarily in the countryside.

It was also these 'gentlemen', as they were called, who were responsible for local administration. The occupants of legal and administrative posts—justices of the peace, sheriffs, and so forth— were appointed by the crown, but established practice had it that such persons were to be drawn from the local gentry. Thus a decentralized amateur administration was built up. The local agents of the state had no training for their position, and they were not paid. This arrangement was a simple one, and cheap for the treasury besides, and it functioned with a tolerable efficiency. These gentlemen-functionaries, who would come to serve as an emblem for republican ideas, had the advantage of strong roots in the local communities they administered. They also had, in Parliament, an institutionalized link to the central power. Those who governed locally were those who dominated the House of Commons. England thus developed a tradition of cooperation between local and central power, and between the state and society as well. The king ruled, but he did so on a consensual basis; he was a king-in-parliament. Parliament, for its part, functioned to a great extent as a meeting-place for the leading persons of the various localities.

Far-reaching struggles took place after the Hundred Years War between different fractions of the higher nobility, in the War of the Roses. This contributed to political disintegration. But once a new dynasty, the Tudors, had been established in the early sixteenth century, the central power came to prominence once more. Henry VIII in particular came to personify the emerging princely power of the New Era. Like his contemporary Gustav Vasa in Sweden, he helped strengthen the central power. The resources for this came above all from the church, the large properties of which were confiscated. Henry also established a central legal organ, the Star Chamber, which curtailed the baronial courts. He set up a secret police, and at times dealt roughly with his opponents—as with his many wives. Yet he never broke with Parliament. The policy of cooperation established during the Middle Ages was in all essentials continued by Henry and the subsequent Tudor monarchs. It was first during the seventeenth century, when a new dynasty from Scotland assumed the throne, that a real struggle between Parliament and king broke out.

The decisive limitation of the English crown was that it lacked the power resources that might have made an autocratic scenario possible. The two components which, in other countries, gave rise to an autocratic 'lever'—a bureaucracy and a standing army, both under the crown's command—were conspicuous in England by their absence. The armies that fought in France during the Hundred Years War had been formed on an ad hoc basis, and they were demobilized when the campaigns ended. This was also the case when, at a later time, Henry and other monarchs sought to intervene in Continental wars. Militias under the control of local officials were responsible for defence on the home front. It was above all the fleet that attended to the outer defence of the realm, and the central power was careful to ensure that it expanded from the 1500s onward. It was an effective weapon. It stopped the Spanish armada that tried to invade England in the late 1500s. A fleet cannot, however, unlike an army, be used for internal political purposes. Despite its growing power, it did not furnish the crown with any trump card in the internal power struggle. The central power was also handicapped in bureaucratic terms. The crown lacked the means to build up a centrally directed administration of its own. Parliament stood in the way of that, dominated as it was by champions of local self-government. The properties of the church, certainly, had provided the crown with a large resource increment, but this was continually drawn on, as sales were undertaken to provide resources 'for today'. The buyers were usually from the gentry, which strengthened its economic position thereby. Nor could the sale of offices, which took place on an ample scale, alter the fiscal situation. When, on a few occasions, the king tried to collect taxes he had imposed without Parliament's approval, the local administration refused to cooperate. The royal power in England had no *intendants* like those in France, nor any *Kriegskommissariat* like that in Prussia.

The struggle for power that took place in the 1600s chiefly concerned the right to tax. But it also contained religious elements. There was a conflict between a Puritan low-church camp, which was strongly represented in Parliament, and a more episcopalian high-church group, with whom the royal power was associated. What is more, several of the Stuart monarchs were Catholics, a fact which sharpened religious antagonisms further. The conflict became acute when Charles I (1625–49) tried to rule without Parliament. A civil war lasting almost ten years ensued; by the time it ended, the king had lost both his crown and his head. The king's economic base lay above all in his unlimited right of taxation in Ireland and Scotland. But this 'free resource' was insufficient, especially since the Scots, groaning under excessive taxation, erupted in rebellion and attacked England. In the long run, the king had no effective weapon against Parliament's capacity to mobilize resources at the local level. Under Oliver Cromwell, Parliament's foremost captain, a republic was established. It lasted for some ten years. With a large army at his disposal, Cromwell was able to govern with harsh and despotic methods. Yet he did not, it is important to note, exceed the mandate given him by Parliament.

The monarchy was restored soon after Cromwell's death in 1658. The old struggles between king and Parliament now resumed. To make a long story short, relations of power between the two sides were basically the same as before. And again, it was the royal power that went down in defeat. The last ruler of the Stuart dynasty was driven from his throne by an invading Dutch army summoned by the leading forces in Parliament. This army was lead by William of Orange, who became the king of England upon his victory. This was the 'Glorious Revolution'. It marked what turned out to be Parliament's decisive victory. The constitutional principles now established, entailing clear limitations on the executive power, formed the foundation of England's future polity. With vigorous rulers on the throne, the royal power could influence affairs awhile yet; but it could not rule without the consent of Parliament.

Later, in the 1700s, it was the parties in Parliament which became the dominant actors in political life. It was the parties which decided, on the basis of their parliamentary strength, the composition of the government. In this way, the system known as parliamentarianism became established in England. The old principle of cooperation between Parliament and the executive power thus found clear expression. And there was no longer any doubt as to which side had become politically dominant. The English state had to a high degree become society's instrument, as society revealed its will in the parliamentary process.

English society had a distinctive social structure. The nobility had not achieved the feudal standing common on the Continent. In the Hundred Years War it was not, primarily, mounted knights that went into battle—which was long the case on the French side—but rather infantryman, who often were mercenaries besides. The military position of the nobility, in other words, was comparatively weak. The aristocracy had also been decimated by protracted internal struggles at the end of the 1400s. What hereafter distinguished the English aristocracy, especially the lower nobility, was its unusually heavy involvement in economic life. Its base was in agriculture, which was commercialized early on. The focus was on the production of wool, which provided the basis for a growing textile industry oriented to export. As Barrington Moore (1967) has noted, a highly distinctive agrarian-urban interest coalition was hereby formed. Between the landed gentry and an increasingly prosperous urban bourgeoisie, there was a connection founded on joint economic interests. It was also primarily these social groups which were represented in Parliament, a fact which further reinforced cohesion.

Under the Norman kings, the church had not been able to achieve the autonomous standing in England that it enjoyed on the Continent. After the Reformation, moreover, it was incorporated into the state. Yet no far-reaching centralization was established in this area either. It was the local gentry who controlled church activities at the parish level. The cities, for their part, had been placed under the central power already under the Norman kings. With the passage of time, however, they became more independent. Many obtained confirmation of their autonomy in the form of charters. The cities had their own administration and legal system, and they were often able to resist crown directives of which they did not approve. As centres of rapidly expanding trade and industry, the cities came to play an ever more important role in English political life.

The changes that took place in agriculture greatly affected the situation of the peasants. In the late Middle Ages, the peasants had achieved a free juridical standing. In contrast to their French colleagues, however, English peasants did not live in dense village communities in which lands to a great extent were administered in common. As agriculture became commercialized, which in England happened early on, the dense village communities were broken up. This had two important consequences. It led, to begin with, to increasing economic stratification among the peasants. Some became tenants, on a larger or smaller scale; others became freeholders, often of a prosperous kind; and still others became agricultural workers. In addition, the peasantry's local organs of decision-making eroded as a consequence of the enclosures. Lacking internal homogeneity, and possessing no organs of coordination of its own, the English peasantry became politically weak. Rather than organizing on a horizontal basis, it developed clientelist ties with the local gentry. As Theda Skocpol (1979) has pointed out, this minimized the risk that struggles on the elite political level would pave the way for eruptive peasant revolts, as happened in France and later on in Russia. England was not a strictly divided society. Through its clientelist ties with the gentry, the peasantry was indirectly linked to the local administration and, more indirectly still, with decision-making on the central level.[12] It was not cut off from

[12] Clientelism is based, certainly, on a relationship of inequality and dependence. Even so, it contains an element of reciprocity and cooperation between the parties. Clientelist networks create links between centre and periphery, and often constitute an initial form of cross-class association. See Chapter 3, pp. 49ff.

other social segments as in France. The fact, moreover, that aristocrats paid taxes—a circumstance unique in Europe—also doubtless facilitated dealings between the different social classes. In addition, the uniform provisions which had been established in the area of civil law served to reconcile the classes. Despite the institutional decay that set in periodically, the people of England were able to achieve gradual, if not always peaceful, changes in their form of government. Relations between the aristocracy and the bourgeoisie were cooperative; nor were the peasants at angry odds with the proprietors who owned a large part of the land and dominated political life.

In the course of time England became, as we know, a great power. Indeed, this long obscure island on the edge of Europe became the nucleus of a world-spanning empire the like of which had never been seen before, nor would be after. This success was based on military victories, on both land and sea, over competing states. These were made possible by two factors in the main. It was in England, to begin with, that the industrial and commercial revolution began. Riches were thereby created giving the state a tax base without peer at the time. In addition, England had a distinctive system of taxation. In contrast to the situation in France, which for long was England's foremost competitor, the English state was able to collect taxes from the richest part of the population also. No privileges obtained in this area. An increasingly well-run tax administration contributed further to fiscal efficiency. England was able thereby to maintain a navy which dominated the seas for centuries, and at the same time equip large armies for upholding the balance of power on the Continent. The country could also provide substantial economic subsidies to other states for the same purpose.

As noted by a famous Member of Parliament, the revenue of the state is the state.[13] In terms of revenue capacity, the British government clearly outranked its foe on the other side of the English Channel. The result was devastating. It was the competition from England that undermined the French treasury, and that paved the way ultimately for the fall of the old regime.

There were many centres of countervailing power in English society. A good many power-seeking kings were forced to discover this. This did not lead, however, to anarchic decentralization and disintegration. For there was also an integrating organ— Parliament—that could vigorously represent the English nation. The representation in question was highly restricted, to be sure. In

[13] See above, p. 136.

the 1700s, only a small percentage of the island's inhabitants could take part in elections. In addition, the borders between the constituencies were drawn in such a manner as to yield a most uneven representation of voters from the different areas. The policies pursued had in large part the character of spoils, the object being to procure narrow clientelistic advantages from the occupancy of office. All the same, this was a political system that functioned unusually well by the standards of the time. It was based on institutionalized cooperation, at both the national and the local level. It was also capable of being gradually reformed over time, and of being broadened to embrace an ever larger share of the population (Zolberg 1986; Palmer 1959: 44ff; Anderson 1978: 119ff; Bendix 1978: 176ff, 218ff; Downing 1992: 157ff; Mann 1993: 112ff; Ertman 1997: 158ff; Finer 1997 III: 1355ff).

Sweden's political history has similarities with England's. In Sweden too, parliamentary forces were able to put a halt to autocratic tendencies, and a 'medieval' state structure founded in constitutionalism could be preserved. But there was otherwise much separating the two states. Swedish society had a wholly different social and economic structure, which resulted not least from the fact that its situation was so different from the standpoint of economic geography.

Sweden's history is that of its peasants. From the beginning, Sweden has been a country of smallholders. As in many other European countries, the peasants lived in small, socially dense village communities. There was a richly developed culture of self-administration based on local cooperation. During the Middle Ages there had been, from the smallest village unit on up to the regional level, institutionally well-developed organs for handling juridical and administrative questions. These organs were under peasant control. About half of the peasants were freeholders; the rest were tenants, usually with secure terms of tenure, on lands owned by nobles or by the church, and, later on, by the crown. The peasants were juridically free and economically largely independent. Through tight peasant communities a strong collective capacity at the base existed in Sweden. In this we see a parallel with France. In Sweden, however, that capacity was not encapsulated, that is, cut off from higher echelons and from other segments of society; the peasantry enjoyed an administrative and political standing without parallel in Europe. The Swedish state, with its king and sundry other positions of privilege, was built atop a peasant society which to a great extent governed itself. Local as well as regional affairs were in all essentials run by the peasants, who had also had their own chamber in parliament—the *Riksdag*—since the late Middle Ages. This latter feature was unique to Sweden. At a very early stage, accordingly, the rank and file—the state's main sources of revenue—could take part in public affairs at the national level, thus interacting with the crown and with other segments of society.

The burghers, the clergy, and the nobles each had their own chamber too. But none of these groups had the same standing in Sweden as elsewhere in Europe. There was a tradition of local self-government in Sweden's cities. But the cities were insignificant, both economically and demographically, until well into modern times. As a political force, the Swedish bourgeoisie was for many centuries conspicuous by its absence. The church was important in the Middle Ages, not least on account of its large landholdings. After the Reformation, however, the church as a corporation was pacified. It was made subject to the crown, which confiscated all of its properties. The Swedish nobility, for its part, was very insignificant by European standards. The squires who had raised themselves above the peasants during the Middle Ages were relatively small in number, and economically their lot were often a meagre one. There was little opportunity, in a sparsely populated country of poor agriculture and vast forests, for any great extravagances. The nobles were exempted from taxes; in return, they had to place a certain number of soldiers at the disposal of the crown. To this extent there was a touch of feudalism. But no more than a touch. No feudal administrative system was ever established in Sweden. The aristocracy possessed no superior administrative or juridical authority at the local level. Nor did it have, notwithstanding its duty to provide soldiers, a feudal standing in the military area. Defence was organized primarily on a militia basis. It consisted of popular militias mobilized by local organs under peasant control.

The Swedish state assumed its modern form under Gustav Vasa (1521–60). Gustav had come to power at the head of a popular rebellion against the Danish supremacy which had obtained since the end of the 1300s, but which had begun as a voluntary union between the countries. He was a vigorous monarch, and at times a ruthless one. The action of his with the greatest importance for the Swedish state was the vast enlargement of royal properties accompanying the Reformation, which Gustav had initiated. The resources now existed to build up a central administration. It should be stressed that, as a state builder, Gustav Vasa was firmly rooted in a constitutional tradition established during the Middle Ages. According to this tradition, the king was subject to the law. He was further enjoined to govern the country in cooperation with the people's representatives. Gustav's royal dignity was founded on the recognition of the *Riksdag*, and all important decisions had to be sanctioned by that body; often, moreover, they received this sanction only with much difficulty. The time-honoured local autonomy also largely survived. It was an overarching administrative structure for national coordination that had been created. But this central apparatus did not primarily function as an 'antipode' to the local civic community. Under the aegis of the new and much firmer state apparatus, cooperation between central and local authorities continued. As in England, parliament—the *Riksdag*—was a sort of clearing house for such contacts.

An important resource for the Swedish crown lay in the rich mineral deposits of silver, copper, and iron found in the country. Sweden became, at the end of the 1500s, the leading metal exporter in Europe; the result was ample revenues for the state from tariffs, production licenses, and so on. Not for nothing did Sweden start establishing itself as a significant military power at this time. On account of the institutional dissolution taking place in Russia and Poland, Sweden was able to send armies of a modest size to the other side of the Baltic Sea. In a short time, Sweden acquired substantial territories in the Baltic lands. This gave the country a springboard for a gigantic military expansion. By the mid-1600s, this small and relatively undeveloped country in the north had converted itself into one of Europe's foremost powers.

The Swedish king Gustav Adolf and his chancellor Axel Oxenstierna were the architects of this feat. The two men built with advantage on Sweden's interactive state, which was able on account of its uniquely popular character to accomplish a highly effective mobilization of national resources; Sweden's *Riksdag* was, it bears recalling, Europe's most democratic parliament by far. By means of a large-scale bureaucratic expansion, the administrative capacity of the state was strengthened, and through skilful political coalition-building, combined with military vigour, Sweden was able to create a resource aggregation of an astonishing scope.

Sweden's transformation into a great power took place during the Thirty Years War (1618–48). As the leading force in the Protestant coalition fighting the Catholic emperor, Sweden fielded enormous armies on German soil. Some of the soldiers in these armies were Swedish conscripts. The lion's share, however, were mercenaries, who were always expensive. How was Sweden able to defray the enormous costs involved? Including the revenues from the Baltic lands, Sweden could itself finance only a third of the costs of the war. The rest was accounted for by subsidies, mainly from France and the Netherlands, and by resources collected on the spot. The latter included resources of two kinds: on the one hand, tributes from German cities and princely houses, which could often be collected on a relatively voluntary basis owing to common religious affiliations; and, on the other, plunder pure and simple, which at times was resorted to on an enormous scale. Germany was, after all, a very wealthy country—up to the war.

With the Treaty of Westphalia in 1648, Sweden acquired still more territory, now on German soil. Yet despite the splendour surrounding the Swedish crown, it was now that the problems piled up. Sweden found it hard to hold these territories in times of peace. Maintaining a military force capable of defending them proved more costly than it was worth. Now there were no more subsidies from allies. Nor was it possible any longer to gather provisions through plunder and similar methods. Now the costs had to be borne by Sweden's own treasury. But the treasury had fallen on harder times. For one thing, mineral exports were now less lucrative than before; for another, the landed properties acquired by the state during the Reformation had in large part been parcelled off. They had been allocated as compensation in kind to the nobles comprising the heart of the Swedish officer corps.

To remedy these financial difficulties, the *Riksdag* decided in 1680 that all lands parcelled out would be returned to the crown, without compensation. The initiative for this measure came from the peasants, who had observed the nobles' gains with apprehension. They won the support of the clergy and the bourgeoisie. The king, Karl XI, also warmly welcomed the measure. Support came from the lower nobility as well, which would be largely unharmed by the measure. It was primarily the higher nobility that was hit— and hit hard. Thus was the so-called reduction carried out, whereby the nobility lost, in a single blow, half of its landholdings. The lands were returned to the crown, which leased them out to ordinary peasants. Thus were state finances strengthened. At the same time, the significance of smallholder agriculture that had been Sweden's distinguishing mark was retained. Another change was the new way of organizing defence introduced by the king: *Indelningsverket*. This institution was peculiar to Sweden. It harkened back to an old tradition of local militias, but now on a much larger scale. The idea was to divide the peasants into small groups, each of which would take responsibility for equipping a single soldier, who also received land for his upkeep. This force of soldier-farmers, recalling that used under the Roman Republic, came to serve as the basis for the Swedish defence system.

On the strength of the popular support he enjoyed, won to a great extent through his measures against the nobility, the king was able to gain the consent of the *Riksdag* for measures substantially increasing his power. The victim in the first instance was the Council, which was dominated by the higher nobility and served as a countervailing power to the king at the central level. This organ was now deprived of all significant influence. The king was thereafter able, through a series of *Riksdag* decisions, to secure for himself an autocratic standing. In other words, the *Riksdag* agreed freely to set its own powers aside. Autocracy reached its full flowering under the subsequent monarch, Charles XII, who ascended the throne in 1697. The elder Karl had continued to convene the estates, but the younger preferred to rule on his own. Charles XII was the only king in the history of Sweden who never convened a *Riksdag*.

His life was spent in the field. Charles XII was the military 'hero king' who accomplished Sweden's definitive ruin as a great power. At the start, however, the wars went very well for Sweden. The newly created Swedish army exhibited, through its size and impressive discipline, a superior striking power.[14] A critical weakness, however, lay in the fact that it was not equipped, on account of the country's limited resources, with an organization for supplying equipment and provisions. As earlier, therefore, the troops had to be provisioned on the spot. That had been possible in rich and divided Germany. It was much harder when the fight turned to the enemy in the east: Russia. Tsar Peter had initiated a vigorous reorganization of the Russian realm. After some initial catastrophes in the struggle with the Swedes, the Russian regime succeeded in creating an army that could match the strength of the enemy. The tsar also applied a tactic the Swedes found devastating: he burned the land in the path of the Swedish army. Little was left on which the latter could sustain itself. The force that met defeat at Poltava in 1708 was an army bled by exhaustion. This was, in reality, the end. To be sure, Karl struggled on with new martial ventures over the following ten years. Now that Sweden had lost its revenue-yielding provinces in the Baltic lands, which Russia had annexed, and also many of its territories in Germany, it was the core area of the Swedish realm that had to bear the entire burden. With heavy taxes and other fiscal drains on an exhausted citizenry, Karl established a veritable

---

[14] By 1700, as Tilly notes (1992: 79), Sweden had passed other states by in terms of troops as a percentage of the population. In Sweden the level was 7.1. In France it was 2.1, in Russia 1.2, and in England 5.4.

war economy in Sweden. Popular discontent grew. In 1713, a *Riksdag* which had gathered without the endorsement of the king called for peace. But peace would not come for another five years, when the king fell victim to a bullet upon commencing an attack on Norway.

Nearly 40 years of increasing autocracy came thereby to a sudden end. The *Riksdag* now vigorously resumed its place on the scene. It was parliament which governed the realm in all essentials during the following 50 years. During this period, known as the 'Age of Freedom', the kings played a very minor role. Parliamentary procedures far in advance of their time were developed. Two parties, the 'Hats' and the 'Caps', alternated in power. Both were dominated by the aristocracy, but the latter usually enjoyed stronger support among the lower estates. Sweden was now a second-rate power, but it was still interesting as a partner in the European balance. The parties functioned to a high degree as the paid agents of external interests.

The year 1772 saw a turnabout. In an undramatic coup, the king, Gustav III, put an end to the rule of the estates. He appealed to popular distrust both of aristocratic dominance and of foreign interference. The *Riksdag* approved a constitution submitted by the king, the stated purpose of which was to re-create the division of powers that had traditionally obtained in Sweden. In reality, however, it was the king who had gained the upper hand—a tendency which became increasingly plain. With the support primarily of the lower estates, won among other things through his curtailing of noble privileges, the king was able to assume virtually autocratic powers. The *Riksdag*, the approval of which was still required on general legislative and tax questions, played a subordinate role. Once again, however, the curve of ascending autocratic power was to be broken abruptly. In the aftermath of an unsuccessful conflict with Russia during the Napoleonic Wars, the king, Gustav IV Adolf, was forced to abdicate in 1809. The *Riksdag* now adopted a constitution aimed at achieving a genuine balance of power between king and estates. The arrangement then adopted would hold good for a long time to come. The great swings that had marked Swedish political life for more than a century were now over. Changes that took place later would assume more gradualist forms.

Sweden experienced, as we have seen, periods of more or less autocratic rule. But these were not especially lengthy; nor did they lead to any fundamental institutional restructuring. The *Riksdag* was retained as an integrative organ of representation, and it was able rapidly and vigorously to re-assume its powers when the auto-cracy came to an end. Despite the concentration of power at the central level, government never took a directly despotic form. In the areas of civil and administrative law, moreover, the practices relating to the rule of law were upheld in all essentials. Nor was the system of local self-government broken[15] (Carlsson 1964; Anderson 1978: 184ff; Downing 1992: 187ff; S. Hadenius 1994: 17ff; M. Roberts 1979; Lindegren 1985; Nilsson 1990).

The means did not exist on a sufficient scale in Sweden to introduce autocracy. A central administration in the service of the king did exist, and a very well-organized one for its time. But only to a limited degree did it penetrate the numerous and geographically scattered local communities of which Sweden consisted. In these communities, an old and popular form of administration had been preserved. Public power was exercised through a collaboration between peasant-controlled local organs and the central bureaucracy. This interaction created a remarkable capacity for mobilizing resources, which in turn yielded competitive advantage. No other country in Europe, in the years around 1700, could place so large a proportion of its population under arms. This pattern of administrative collaboration between peasants and crown is an abiding fact of Swedish history. It was this unity, together with a common fear of aristocratic rule, that furnished the basis for the constitutional changes that yielded periods of royal autocracy. This was, however, an administratively circumscribed autocracy. Governance was still based on cooperation with autonomous local organs, which were linked together on the national level through representation in the *Riksdag*.

There were distinct limitations in the military area too. Sweden had a standing army, to be sure. This was not an army of such a character, however, as commonly promotes autocratic government. As Weber, Hintze, and many others have observed, there is a clear correlation historically between military arrangement and form of government (Downing 1992: 25, 58). A people under arms, it has been claimed, is what makes popular rule possible: the 'soldier-citizen nexus'. An oft-cited example is the hoplite army of ancient Athens, which consisted of armed citizens who successfully defended their state and took part in its government as well. Armed forces of a sort excluding the common people—the mounted armoured hosts of medieval times, for example—have an

---

[15] Attempts were made in the last years of Charles XII to establish a far-reaching central control over local activities. The traditional order was restored, however, when this warrior-king passed from the scene.

unfavourable impact from the standpoint of popular participation. The infantry is the military branch of the common people. Armies based thereupon can be structured, however, in a variety of ways. The particular manner in which they are structured can have great importance. The idea behind the 'soldier-citizen nexus' is that a citizen who is also a soldier tends to claim the right to political participation; if he is granted that right, moreover, he is unlikely to turn his weapons on the government which he and his fellows have taken part in choosing. This presumes, however, that the members of the military remain on intimate terms with ordinary citizens. If the military becomes, as a professional army, detached from the rest of society, a distinct military identity can arise, creating a fracture between the members of the military and the rest of the population. This tendency is most palpable, of course, in the case of a professional army of a mercenary character, that is, one consisting of soldiers who come from other countries and thus have no affinity with the population of the country in which they operate. Such troops have always furnished oppression with its best weapon. An army of conscripts, by contrast, is the most favourable from the standpoint of popular rule, since it normally means that all men capable of bearing arms do military service, and usually for a brief period only: thus the men are not socialized into a 'barracks life' cut off from the rest of society.

Another distinction bears stressing as well. It concerns whether soldiers are recruited and equipped on a local basis by the population, or whether instead they are organized on a more centralized and bureaucratic basis. In the first case, defence is organized on a militia basis. Such a system gives the troops a local connection and a closeness to the ordinary life of society. They are not demarcated as distinctly as in the more bureaucratic model. A militia system is implemented, furthermore, with the assistance of local institutions, and thus has a more pluralistic structure.

What Sweden had created was a professional army of a militia character—mercenaries were certainly used in the wars, especially in Germany, but they did not operate on Swedish soil. The Swedish professional soldier was a peasant. When he was not in the field or on military manoeuvres, he lived the life of an ordinary citizen. A soldier of this type would scarcely have been the most suitable to use in overturning the popular influence that had developed in Sweden. Indeed, no monarch ever made a real attempt at using the armed forces against the *Riksdag* or the local organs for self-rule, as often occurred in countries where autocracy emerged victorious.

The Netherlands was like Sweden, inasmuch as it too had a very small population: somewhat over a million in the years around 1600. It also had a weak aristocracy, substantially weaker even than Sweden's. In social, economic, and geographical terms, however, the two countries were each other's opposite. While Sweden was a geographically extended and sparsely populated agrarian society, the Netherlands was small in area, and very densely populated. It was also a pronouncedly urban society. Trade, commerce, and industry were the leading sectors of the economy already at the outset of the New Era. The urban bourgeoisie, moreover, was the wholly dominant segment of the population, both socially and politically speaking.

During the Middle Ages, the areas now comprising the Netherlands, together with what today is Belgium, were governed by the duke of Burgundy. These territories then fell to the Spanish crown in the early 1500s through inheritance. In both cases, however, the rule from without was largely nominal. The areas in question governed themselves to a high degree, and their administration took highly decentralized forms. They were divided into provinces— 17 at the time—which had acquired relatively uniform juridical and economic institutions during the period of Burgundian rule. In political terms, however, each province ran its own affairs in the main. In return for the taxes they paid, the cities and provinces had acquired a far-reaching autonomy. The provinces had representative organs, *States*, the approval of which was needed for promulgating laws and collecting taxes. The provinces also had their own administrative organs. In addition, a national representative organ was convened on occasion, known as the States-General, to which the provincial assemblies sent representatives. Like its counterpart in France, this was a rather weak organ, since the representatives sent to it often had very restrictive mandates. The executive power was represented by a *Stadtholder*, who was normally drawn from the local nobility. The powers of this official were very limited, however. The provinces were governed by their local organs. It often happened, in fact, that these organs denied requests by the princely power for higher taxes.

The Spanish rulers of the region sought, in the latter part of the 1500s, to change this state of affairs. A revolt thereupon followed, beginning in 1572. These struggles lasted almost 80 years. Peace was concluded at Westphalia in 1648, when the Dutch Republic was recognized as an independent state. The ambition of the Spaniards had been to destroy the prevailing constitutional order and to replace it with a centralized and autocratic one. Taxes were collected without local consent, and representative organs were abolished. The crown also sought to acquire a firmer control over the localities. In the religious area, furthermore, the Spaniards had far-reaching ambitions. This was the time of the Catholic Counter-Reformation, and the Spanish monarch, Phillip II, was its foremost champion. The Low Countries, which were in large part populated by Protestants, mainly of the Calvinist branch, now got a taste of the harsh and lawless methods of the Inquisition. Protests from the population were met by severe punishment.

The Spanish king sought to acquire for himself a new Castile. In the southern provinces he largely succeeded. But in the north he encountered a new Aragon, and a worse one. In that region, seven provinces united in common defence. This was the Union of Utrecht. It is this union, in fact, which forms the basis of the present Dutch state. Under the leadership of their *Stadtholder*, William of Orange, who had taken the side of the provinces, a war was prosecuted that affected the population severely, and that drained Spain's military and fiscal capacity badly. The rebels were aided by geography. The land, which was protected by a great many dykes and could be easily flooded, was not appropriate for the type of warfare in which massed troops clashed in large numbers, for which the Spanish army was suited. The many cities were extremely well-fortified besides. A further important precondition for the success of the rebels lay in the highly favourable economic position of the Dutch cities. With Amsterdam at their head, the cities in the area had become the trading centre of Europe. Following the decline of the Hanseatic League, it was Dutch vessels that controlled navigation in the North Sea and the Baltic. The Dutch cities also had colonies and commercial connections in the Caribbean, South Africa, and Asia. Over the long run, the rebels disposed of much greater resources for the making of war than did the colonial power.

After the Peace of Westphalia, Spain was a great power in sharp decline. Its finances were broken, and thus its military capacity too. The Netherlands enjoyed the opposite situation: it stood, in the mid-1600s, at the summit of riches and well-being. Its like was not to be found in Europe. Relatively well-administered and endowed with an excellent tax base, the Dutch state was able to collect revenues as large as the French state, the population of which was almost ten times as large. The new state was therefore able to act as a great power in military terms also. This was a position, however, which its leading class, the commercially oriented bourgeoisie, exploited only with great care. Foreign policy was largely defensive in character, and was accomplished in great measure through financial subsidies to allied states.

We touched briefly on the social and economic composition of the country earlier. The noble families were few in number, and their economic position was rather insignificant as compared with that enjoyed by their counterparts in other countries. The importance they could in certain cases acquire was based first and foremost on their occupancy of public office. The great majority of peasants were freeholders, and they had enjoyed full juridical rights since the Middle Ages. In their village communities, they practised a vigorous self-government. The clergy, for its part, was rather insignificant as a corporation, although like the nobility it had its own chamber in the representative body, the States-General. The important estate, however, was the third. It was dominated by the rich urban bourgeoisie.

The state was highly decentralized in its structure. It was an association of provinces, and at times it functioned more as a confederation than a true federation. Attempts were made during the war of liberation to concentrate powers in the hands of the States-General, but in the end this was never done. The essential decision-making functions remained in the hands of provincial organs. Each province might have a *Stadtholder* of its own, who was usually the supreme military commander and foreign-affairs representative. The right to make certain appointments might devolve on the *Stadtholder*. For long periods, however, the most important provinces—Holland, Zeeland, and several others—left this post unoccupied. The leading burghers, or 'regents' as they were known, indicated thereby their ambition to counteract every tendency towards military and administrative centralization. This arrangement functioned well enough during peacetime. When, however, the country was attacked at the end of the 1600s, and again in the mid-1700s—the threat in both cases issued from France—these provinces too were obliged to procure the unified executive authority afforded by the office of *Stadtholder*. It is an interesting fact, however, that the republic never had a *Stadtholder* for the country as a whole. Only when each and every province appointed the same person did the several offices devolve upon a single incumbent; when this happened, the charge fell to the House of Orange.[16]

---

[16] It might be wondered at that such a loose state formation was able to hold together and, indeed, to lay the basis for a state still existing today. A comparison with the Italian city-states and the Hanseatic League may be instructive here. As Hendrik Spruyt (1994: 130ff) has shown, the city-states of Italy were riven by conflict, both within and among themselves. Noble families were strong in these cities, and such families, which were organized along lines of clan, often feuded with each other. Among the common people, moreover, sharp class antagonisms

The *Stadtholder* was often regarded by the lower strata of the population as a counter-weight to the oligarchical regents. This official also frequently functioned as a moderating factor in the tensions prevailing between the different religious segments in the country, mainly between Protestants and Catholics. The powers attached to the office were limited as a rule, but its occupant could allocate privileges on a clientelist basis through his right to appoint certain officials. The cities and provinces maintained their own militias. They also hired mercenary armies in their defence, and these could reach a great scope in time of war. Even so, no trace could be found in the Netherlands of the '*condottieri* syndrome' that plagued the city-states of Italy, whereby the commanders of mercenary troops entered the political contest themselves, and at times assumed political power. The decentralized structure and the great political cohesion, both within the cities and between them, counteracted tendencies of this sort.

One factor that contributed heavily to social and political harmony was the extremely rapid rate of economic development. The Dutch Republic was, in the mid-1600s, the richest country in Europe by far. These favourable conditions continued for another 100 years. After that, however, a striking change took place. In the latter part of the 1700s, the Netherlands suffered a palpable economic decline. The industries that had earlier existed in large part went under, and the role of Amsterdam and its surrounding cities as the trading centre of Europe could no longer be maintained. A series of factors contributed to this: mercantilist and protectionist policies on the part of surrounding states, a high wage and tax level in the country, and a loss of dominance at sea, where England had

prevailed. The different segments of the urban population often lived separately from one another, and they had their own military units. In conflicts between the cities, as well as in fractional struggles within them, the warring parties often kept close contacts with external powers, which were only too happy to get involved. Defence pacts between cities were sometimes concluded, but as a rule these were short-lived. In northern Europe, by contrast, the cities were more homogeneous, socially speaking: the bourgeoisie was completely dominant. This facilitated cohesion both within and between cities. The Hanseatic League, which lasted for several centuries—up to the mid-1600s—was a pure confederation. It possessed organs for coordination but lacked an overarching executive agency. Cooperation was also made harder by the great geographical spread and the absence of standardization in respect of legislation, currency, weights, measurements, and so on (Spruyt 1994:109ff). In these latter respects, the Dutch cities were more uniform. They also lay close by one another, and for long periods they had, in the common *Stadtholder*, an overarching executive agency. Cooperation was also surely facilitated by the fact that one city, Amsterdam, was so clearly dominant: it accounted for two-thirds of the republic's income (Spruyt 1994: 260; see also Burke 1986).

taken over. The role of the Dutch cities as a financial centre remained, to be sure. All things considered, however, the resource base no longer existed for the economic and military great-power status which the country had had. The state became ever poorer. For many years now, it had not maintained a national defence force, and it found other public expenditures difficult to sustain also. At the same time, a marked increase in social inequality within the population had taken place. A 'patriotic' movement emerged in reaction to this state of affairs. In a nationalist and democratic spirit, it turned its ire on the oligarchical form of government, which had become ever more exclusive and closed. The patriots also opposed the House of Orange, with its close ties to the English crown. This movement had its social roots in lower bourgeois and professional strata, and it was inspired by the principles of the American Revolution. Full-scale insurrections took place in the mid-1780s. These, however, were suppressed through foreign intervention.[17] The old order was thus restored. But it did not last long.

When, in the aftermath of the French Revolution, French armies attacked the country in 1795, they met with no resistance. On the contrary, the radical movement welcomed them. A new state, the Batavian Republic, was established. In cities and in provinces, the old regents were turned out in favour of patriots. A national convention was chosen to work out a new constitution. The suffrage was extended to all adult men save for paupers. Those loyal to the old regime were excluded too. Discord arose in the convention as to whether a federal or a unitary state ought to be established. Despite far-reaching compromise, it was not possible to gain popular support for the proposal put forward, which was rejected in a referendum. After a period of political deadlock, the occupying power intervened. French troops drove out the federalists from the convention. A new constitution providing for a broad suffrage and a unitary form of government was now able to win acceptance in a referendum, from which, however, the opposing side was excluded. The radicals were now in power. Compared with the French Jacobins who inspired them, however, the Dutch radicals conducted government affairs in a strikingly modest manner: 'They did nothing really drastic; there was no attempt at social revolution, general confiscation, or terror' (Palmer 1964: 202). The French presence made itself increasingly felt after Napoleon assumed power. Several changes of regime were carried out, and for a time the Netherlands

---

[17] The consort of the prince of Orange called upon her brother, the king of Prussia, who sent help in the form of a military force.

was made a part of France itself. Despite the turbulence, however, a conciliatory spirit was retained in political life. After the fall of Napoleon in 1815, the Dutch were able to re-establish a national regime in a calm and peaceful manner. The choice was now made to establish a parliamentary monarchy—William I of the House of Orange became the first sovereign—and to return to a more federalist order. For a brief time—up to 1830—the country was in union with what today is Belgium. It proved possible, however, to separate the two countries in a fairly undramatic and conciliatory fashion. After centuries of parliamentary practice, a fertile soil existed for the peaceful resolution of conflict (Palmer 1959: 324ff; Palmer 1964: 177ff; Downing 1992: 212ff; Jacob and Mijnhardt 1992; Israel 1995).

We have now looked at three nations in Europe—England, Sweden, and the Netherlands—where an old constitutional and parliamentary order could be preserved. The case to which we now turn is of a more recent provenance. The country in question lies outside of Europe, but has in large measure derived its institutional impulses therefrom. I have in mind the United States. The form of government there developed can be considered, as Samuel Huntington (1968: 96–7) has stressed, an offshoot of medieval European practices. We can see it as an old plant set in a new soil. And in this special soil, the plant took on forms contributing greatly to the spread of the idea of popular government. It was to this country that Tocqueville made his way. He had been sent there to study the prison system. He returned with a report on the practice of democracy on the new continent.

The immigrants from England who started building a new society on North America's east coast in the 1620s were subjects of the British crown. For a long time, however, their colonial status was mainly a formality. Like their counterparts in the various agrarian frontier areas of Europe, the settlers were able to apply such forms of government as they saw fit. The first wave of settlers went mainly to the area later known as New England. The communities there were in large part modelled on the Calvinist religious denominations to which the population belonged. These denominations were suffused with a low-church and congregrational spirit. The people, that is, the congregations, chose their religious officers and could dismiss them. Similar procedures were applied in secular public life; indeed, the distinction between the two spheres was sometimes highly fluid. Government was to a great extent locally rooted. It was commonly conducted in the form of general meetings in villages or in cities, in which all property-owning men could take part. And since property was widely dispersed, the great majority of inhabitants being freeholding farmers, an extremely broad popular participation was possible. The public 'apparatus' was very small as a rule. The primary institutions of local governance were the courts, which had juries, in accordance with English practice. The primary function of the courts was to adjudicate legal disputes between citizens. But like the old Germanic *ting*, which had developed in a comparable manner (Berman 1983: 62), they assumed responsibility for administrative tasks as well: building roads, organizing poor relief, and so on. Their responsibility was often restricted, however, to supervision, to ensuring that things got done. The implementation of the tasks in question took place largely outside of the public domain: it was typically the citizens themselves who performed these tasks, on a voluntary basis. There were, to be sure, officials charged with matters of enforcement, like the Sheriff, and there were military units in the form of local militias. Such units were small, however, and subject to popular control. In the British colonies of America, the state operated with a very low degree of coercive power. It functioned in all essentials through the legitimacy it enjoyed among the citizens, and through their active assistance. On account of its close ties to the citizens, the settler state was highly interactive in character. This coordination capacity, to which citizens had long been trained, awakened great admiration in Tocqueville: a relation of this kind between the state and society, one marked by mutuality and united action, was beyond his experience.

From the standpoint of popular participation, however, there is no straight line between the Puritan farmer society of the 1600s and the country visited by the French observer. The development in question took place, rather, in waves. A gradual process of social and economic stratification occurred among the colonists. This was especially the case in the south, where large-scale plantation agriculture based on slave labour was built up. But in the north too, where freeholding farmers remained the wholly dominant population group, a stratum of large landowners crystallized. Roughly as in England, this local gentry came to dominate social and political life. It was these gentlemen who were usually appointed to public office, but with the difference that, as against the situation in England, they were chosen by the local population, not appointed by the crown. And when an overarching representative body was created, it was mainly persons from this stratum who took the seats therein. This pattern of selection reflected the fact that the various offices brought, as in England, no financial compensation. On account of this, it was primarily persons of means who were able to devote themselves to such tasks. However, political legitimacy was also sustained through networks of patronage. Through their own economic resources, and through their control of assets derived from the occupancy of office, the politically dominant figures were able to furnish their supporters with particularistic advantages of various kinds: loans, licences, the right to buy land, and so forth. The system was facilitated by the fact that prevailing practices within the administrative structure left considerable room for nepotism and corruption.[18] Yet, as in England, the clientilist networks thus established served as ties of exchange and mutuality between the upper and lower segments of society.

The English crown was represented in the colonies by its governors. On paper, these officials had considerable authority. In practice, however, their power was highly restricted. Each governor surrounded himself with a council, which functioned as a sort of government. This organ was also the highest court in the province. Its members were appointed by the governor, and usually recruited from the leading families of the province. In addition, there was a popularly elected assembly. The terms of the suffrage varied from province to province; in the mid-1700s, however, some 50–70 per cent of the adult white male population could usually vote in elections to the representative assembly. As compared with conditions in the mother country and elsewhere in Europe, this was a remarkably high figure. And this organ was completely unstratified: there was no upper house, and no separate representation for 'higher' estates, as was common in Europe. It bears noting as well that the provincial assemblies had acquired a position of considerable power. They were the decisive decision-making organ on most significant questions. It was often the assembly, moreover, which in reality appointed the members of the governor's council. A parliamentary order of sorts had thus been adopted. The governor, furthermore, had few resources of his own. He commanded no military forces, and

---

[18] Gordon Wood (1991: 77) provides the following report: 'When Benjamin Franklin was made deputy postmaster-general of North America in 1753, he wasted no time in appointing all his friends and relatives to positions under his control. His son became postmaster in Philadelphia. One brother was made postmaster in Boston; when the brother died, Franklin gave the office to his brother's stepson. He made his nephew postmaster in New Haven, appointed a son of a friend postmaster in Charleston, and made another friend in New York controller. A year or so later he promoted his son to be controller and moved the husband of his wife's niece to the vacant Philadelphia position. When this office again became open, he brought another brother down from Newport to fill it. Such patronage politics was simply an extension into governmental affairs of the pervasive personal and kin influence that held the colonial social hierarchies together.'

no bureaucratic apparatus stood at his disposal. He lacked the means to pursue a policy contrary to the will of local representatives. To get anything done, he had to cooperate with the representative organs. The influence he could exercise derived first and foremost from his right to appoint persons to certain offices, and from the patronage he thereby controlled. In these respects, conditions in the British colonies resembled those obtaining between monarch and parliament in the mother country.

Notwithstanding the dominance of the gentry in political life, the form of government obtaining in colonial North America was without doubt, on account of the broad suffrage, the far-reaching political freedom, and the extensive decisional competence achieved by the elected organs, the most democratic in the world. This arrangement came under serious threat, however, in the middle of the eighteenth century. The threat arose from the fact that the English government now chose to abandon the mild system of colonial government prevailing to that point. Following the successful Seven Years War with France (1756–63), which among other things concerned dominance in North America, the government sought to maintain a permanent standing army in the colonies. New taxes would be introduced to defray the costs involved. There was nothing strange about this proposal, as matters were viewed in London. The colonies had been extremely lightly taxed. All that was now proposed was a tax take comparable to that in England. In a display of unity, Parliament promulgated a series of laws to that effect. On the other side of the Atlantic, however, the laws provoked a great hue and cry. In arguing against the new taxes, the colonists adduced the principle of 'no taxation without representation': a principle for which the English parliament itself had fought a century before! Concretely this meant that, in order to come into force, tax increases first had to be approved by the provinces' representative organs—which they would surely have not been, had they been put to this test.

A congress representing the assemblies of all the different provinces was convened. The express prohibition of such gatherings by the governors had little effect. A national arena thus began to take shape. Coordination was facilitated by the small size of the politically dominant stratum, and by the close ties existing between the leading families of the different provinces. As in France, a vital collective capacity existed at the top of society. In America, though, the elite actors could join forces with lower strata. Contrary to France, vital local arenas of decision-making had for a long time bred class interaction. No legal privileges, moreover, separated the economic and political elite from ordinary people. This state of affairs should constitute a big difference between the two revolutions.

The protests generated a lively response among the broad mass of the people. Local organs arranged mass meetings and issued proclamations; committees and associations were formed to obstruct official decisions and to organize boycotts of English goods. Local mob riots broke out as well. America seethed with civil disobedience. In response, the British government sought to gain a firmer administrative grip over the territories. An office for the coordinated management of affairs throughout British North America was established. Tax collectors directly subject to the crown were sent out into the field—one recalls the French *intendants*—and attempts were made to replace popularly chosen local judges with jurists selected by the colonial power. But all to no avail. The provincial governors reported back to London that the territories were in reality ungovernable. Time and again, the British were forced to back down and to annul decisions introducing new taxes. But such retreats were largely tactical. The ambition to put an end to American autonomy remained. The situation became truly critical when, at the beginning of the 1770s, the British government decided to revoke the constitution of the province of Massachusetts. This was in answer to the 'Boston Tea Party', when denizens of that city had dumped a cargo belonging to the British East India Company into the water in protest at the new taxes and trading restrictions imposed by Parliament. The new constitutional order would have entailed a substantial weakening of the provincial assembly and a corresponding increase in the power of the governor. The powers of local organs would have been sharply curtailed besides. This was an alarm bell: if it could happen in Massachusetts, it could happen anywhere. A Continental Congress representing the assemblies of all of the different provinces was convened. This famous congress issued, in 1776, the Declaration of Independence, whereby the United States proclaimed itself a sovereign and independent state. A declaration of rights based on the principle of popular sovereignty was adopted as well. Certain 'natural' or 'inalienable' rights of the citizen were averred, and the legitimate powers of government defined. This document came, on the normative level, to shine like a beacon the world over.

But for the rebels gathered in Philadelphia, the first order of business was the struggle with England that had now started. The methods of administrative obstruction already in use were one thing. For these the population was extremely well-equipped. Its long-standing habituation to the practice of local self-government, together with its access to a rich network of intermediate structures, furnished it with a civic coordination capacity, involving most segments of society, that was too much for the colonial power. But now there was a war on. And for that the colonists were much the worse prepared. The local troops which had taken part in the Seven Years War had truly not distinguished themselves: it had scarcely been possible to collect them at all. The Continental Congress succeeded, however, in establishing a national army. George Washington was made its commander.

A powerful mobilization of the people took place; nationalist sentiment was fanned not least by the fact that the English army was composed primarily of German mercenaries. Another factor contributing strongly to tipping the balance of forces in favour of the Americans was the large-scale assistance from France, which took the form of funds, equipment, and troops. In 1783 the war was over: the rebellion had succeeded. The American Revolution was a fact.[19]

A new constitution was adopted in 1787. It established the framework for a federal and highly decentralized state. It was based on the separation of powers, and founded on the notion that government must rest on the consent of the governed. Virtually all of the 'Founding Fathers'—the men who had led the revolt and framed the constitution—were from the gentry which had dominated the political scene earlier. The war, however, had made an impact on the forms of government applied. In a bid for popular support, property qualifications for voting had been reduced in most of the States. Among white men, some 60–90 per cent now had the vote. Constituencies were also redrawn in most cases, the better to reflect population size.

Through the popular mobilization that had taken place during the war, a broader participation in the political process had already made itself felt. This tendency continued. The lower strata, who had usually stayed out of politics before, were increasingly activated and involved. This development was facilitated by the build-up of national parties and by improvements in communications, both physically and in terms of information. The aristocratic form of clientelism that had prevailed previously was successively broken down. A more participatory and populist politics became common in the early 1800s. The new spirit was particularly evident during Andrew Jackson's presidency in the 1830s and 1840s. Through

---

[19] The armed forces were demobilized after the war. The United States has never had a standing army.

direct mobilization, Jackson and his Democrats sought support from the broad mass of the people, and with great success. The electoral participation rate in the presidential election of 1840—80 per cent—must be judged astounding. The old 'gentleman era' was now definitely over. A far-reaching system of spoils and an increasingly corrupt culture of administration had become the order of the day. In this context, notorious political machines of clientilist character were later able to spread.[20] The United States was a young democracy, and it experienced a good many growing pains (Nettels 1963: 106ff; Palmer 1964: 143ff; Lawrence 1972; Bridenbaugh 1981: 167ff; Wood 1969; 1991; Morone 1990: 33ff; Mann 1993: 137ff; Finer 1997 III: 1394ff, 1485ff).

Two Paths of Political Transformation

The American Revolution came before the French Revolution, and indeed it inspired the latter. Both events saw magnificent declarations of rights and the establishment of new constitutional arrangements. Few political events have had, where popular government is concerned, so great an influence over our minds. In practical terms, however, the two revolutions had strikingly different outcomes. In the United States, the political reforms proved abiding. The institutional structure established by the Founding Fathers provided the framework for future development. Under the aegis of the constitution, gradual changes in the patterns of political life could take place. New population groups were drawn into the process. A broader and more active popular government could thus take form. The American Revolution was a revolution against British rule. But internally it marked no break. It was a continuation—and in many respects a codification, constitutionally speaking—of long-established political practices. In America, institutions of popular rule had been in use for generations. Here was a people instructed long and thoroughly in the school of democracy. Americans were accustomed to performing the role of citizen presumed by the idea of popular government through peaceful resolution of conflicts. This was not the case in France.

The latter country had no legacy of constitutionalism. Royal rule had been marked by an absence of legal structures regulating political affairs. There was no existing rule of the game that the actors could draw upon. In France the project of institutional design

[20] See Chapter 3, p. 53.

started practically from scratch. As Tocqueville has pointed out, moreover, French society lacked experience of inter-segmental interaction. Neither in social and economic life, nor in political life, had routines of collaboration between different segments of society been developed. This was manifested in a complete lack of tolerance and respect for minority rights among the French revolutionaries. A political culture scarred by implacable conflicts, and a legacy of social and political convulsions, thus took shape.

The century following the French Revolution was marked by great and dramatic swings, in which popular revolutions, which had great resonance internationally, alternated with periods of authoritarian government. Established through force and with a continuous redrawing of the institutional map, the various regimes faced a constant problem of legitimacy. During periods of republican rule, the monarchists were up in arms, and the converse circumstance obtained when a king or emperor ruled the land. The long periods of authoritarianism, furthermore, had a detrimental effect on the development of the party system.

It was first in the late 1800s that France was able to start moving towards a more stable parliamentary system, which over time has extended its roots. The constitutional order has been marked by turbulence, however. Owing to the weakness of political parties and of the organizational sphere in general, political life was charecterized for a long time by high degree of fragility. One republic followed another, and governments often succeeded one another with an astounding frequency. This was the result of a highly fragmented party system, which at the same time maintained the old legacy of strong ideological polarization. Long marked by a high degree of administrative centralization and a low degree of civic organization,[21] France retained in large part its character as a protest-and-barricade society. More often than in other countries, 'the voice of the people' has tended in France to make itself heard in irregular forms, a tendency classed by Kornhauser among the expressions of an atomized 'mass society'.[22]

The national trauma of decolonization has also left its mark. Through a desperate attempt at maintaining its colonial *'gloire'*—a militarily hopeless endeavour—France fell into political chaos in the 1950s. Faced with the threat of a military intervention in order to oust the government, a paralyzed National Assembly endorsed

[21] The fact that popular associations were forbidden for a long time from the French Revolution up to the end of the nineteenth century—has contributed to this.
[22] See Chapter 1, p. 10.

the take over by General de Gaulle in a coup-like manner. Thus was the Fifth Republic created, which exists in France today. New institutional structures—the introduction of a semi-presidential system in tandem with a majoritarian electoral formula—have given incentives for political groups to come together and form more unified and enduring party blocks. This has strengthened the representative system and has stabilized too the governance capacity of the executive. These measures, together with steps in the direction of increased regional and local autonomy, seem to have established a more solid ground for democracy in France (Kornhauser 1960: 84ff; see also Tarrow 1994: 74ff; Sulieman 1994; Demker 1996).

In Spain, the process of transformation was still more protracted, complicated, and turbulent. Revolutions, coups, and counter-coups took place constantly during the nineteenth century. Royal rulers, popular leaders, and military commandants alternated in power. Severe ideological antagonisms rent the land. Republicans squared off against monarchists; liberals and clericals contended. A strong socialist movement hostile to the system emerged over time as well. In addition, a gulf separated the central power from the various regions; the latter had not, in a good many cases, been integrated under the crown, despite the many centuries spent in the same kingdom. Finally, there was of tradition a sharp conflict of interest between a powerless, isolated, and poverty-stricken peasant population and a thin stratum of large landowners, who owned a great proportion of the arable land. Nor did the recurrent colonial wars, with the constant setbacks they entailed, make the exercise of government any easier. The army, moreover, was often an actor in the political game. According to a common pattern, units in the army would join forces with certain popular and regional groups to make a rebellion, which, if successful, might be followed by a new revolt of another composition. Parliamentary practices could not easily take root, especially since the electoral process, when it was upheld at all, was highly corrupt. In the administrative area, Spain had maintained the heavy centralism established in the 1700s by the Bourbons. Governors and mayors were all subject to the central government. Local arenas for popular participation were conspicuous by their absence. The game of power was usually played with extraparliamentary tools, especially military ones. 'Generals remained the surest instrument of political change' (Carr 1982: 525). Spain was a country marked by revolts and sharp antagonisms. The capacity for the conciliatory and peaceful resolution of conflicts was slim. This conflictual political culture found its fullest expression in the brutal and wide-ranging civil war fought in the

1930s. This was followed by several decades under a politically paralyzing one-party state, with vaguely fascist features, under General Franco. It was in the 1970s that developments first moved in a—by European standards—normalizing direction. A relatively soft transition to democracy could be set in motion following the death of the general. Notwithstanding coup attempts, of a limited scope, on the part of opponents of the new order, it appears now that democracy in Spain can be stabilized. It bears noting, however, that Spain has lost a good many years. For generations, its population was subject to great trials from which other European peoples were spared (Rueschemeyer, Stephens, and Stephens 1992: 119ff; Brooker 1995: 129ff; Carr 1982; Bonime-Blanc 1987).

In Russia and in Prussia/Germany, the old authoritarian order could be maintained much longer. As a consequence, it was not until the twentieth century that the great break came. It was the World War I, in both cases, that brought the old regime to ruin.

Serfdom was not abolished in Russia until the mid-1800s, at which time a certain allocation of lands to the peasants took place. The property thus acquired was in all essentials collectively administered, within the framework of the traditional village community. The village community was also strengthened by the fact that it was now charged with new administrative duties. The cities and the local aristocracy, for their part, also acquired organs through which a degree of self-government was possible. In this way, the store of local social capital was reinforced. Yet isolation and atomization were not broken for that. A degree of collaboration could take place, to be sure, between the various village communities. However, upward links into the highly centralized state apparatus were lacking. Nor were there any institutionalized links between the various social segments, which lived, socially and economically speaking, in different worlds. The large land-hungry population of peasants had traditionally nourished a great hatred for the privileged nobles. It was the iron hand of the state that had checked such aggression for centuries. This state was not, in its autocratic core, much changed at the start of the twentieth century. Up to the end, the tsarist regime was an autocracy in which political organization and freedom of expression were strictly limited. A legal system modelled on liberal principles had been introduced as part of a reform package in the mid-1800s. Soon thereafter, however, another tendency prevailed. An emerging opposition movement called attention to itself, deprived as it was of other means of expression, through far-reaching terrorist actions. These was met by harsh measures on the part of the state. In the late nineteenth century, Russia became a veritable police state. On the basis of vague criteria of state security, governors and police officers could imprison or deport any citizen by administrative decree. It was the political police, whose actions were subject to no legal restrictions, that henceforth supplied the main muscles of the regime.

A constitution providing for a representative assembly based on a narrow suffrage had been introduced after the popular revolt occurring in connection with the disastrous war with Japan in 1905. After the rapid conclusion of this war, however, the regime was able to turn its military forces inward and subdue the revolt. The representative assembly—the *Duma*—that had been established was thereafter a powerless organ. The tsarist regime fell in 1917. This happened through the same kind of spontaneous uprising, in both city and countryside, that had rocked the regime in 1905. The difference now was that the regime had lost the capacity for the exercise of force necessary for its survival. Engaged in a great and protracted war, in which Russian forces had suffered devastating losses, the regime could no longer control the internal front. The *Duma*, which despite its powerlessness had become an arena for opposition, demanded a government responsible to it. Rather than yield to such calls for reform, the last tsar, Nicholas II, abdicated. The parliamentary government which thereupon followed could not, however, do much about the popular uprising either. Social and political tensions suppressed for centuries were now let loose. The institutions of the state fell apart. The socialist/liberal government soon discovered that it lacked any real capacity to govern. Just half a year later, the Bolsheviks of Petrograd under the leadership of Lenin were able to overthrow it, with the use of simple means. Seventy years of oppression under a communist one-party state would now follow (Skocpol 1979; Pipes 1991; 1995).

In Prussia, a far-reaching project of reform was undertaken on the heels of the devastating military defeat at the hands of Napoleon. The state administration was enlarged, reorganized, and centralized still further. Serfdom was abolished in the countryside. The peasants now became independent smallholders, or workers on the ever more prevalent *Junker* estates. Local administration remained in the hands of the *Junkers*. Constitutionally, the autocratic order was retained. The reforms, which throughout were conducted from above, were limited to administration and economic life. The purpose was to endow the Prussian military state with greater staying power.

The revolution in France in 1848 had reverberations in many countries, Prussia not least. In the aftermath of the urban unrest that now followed, constitutional reforms were implemented.[23] A *Landtag* with two chambers was introduced. One was reserved to the aristocracy. The other was elected on the basis of universal but unequal manhood suffrage; voters were divided into three classes according to economic criteria. Persons of great wealth were strongly over-represented. Thus were the *Junkers* and the emergent class of rich industrialists favoured. When Germany was united in 1871, and the king of Prussia was proclaimed emperor of Germany, a parliament—the *Reichstag*—was established on a more radical pattern. Universal and equal manhood suffrage obtained in elections to that body. Much remained of the old order, however, and this substantially limited the impact of the suffrage reform. It was the emperor who appointed the government, and the latter was not responsible to the *Reichstag*. The core of the state—the aristocrat-dominated military and administrative agencies—was firmly under the emperor's control. In Prussia, moreover, the old constitution, with its divided and unequal suffrage, was retained; it would not be changed until the monarchy's fall.

Chancellor Otto von Bismarck dominated the political scene in Germany during the latter part of the nineteenth century. Bismarck introduced a scheme of social legislation, very advanced for its time, which favoured the expanding working-class population; Germany underwent rapid industrialization during this period. At the same time, the regime proscribed workers' organizations and persecuted them. The purpose was to render the masses, who had been given the vote, passive and inert. This was a policy of 'negative integration', as Guenther Roth (1963: 8) has put it. The door to a broad participation was opened, but access to the centres of power was denied. The primary institutions of the state were still controlled in all essentials by the old power bloc: the emperor and the *Junkers*.

In the autumn of 1918, the war, which had continued on for four long years, and for the outbreak of which the emperor bore a heavy responsibility, had reached a definitive deadlock. In exhaustion, the regime collapsed. The emperor abdicated. A democratic republic—the Weimar Republic, as it came to be known—was now installed. It was born in an atmosphere of severe political alienation and distrust. A lack of legitimacy dogged the republic throughout its brief life. Already at the start, left socialist groups attempted, in the

[23] Prussia had been awarded the Rhineland following the Napoleonic Wars. This area, which had a larger population than old Prussia, had a highly urban stamp. It was in the Rhineland that the great industrial expansion took place in the 1800s, improving the revenue base of the state considerably. It was also there that the opposition in 1848 was the strongest.

mould of their Russian counterparts, to seize power by force. In the early 1920s, moreover, right-wing nationalist parties tried to over-throw the republic by the same means.

The groups that had sustained the old order nourished a myth of national betrayal: the democrats, after all, had agreed to Germany's capitulation and to the onerous peace terms. Fertile soil existed in such circles for revanchism. In addition, there was an unusually powerful communist movement; it opposed the parliamentary sys-tem also, proposing to replace it with a state on the Soviet model. The space for the forces of moderation became ever narrower. The Weimar Republic developed a culture of political polarization, which became ever more intense with the worsening crisis in the economy. It was in this setting that Hitler and his Nazis were able to enter the stage and to gain popular support quickly. Badly struck by the world depression, Germany was a bitterly divided nation in the early 1930s. The political dialogue had become a fist fight, both figuratively and literally. In one of the elections of 1932, the Nazis and the communists together received the support of a majority of voters. The two parties were each other's main rivals, but they had one thing in common: both were expressly in favour of democracy's abolition. In the hope of 'taming' the Nazis, and of marginalizing them thereby, one of the parliamentary conservative parties took the initiative for a coalition government, with Hitler serving as chancellor. This proved a costly mistake. Once well at the head of the government, Hitler was not slow to abolish the Weimar Republic, and so democracy too, through a coup. His assumption of power took place in 1933 (Moore 1967; Anderson 1978: 286ff; Scocpol 1979: 104ff; Stern 1997; Linz 1978).

As Sheri Berman (1997) has shown, Germany suffered no lack of popular associations during this period. From a Tocquevillian standpoint there was, it might therefore be thought, a favourable basis for the establishment of democratic practices; and Berman points out precisely this connection. The problem, she notes, was that these associations were strongly tied as a rule to the polarized political groupings. Despite the multitude of organizations, strong patterns of encapsulation prevailed. Instead of serving as a meeting place where people of different camps could mix, the associations helped to strengthen sharply antagonistic identities. Democracy requires, as we know, more than just a capacity for popular mobil-ization. It also presupposes a desire for compromise and concili-ation. In the Germany of the Weimar Republic, this desire was present in too limited a measure. In the shadow of national and economic crisis, a spiral of ever more intensive struggle between political fractions developed, and the Nazis managed to come out on top. In his efforts to install a totalitarian Third *Reich*, Hitler enjoyed two critical advantages: he controlled paramilitary forces of his own, and he faced military and administrative agencies staffed by persons nostalgic for the 'old regime' and accustomed to following orders. Sharply divided as it was along political lines, civil society could offer little resistance.

In such countries as England, Sweden, the Netherlands, and the United States, the course of development was substantially calmer and, from a democratic standpoint, more successful.

Through a gradual constitutional transformation, it proved possible in these countries to include new population groups in the political process. In England and in Sweden, these changes could be implemented through well-established parliamentary practices. The fact that the population in both countries was highly homogeneous, ethnically and religiously speaking, naturally facilitated the process. The absence of severe economic fractures was helpful too. In the Netherlands, on the other hand, strong segmental tensions of a religious character long presented a problem. As Lijphart (1977) has shown, however, Dutch political leaders found, through a compromise-oriented policy of a consociational nature, a basis for interaction through which conflicts could be restrained and successively alleviated. The big dilemma in the US, finally, has been the race question: specifically, the standing of the African-American minority. In the southern States, where the main part of this population lived, slavery prevailed up to the 1860s. It was only after a devastating civil war that this condition could be eliminated and blacks given the vote. For many years, however, discrimination against black citizens continued in many southern States, albeit now in a more restricted form. It was not until the civil-rights legislation of the 1960s that these conditions were thoroughly changed.

The broadening of participation has usually been pushed through by politically excluded groups in the population. As Stein Rokkan (1970) has shown, on the basis of several historical examples from Europe, this process may be facilitated by a struggle for power within the governing elite. In such cases, rival fractions in the elite have had an incentive to draw in new groups, in the hope of widening their basis of support. These new strata could then be socialized, in the successful cases, into a culture of peaceful conflict resolution built up over a long period earlier. In such cases, a stored-up 'capital' of conciliatory capacity has been present, making it possible to handle political conflicts in manageable forms. This is a capacity which normally takes a long time to develop. For it emerges out of a process in which preferences are changed: a process of learning by doing, in which trust and new identities are slowly built up. Robert Dahl (1971) has pointed out the advantages ensuing when, of the two principles on which popular government is founded—broad citizen participation and open competition for power—it is the latter which is introduced first. For it is this which is democracy's explosive side. The contest for power has a strongly polarizing tendency. Hence it can issue in conflicts destructive to all. Societies have often needed many generations to learn the art of restraining intolerance and monopolistic tendencies in the open contestation entailed by pluralist government. Those who began the process early on, and have been able to keep it going without long interruptions, have quite naturally enjoyed an advantage.

The fact that, for a long while, it was only an elite that took part in politics was naturally an important drawback from a democratic standpoint. But from the standpoint of cooperation it was an advantage. It is easier to establish trust and understanding in a small group. The process is still simpler if the group in question is relatively homogeneous. A narrow circle of elite actors, normally unified by a common educational and economic background, was able to found a structure for collaboration in ordered forms which could be applied by other population groups later.[24] A culture of reconciliation had been created. Institutions were erected which proved able, in step with increasing popular mobilization, to integrate ever-wider sections of the population into this culture (Dix 1994; Gallagher, Laver, and Mair 2001).

During long periods, it should be noted, 'soft'—patrimonial—forms of governance were the predominant model of pluralist government. In the early years of popular rule in such countries as England, the Netherlands, and the United States, it was access to clientelist channels into the state apparatus that constituted the main prize of the political game. For a political system presided over by a relatively homogeneous elite, an arrangement of this sort may occasion little worry. Interaction within the elite is facilitated by the business-like logic of the system. Access to spoils, furthermore, helps the elite actors uphold a representative function to the extent that they can deliver advantages to their followers. What holds the system together, in the absence of official rules, is the informal 'gentleman-norms' grounded in the close social bonds within the

---

[24] A striking example may be seen in the case of the so-called Founding Fathers, the men who signed the American Constitution in 1787. This group consisted of just 129 persons. Almost all were drawn from the wealthiest and most prominent colonial families (Mann 1993: 150).

governing stratum. This state of affairs becomes difficult to maintain, however, when mass politics enters the scene. When the actors become more numerous and heterogeneous, the soft state's lack of rule-governed governance becomes a complicating factor. Complexity and conflict usually increase during this phase. This makes a more fixed institutional framework necessary. Traditional 'gentleman' administrative forms must now be discarded and replaced by an administration structured in accordance with the principles of professionalism and the rule of law, such as happened in England and the United States in the late 1800s and early 1900s (Theobald 1990). If this does not occur, there is a risk that popular organizing will take a form which, in a 'symbiosis' with the institutions, helps cement the prevailing patrimonial order, resulting in a fragile democracy.

A general trait of the successful cases here reviewed is a substantial degree of political and administrative decentralization. To be true, popular involvement in the running of local affairs was often constrained, and the practices marred, moreover, by corruption and low degree of managerial capacity. Historically, the positive effects of decentralization have flowed mainly from division of powers and in a broader access to public offices. It has been important besides that there were channels of interaction with the overarching political system. Influence was not restricted merely to the locality. Such isolation is the mark of an 'hour-glass society'. China, Russia, and France are classic examples. In these countries, organs existed for participation at the local level, but such participation took place in highly atomized forms. Influence was limited to the village level. There were few contacts between the different local units, and there were no upward links into the national political sphere. In such societies there is ample social capital, but it is suppressed and dispersed. When the inhibiting conditions are removed, such societies may be shaken by enormous explosions of popular protest. As a result of the prevailing structures of political exclusion, these actions can be highly aggressive once they are let loose. To gain positive effects democratically, in other words, arenas of local involvement should be coupled with access to channels of influence that can connect the periphery with the centre.

A Counter-argument

Finally, an argument that runs contrary to a central thesis of this book deserves to be addressed. This argument holds that authoritarian rule may serve as a fruitful breeding ground for democratic development. Otto Hintze was an early exponent of this view. Political development in Europe, as he saw it, could substantiate such a stance.

As we know, an historically unique system of estates and constitutionalism was established in Europe in the Middle Ages. In the period between 1500 and 1700, however, representative bodies and constitutional liberties were done away with in a great number of countries. This autocratic phase lasted for several centuries. According to Hintze, however, it was just a temporary pause in the development towards constitutionalism.

This was only a transitional state resting on the fact that the Estate system had in many places become a hindrance to the development of greater states. As soon as this development dictated by political necessity had been completed, we find a revival of the representative principle, together with the awakening of a national political consciousness within these centralized great states, in the form of a constitutional system. (Hintze 1975: 347–8).

What absolutism helped to do was to integrate population groups which had earlier been divided, thereby contributing to national cohesion. By coercive and centralist methods, the different groups were thrust into common institutions and governed in accordance with uniform rules. This created 'a sense of political cohesion, the rudiments of a common political interest . . . The individuals became conscious of being a people' (Hintze 1975: 175).

Huntington has put forward similar ideas. A heavy concentration of political power was necessary, he argues, in order to modernize the state. 'The opposition to modernization came from traditional interests: religious, aristocratic, regional and local' (1968: 126). The autocratic model was the instrument needed to break down the old order. In this, Huntington sees a parallel with the regimes, especially of the one-party type, which have been common among new states established in our time: 'in the seventeenth century the absolute monarch was the functional equivalent to the twentieth century's monolithic party' (1968: 102). In pursuit of the same objectives of modernization, these regimes have instituted a strong central power free of society's control. These often backward and parochial societies had to be changed fundamentally, and this could only be done through vigorous rule from above (1968: 137).

On this point, Huntington has a lot of company. Autocratic rulers have often justified their methods as necessary to achieve 'modernization'. Whether the regime has been a one-party state or a military junta, the melody has been much the same (Zolberg 1966; Hadenius 1994*a*; Horowitz 1991; Brooker 1995). An important component in the process of political modernization, according to Huntington and others, is the national homogenization mentioned by Hintze. The new states of today are often sharply divided, as once were the old states of Europe, along ethnic, religious, and regional lines. The task is now, as it was then, to create national unity out of the disparate population groups. It is first on such a basis that popular participation in pluralist forms can be implemented. If popular government is instituted when the population is still too heterogeneous, the antagonisms can become so severe that the system collapses. This notion links up with an argument proffered by Dankwart Rustow (1970): popular government requires for its preservation that there be a cohesive *demos*: a population characterized by a high degree of homogeneity.

We find similar notions in the work of Stein Rokkan (1975). In Rokkan's view, that phase in the state-building process during which popular influence expands should be preceded by two others: first, a phase in which the state is established and gains control over its territory; and second, one in which various policies of standardization are undertaken in order to create a common identity within the state. It is important, Rokkan argues, that these different phases occur at points well separated in time. If they take place too closely upon one another, or even simultaneously, as has sometimes been the case in the new states, there is a risk that unsustainable tensions will arise.

The argument for autocratic homogenization is based on two assumptions. First, its exponents claim national unity is a necessary condition for a functioning democracy. Second, they argue, such unity is created most effectively by authoritarian means. I would object to both assumptions. The autocratic method is based on the conjecture that national integration can be driven through by administrative means. In the same way that one standardizes measurements and money, one can make the population uniform. By incorporating the population into uniform institutions, and by subjecting it to various kinds of 'nationalizing' policies—education and so on—state leaders can call forth a spirit of common belonging, a sense of being one people. This idea is certainly not unrealistic. It has often worked this way historically (Anderson 1978). But this method usually requires a long time, as well as the use of significant elements of repression. Since it involves the denial of segmental identities or the prohibition of their expression, and the simultaneous imposition of another identity, this approach has the potential

of generating extremely serious conflict; people are not standard-
ized as easily, after all, as are measurements and money. The
method requires that the open display of tension be constantly suppressed. If, however, the regime is weak or collapsing, which under
such conditions is not unusual, the result can be a devastating
release of antagonisms which were previously suppressed. From
Africa and eastern Europe—the former Yugoslavia not least—we
have had many reminders of the explosive power that can be
released, sometimes with ghastly results, upon the sudden relax-
ation of a 'nationally integrating' political order based on the sup-
pression of segmental identities. The model entails, in short, great
risks: it can have highly counterproductive effects. This is one side
of the matter. The other is that, even if the model succeeds, it does
so through the long-term preservation of an authoritarian institutional structure, which in itself has a negative effect on democratic
development. It achieves one important objective—national integration—which can certainly provide a favourable basis for democracy. But it achieves this at the cost of great damage to democracy's
prospects in other respects.

It should further be recalled that troublesome ethnic and religious divisions have marked several old democracies. The
Netherlands and Switzerland are cases in point. In the non-
Western world, India is a striking example. Through the upholding
of pluralist practices, it has been possible in these countries to reconcile existing divisions and to render them politically manageable.
While not easy to carry out, this approach would appear to offer, as
Lijphart (1977) argues, the most effective strategy for resolving segmental conflicts.

9

States and Development

In this chapter, the development of states and their effects in the social realm will be further examined. It is therefore natural to draw on the history of Europe. It was on that continent, after all, that new developments took place which spread eventually to other parts of the world. How can this dynamic be explained?

Barrington Moore has presented an oft-quoted approach to explaining this matter. Changes in the economic sphere, especially in the formation of classes, provide his point of departure. According to Moore, it was the bourgeoisie's destruction of aristocratic economic power which paved the way for political pluralism and democracy. The critical elements in this process were the transition to a more commercial agriculture and the increased dominance of the cities. In countries where this did not happen, the introduction of democracy met with grave difficulties. 'No bourgeois, no democracy', Moore concludes (1967: 418).

The thesis unquestionably has a lot going for it. The cities that developed in the Middle Ages furnished a counter-weight to the previously dominant feudal aristocracy. This contributed to pluralism and the dispersion of power. In their internal governance, moreover, the cities applied a constitutional order which, at times, provided for far-reaching participation by the people. A closed and oligarchical form of government became, to be sure, the typical urban pattern in time. Nevertheless, the bourgeoisie has contributed to a high degree to the establishment, on a firm basis, of institutional structures founded on pluralist and constitutional principles. The Netherlands, of course, is the classic example: this state was a burgher republic in its beginnings, and so it long remained. In England too, a vigorously expanding bourgeoisie was closely involved in the stabilization of the parliamentary order. Parliament was dominated, to be sure, by the rural gentry up to the 1800s; but as Moore has stressed, this class took part in commercial activities too.

Sweden and the United States, however, make for theoretical difficulty. There were no cities and no bourgeoisie of any significance in Sweden. In both demographic and economic terms, Sweden was essentially an agrarian society. The same can be said of the United States. At that time in its history when political rights were extended to include almost the entire male population, the US was inhabited mainly by farmers. It was in the simple population of the countryside that popular government had its original roots.

In Sweden, an ancient peasant democracy was retained. This system prevailed, at the local level, in many places in Europe during the early Middle Ages. Its origins can be traced to the forms of government applied by the Germanic peoples during their migrations (Hintze 1975: 113ff). With the spread of feudalism, however, the peasants' autonomy and self-government were curtailed. But where feudalism was weak, this break did not take place. Such was the case in the forested and sparsely populated region of Scandinavia.[1] In that part of Europe, the system of local peasant self-government formed the basis for the states established later. The aristocracy, which originally was extremely weak, could at times assume an important role on account of its position in the state apparatus. Yet through their representation in the Swedish *Riksdag*, and through their ability to conclude alliance with other estates, the peasants were able to wield significant influence.

In the United States, as in many other settler communities, a vigorous system of local self-government was implanted during colonization. A long-passive colonial power allowed the population in all essentials to govern itself. Due to the absence of a feudal noble stratum, the original system of popular self-government could be kept and, in time, broadened to embrace ever wider sections of the population. In addition, the popular mobilization in the war of independence contributed heavily to the enfranchisement of the lower classes.

The cases of the United States and Sweden indicate that Moore's thesis requires modification. The bourgeoisie's role as a 'battering ram' was necessary only in those cases where a feudal economic power structure was already firmly established—Moore would almost certainly agree to this modification, incidentally. This reminds us, however, that broad-based popular government is not a modern invention. It emerged, in varying forms, far back in time. This tradition was in some cases able, moreover, to survive into modern times. This has implications in turn for our understanding of the role capitalism has played in the tale. If by 'capitalism' we

[1] Switzerland is another example. It illustrates the device that mountains are the terrain of liberty (Burke 1986: 152).

mean an economic arrangement associated with urbanization and the factory system, then it is clear that capitalism is not an altogether necessary condition for democracy. If, on the other hand, our argument is that democracy presupposes a considerable measure of private ownership in the means of production, together with a wide dispersion of this ownership in the population, then the thesis would appear more tenable. For it can be applied in that case to countries in which smallholding farmers are primary actors in the economy. The young United States was such a country, and similar conditions prevailed in Sweden.

Other scholars have sought to explain the special character of political development in Europe by reference to the state system which arose there during medieval times and continued up to the modern times (Hintze 1975; Poggi 1978; Jones 1987; Tilly 1992). This argument takes the existence of competition among states as its starting point. It was the inter-state rivalry prevailing in Europe that was the root cause of the continent's special advancement. The historical course of events does indeed provide much support for this thesis. Nevertheless, it is not a fully satisfactory explanation. Besides the relationship *between states* that accompanied European development, we must also take notice of the *special nature of the state* which, due to other conditions, emerged in Europe. Such is the argument I will try to substantiate. Let us start, however, with the conventional view, which focuses on the interplay between states in Europe.

In Europe, it has been remarked, no empire of an abiding kind arose after the time of the Carolingians. What came to prevail instead was a constant competition among a wide range of states, in which perpetually shifting coalitions prevented any one state from definitively securing the upper hand. At the same time, a constant elimination took place of actors unable to hold their own in the ongoing struggle for survival. In the early sixteenth century, for instance, there were about 200 states in Europe. By the start of the twentieth century, this number had fallen by almost nine-tenths, to somewhat over 20. The states which survived were, as Charles Tilly (1975; 1992) has stressed, those which had been able to build up a suitable institutional structure. It was necessary, in the rivalry that prevailed, to have access to military forces of the foremost sort. This presupposed in turn an administrative apparatus that could collect taxes efficiently, and use the resulting revenues in a suitable and rational manner. An ample tax base—that is, a society capable of bearing the burdens placed upon it—was necessary too. For in a state system in reasonable balance, each state must rely mainly on such resources as can be mobilized internally. External exploitation on a large scale requires, after all, the establishment of a stable empire.[2]

In a state system characterized by competition and the elimination of weaker actors, the incentive is strong, as in any market, to copy such methods as show themselves profitable: 'the rules of the state competition meant that imitation remained the price of survival' (Hall 1986: 169). Military innovations tended to spread quickly. The various European states quickly adopted, for instance, the new military technology and recruitment methods which had demonstrated their superiority on the battlefield at the end of the Middle Ages. Large armies of infantry, manned mainly by mercenaries, became for 200 years the winning model in Europe. Sweden, however, introduced a conscript-based army of sorts at the time of its greatest military power. But since that nation was small, the military force thus collected was of a modest extent. All the more effective did this model therefore become when, in the years after the revolution, France made it its own. The enormous popular armies under Napoleon's command, which were composed of soldiers infused with a national ethos, were able to crush all resistance in Europe. In Prussia, the catastrophic defeat at the hands of Napoleon led to a thorough reorganization of the military system. The abolition of serfdom was an element in these reforms: an effective conscript army requires free citizens. Tsar Alexander II drew the same conclusion after Russia's humiliating setback in the Crimean war. It was military necessity that led to the abolition of serfdom in Russia (McNeill 1982; Tilly 1992).

In the area of administrative reform, Sweden was a leading country. A well-functioning administrative apparatus had been introduced in that country already in the first half of the 1600s. Tsar

---

[2] In the history of Europe, it was above all Spain which was able, on account of its highly lucrative possessions in America, to make use of the imperial financing form. Sweden, for its part, tried to apply a similar model on European soil. But this attempt was short-lived. In the state system existing at the time, the defence of external territories cost more over the long run than the possession of these territories yielded to the Swedish treasury. Another brief example was the French empire created by Napoleon, which was based to a great extent on the plunder of defeated states: 'The sums acquired by the administrators of [the] *domaine extraordinaire* in the period of France's zenith were quite remarkable and in some ways foreshadow Nazi Germany's plunder of its satellites and conquered foes during the Second World War . . . All this had the twin advantage of keeping much of the colossal French army *outside* the homeland, and of protecting the French taxpayer from the full costs of the war. Provided that the army under its brilliant leader remained successful, the system seemed invulnerable' (Kennedy 1987: 133).

Peter of Russia, who in his efforts to modernize his country was the imitator above all others, established a central bureaucracy in large part modelled on that of Sweden. But the country which subsequently set the standard in matters of bureaucracy was of course Prussia. It was first under Napoleon that France, for example, acquired a professional administration able to compete with Prussia's. And in England, similar changes, from a largely patrimonial administration to a stricter and more rational one, had to wait until the latter part of the nineteenth century (Tilly 1992; Skocpol 1979; Theobald 1990; van Crevald 1999).

Due to the openness of borders in Europe, technological advances of importance for economic development could spread relatively freely, through migration and the exchange of information. State leaders, moreover, were actively involved in the diffusion process. The most striking example was when Tsar Peter stayed in the Netherlands in order to learn shipbuilding. Another method used by Peter—enticing skilled foreign workers to settle in the country with favourable terms of employment—was more common. State support for the expansion of trade and industry was common, and a good many institutions devoted to such purposes spread among the countries of Europe. Examples include a legal system providing clear and effectual rules for economic actors—such rules are critical for the progress of commerce and industry—and a reasonably fixed and predictable tax system, which must exist if incentives to make long-term and productive investments are to arise. It was the Netherlands and England, in particular, which showed the way in this area (Rosenberg and Birdzell 1986; Jones 1987; North 1990). In these two countries, a flourishing economy emerged in the cities early on. In fiscal terms this had, as Tilly (1992) has shown, several distinct advantages. First, on account of the higher productivity of the urban economic sector, a substantially richer tax base was available than existed in agrarian societies. Second, the urban economy was much more easily taxed, administratively speaking, since revenues could be raised through tariffs and other levies on trade; these could be collected with the use of relatively minor mechanisms of control. Urbanized states could make do, in other words, with a much smaller administrative apparatus than could agrarian states. Furthermore, the accumulation of riches often found in the cities furnished the basis for banking activities on a large scale. This was a source of financing coveted by a good many warring princes.

On account of the constant competition, it has been alleged, there was a constant upward pressure on state performance. It was this that provided the foundation for the 'take-off' that took place in Europe. An exceptional rate of economic, technological and administrative development followed, paving the way for Europe's military and cultural dominance. One result of this was an appreciably higher social and material standard for the broad mass of the people. This rapid development formed a contrast, moreover, to the stagnation characterizing the contemporary empires of the east. In the latter region, state leaders were assured, through their military hegemony, the tax revenues needed to sustain their regimes. A striving to preserve the existing social and political order was the dominant pattern here. No promotion of commercial activities was to be seen in these empires. On the contrary, the growth of an urban economy was obstructed, for it might have led to an erosion in the political power of state leaders, which was based on their control over vital economic resources. A protracted fiscal and administrative decay could furthermore take place without any vigorous counter-measures being taken. Possessed of a very low governance capacity, such states were restricted in their functions to tasks having to do with the military and police. A rudimentary social peace could thus be upheld, but no more. The states of Europe, by contrast, developed an increasingly broad array of services for their citizens during this period: public education, disaster relief, functioning legal institutions, assistance to the poor, and so on. The great empires of the east offered their population virtually none of these things (Hall 1986; Mann 1986*a*; 1993; Rosenberg and Birdzell 1986; Jones 1987).

Political fragmentation in Europe was accompanied by economic growth, military strength, and increased prosperity for the population. And not just that. In addition, it has been argued, the processes generated by the prevailing state system also helped increase the political influence of the people. The higher taxation necessitated by military competition made state leaders more dependent on the taxpayers. For each state found it necessary, in all essentials, to aggregate its resources internally: to induce its own population to defray the costs of the constant wars. This forced state leaders to negotiate with the representatives of society. The price to be paid for this, often, was increased political rights for citizens. This logic—an outcome of 'the constant rivalry among the states'—was a precondition, according to Otto Hintze (1975: 346), for the unique representative systems established in Europe:

In the constant battles . . . the rulers found themselves thoroughly dependent on the good will of those strata of the population capable of military and financial contributions. The good will naturally had to be rewarded or even bought by giving full compensation to their economic and social interests but also by giving concessions and liberties of a political nature like those enshrined in the privileges of the Estates—the basis of the Estate system ... The active elements of the population who helped to build the state also gained a share in its government.

Tilly (1992: 102), for his part, summarizes the matter as follows:

The core of what we now call 'citizenship', indeed, consists of multiple bargains hammered out by rulers and ruled in the course of their struggles over the means of state action, especially the making of war.

The explanation for the early emergence of popular government in Europe thus lies, according to this line of reasoning, in the military competition between states. And, indeed, the absence in Europe of an empire has been a favourable factor. Only in such a context is the state leadership dependent on the population in its own core region: it cannot defray the costs of its regime to any substantial extent through external exploitation. Herein lies an incentive for negotiation, and an impetus to the growth of an interactive relationship between the state and society. Yet this has far from always been the result. A goodly number of states have been involved, at various places and times, in protracted martial competition with each other, without the aforementioned effects having arisen. An example is India. For the greater part of its history, this vast country was divided into a great many states, many of them in conflict with each other. Yet no pattern of development resembling that in Europe ensued for that (Hall 1985; Jones 1987; Kulke and Rothermund 1997).[3]

The unique course of events in Europe arose for special reasons. Given the pluralist relations of power that prevailed, for military and economic reasons, in the medieval states of Europe, the princes had a strong incentive to seek support from society. For the sake of such support, an institutional order was established for which very particular conditions were needed—conditions found only in Europe. In that continent, as Hintze clearly shows, a fusion took place between a Germanic tradition of popular participation and a formalized structure for immunity and representation developed by the church. This was an order founded on constitutional rights. On the one hand, these rights guaranteed a

---

[3] In the Islamic world too, a high degree of competition between states prevailed during the Middle Ages. As John Hall (1986: 159) has emphasized, however, the prevailing fragmentation simply resulted in state structures of a purely predatory type.

certain autonomy for the most important groups in society; on the other, they furnished those groups with a right to participate in affairs of government. The result was to establish a reasonably fixed institutional framework for an interactive state. Between the state, as represented by the prince, and the upper strata of society, a formal or *de facto* contract of partnership was concluded. The arenas and channels for interaction thus introduced had a twofold impact on the development of popular government. The main function of these arenas and channels was to serve as links between the state and society. But they had an indirect effect too: they strengthened society's capacity for internal coordination, thus increasing its capacity for collective action. This effect arose partly because the immunities and systems of representation reinforced group identities, and partly because the participation of different groups in representative organs resulted in an improved capacity for cooperation between different segments of the population.

In the New Era, however, the European state system gave rise to a movement in the opposite direction: a movement away from the separation of powers which had earlier been the dominant pattern. This tendency was due, as Brian Downing (1992) has thoroughly demonstrated, to military causes. The new techniques of warfare put a great premium on scale. The conditions of competition became much more severe. Only those states able to meet the new demands had prospects for survival. This particularly applied to states located in geographical areas which could be relatively easily invaded—which was the case in the greater part of Europe. In most cases of this sort, a pronounced militarization of the state took place, most markedly in the garrison state of Brandenburg-Prussia. Autocracy, in combination with a centralized and professional bureaucracy, made it possible to devote a large part of society's resources to military objectives. In Russia, in Castile, and in France—and in many other countries besides—developments took a similar course. It was only such countries in Europe as were endowed with natural geographical protection, in the form of water or high mountains, which were able to preserve the medieval institutional structure. In other words, the only states able to do this were those which were spared the military pressure otherwise engendered by the state system. This category included England, the Netherlands, Sweden and Switzerland. In these countries, no militarization of the state apparatus occurred. Constitutionalism and the separation of powers continued to prevail. Much of the old decentralized administrative structure was likewise retained, as was the largely local organization of defence tasks.[4]

A 'medieval' institutional structure also formed the framework for the settler society established in North America. That society was further stamped by the institutional pattern developed within the Puritan congregations, with their high degree of popular participation. The new society was also free from all serious external threat: the military resources of the indigenous population, which had been forced out, were wholly inferior. For a long time, moreover, this society was extremely homogeneous in class and ethnic terms.[5] Taken together, these factors provided the basis for a lively participation on the part of the common people. It was here, far from the struggle for survival raging in the European state system, that popular rule could take root in a more developed form.

---

[4] The geography-military thesis was launched by Hintze (1975), and it was later substantiated by Downing (1992) in particular (see also Tilly 1985; 1992). In opposition to this view, Thomas Ertman (1997) points to Spain, Hungary, and Poland; these countries, he argues, do not fit the theory. In the case of Spain, he remarks, the country was protected by a formidable geographical barrier, the Pyrenees, which protected it from the rest of the continent. Yet, I would object, it proved possible, on several occasions, to breach this barrier. More importantly, though, the Iberian Peninsula has no natural protection in the south. For more than 700 years, the country was occupied by Moorish invaders from North Africa. The Spanish, and chiefly Castilian, garrison state was formed during the struggle with the Moors, who were finally driven out in 1492. In that same year, Columbus was sent to India but ended up in America. Hence the Crown gained important economic resources, which lubricated its autocratic machinery for centuries to come. Hungary and Poland, on the other hand, are truly deviant cases, in that they were indeed geographically vulnerable, yet did not establish a military state. Ertman's own solution to this puzzle is that Hungary and Poland, along with England, applied a coherent territorial form of parliamentary representation, as opposed to estate representation, with the diversity and weakness on society's part to which it presumably leads. This argument does not make sense, however. It renders the constitutional development of Sweden and the Netherlands, both of which applied estate representation, incomprehensible. Coming to grips with the cases of Hungary and Poland requires instead, I would suggest, a look at the specific social composition of those countries: in particular, the lack of counter-weights to the nobility, and the constant rivalry among the various aristocratic fractions, which to a great extent followed clan divisions (cf. Hintze 1975). The aristocrats had but one interest in common: blocking the evolution of a central state machinery. Hence both countries proved an easy prey for neighbouring states, which were better organized in military terms. Hungary and Poland suffered from a weakness similar to Japan's—see Chapter 7, pp. 157–8—but the geographical conditions were different.

[5] Religious antagonisms, on the other hand, rent the area for a long time; the Puritans were not tolerant on this point. Ethnic diversification eventually took place too, and on a large scale.

The 'system logic' that came to dominate the European continent involved the abolition of the interactive order, based on institutionalized collaboration between the state and society, which had been established during the Middle Ages. In country after country, state leaders abolished the representative organs and guaranteed freedoms, or immunities, which had formed the basis of the interactive order. In many such autocratic countries, moreover, the state assumed a more active role. Due to the military threats to which they were subject, the garrison states required heavy public outlays for their survival. The overall tax level in Europe was accordingly higher than elsewhere. As a result, European states were able to get more accomplished as a rule. This applied in the 'social' area too. Prussia was a pioneer in this regard (Dorwart 1971). The oppressed serfs of that country had already been granted certain statutory social and economic rights in the 1700s. The purpose was to assure the state a solid foundation for the recruitment of soldiers and the collection of taxes. In addition, the regime sought by this means to win the loyalty of the population.[6] In a paternalistic spirit, Prussia took care of its subjects to a certain extent; and other countries did likewise in time. The price for this, however, was an absence of freedom and a circumscribed influence for citizens.[7]

The objective of the garrison model was to organize society for military purposes. Despite its well-ordered character, however, this model could not hold its own in coming trails of strength.

Four Modes of State

Tocqueville's report from America was a signal of a new current. The form of government practiced in the 'New World' struck Tocqueville with wonder. It was not just the breadth of participation which struck him, but the strong interaction between the state and society as well. The French visitor saw scarcely a trace of that top-down rule of which he had seen so much in his homeland. What he observed instead were citizens who took charge of a series of common concerns independently, while taking active part in the public

[6] The same strategy for safeguarding the recruitment of soldiers and the collection of taxes has been applied by many successful garrison states in history. Rome is one example, the Ottoman Empire another.

[7] A similar method was used in the late 1800s against the growing working class. Chancellor Bismarck introduced sweeping social legislation on behalf of the workers. At the same time, he undertook measures suppressing the workers' organizations; see Chapter 8, p. 229.

organs at the same time. Through developing their own coordination, and through the institutions of their state, the citizens of America had developed an unusually great collective capacity.

What Tocqueville described in his report from America was an interactive state: a state that worked closely with its citizens. This endowed the American state with a special character. It was not large in scope; indeed, it was clearly smaller than the French state. Yet it could get a good deal done. It had great governance capacity. This phenomenon was not altogether new, however. In a more restricted and elitist form, the interactive model has shown its strength in Europe too. Despite a relatively small population, and with no natural resources to speak of, both England and the Netherlands had developed a remarkably great state capacity. It was based essentially on two factors. Due to a favourable institutional framework, trade and industry developed in these countries early. Great riches were created thereby, providing the state with an excellent tax base. The economic elite, furthermore, was closely involved in running the state, yielding additional benefits. There was not just a better tax base in England and the Netherlands. There was also a greater willingness to be taxed.

There were many in France who looked with envy on these countries. England in particular served as an inspiration to many within the aristocratic opposition to the monarchy, as the writings of Montesquieu testify. Subsequently, the mobilizing force demonstrated in the American Revolution imparted a strong impetus to the more radical opposition groups. In his fiscal need, the king was forced at last to allow society to take part in decision-making. A very broad electorate could now suddenly express its will. The result, as we know, was the overturning of the old order. The lower social strata who took power carried out a social transformation. The political consequences were soon chaotic. From an unchecked policy of confrontation followed terror and administrative decay. The state's governance capacity became progressively more curtailed. Soon the authority of the central power could be maintained only with the help of the army, which had grown to an enormous size after the revolution. In the end, one of the army's generals, Napoleon Bonaparte, assumed power and declared himself emperor. The absolute state had thus returned. In the choice between anarchy and Leviathan, most people preferred the latter. As a brilliant commander, and with a restored centralist state at his disposal, Napoleon made himself master of Europe for a decade. But he could never break the resistance of England. Despite a gigantic exploitation of the vast areas under occupation, together with a far-reaching trade boycott against England, France could not hold out against the state capacity which its adversary could muster.

In this instance, as in the great wars that followed in the twentieth century, the centralized militarist state lost out against the freer interactive state (Lake 1992). These victories have decisively reinforced the principles of constitutionalism and popular rule. At long last, in other words, the states of 'medieval Europe' have defeated the militarist autocracies of the New Era. As the twentieth century has closed, it is the interactive model which has become dominant. It does not, to be sure, extend over the entire map of the world. But it is this model which has proved, in a longer perspective, to possess the greater power.

We have just touched on one of the well-known alternatives. It is the *Leviathan state*. This is a state with a high degree of autonomy from society. Through its control from above, such a state can penetrate and control social life. Society, for its part, has neither autonomy nor an independent coordination capacity: it is dominated and directed by the state. To the degree popular organizing is allowed to take place, it is tied to the state and subordinate to it. Popular 'participation' takes place only in controlled forms. A common variant of the Leviathan state historically has been the militarist garrison state. Many of the great empires were so structured in their heyday. They were based on an intensive extraction of resources for the pursuit of militarist goals. The entire society was organized for this purpose. Prussia was an example of such a state during modern times. The Soviet Union too gradually acquired the features of a garrison state.[8] Another and more modern variant is the social-transformation state. Lenin was the great innovator here. The primary aim of the Soviet state he founded was to achieve a thoroughgoing transformation in the social and economic structure. The goal was to carry out a radical redistribution, leading to a classless society, and at the same time to advance economic development. This would take place through strict central control exercise by a state enjoying autonomy from society. This model had many successors. The so-called developmental state, which was established in many countries from the 1950s on, not least in Africa, often took the Leninist state as its model, albeit with varying degrees of explicitness. The Leninist approach was long thought to yield a superior statecraft; it was believed capable of creating both social justice and great economic progress (Migdal 1988; Leftwich 1995).

---

[8] See Chapter 6, footnote 10.

The objectives of the Leviathan state—to penetrate society, while at the same time being autonomous from society—require a well-developed repressive and administrative capacity. Governance is accomplished in large part through coercion, which is exercised best when combined with extensive controls on the activities of citizens. Access to an effective intelligence organization, like the *Stasi*,[9] for example, is a great advantage from the standpoint of this model. Efforts at normative control also normally form part of the repertoire. An intensively propagated state religion, or other comparable ideology, can facilitate the subordination of citizens to the state. This model has been most long-lived and efficient when it has been built up with the support of a well-ordered and rationally recruited bureaucracy working in the service of the state. The Chinese Empire is the classic example here. This form of government is more brittle, by contrast, when it relies on a heavy use of despotic and repressive methods. In the extreme case, this can take the form of a purely terroristic government, Pol Pot's Cambodia being a recent and horrifying example. The interest here maximized is that in political control and dominance. Society is paralyzed. The drawback from the standpoint of the Leviathan model is that the state machinery also runs the risk of paralysis over the long run, with a concomitant loss of governance capacity. Despite its hectic use of despotic methods, then, such a state scores poorly in terms of infrastructural power.

When the state autonomy and dominance signified by the Leviathan model cannot be sustained, another form of state has often arisen in its stead. This is a state which surrenders more and more of its autonomy, which associates with society and blends with it. From having governed from above on the basis primarily of coercion, the state now resorts to governance mainly through incentive—through allocating the benefits arising from the occupancy of state office. The *predatory state* is the result.[10] This is a state founded on the logic of rent-seeking. Its control over the various activities of society is dependent on its 'buying power', that is, its capacity to marshall support through providing access to spoils. By allocating privileges and sundry particularistic advantages through cooptation, corruption, and policies of privilege, the regime can keep itself going. This model presupposes that the state has the ability to acquire the kinds of resources in

[9] 'Stasi' was the name of the vast East German intelligence organization. It employed several hundred thousand functionaries, and it had networks in every nook and cranny of society.

[10] For an overview of the literature, see Lundahl (1997).

which societal actors are interested. The more fully the state leadership can monopolize the control of these resources, the more closed and top-down the system of rule can become. Through strategies of 'divide and rule', society's coordination capacity can be inhibited. While the Leviathan state makes a clean sweep of independent organized interest groups, the predatory state leaves substantial room for competition between different groupings rooted in civil society. Political practices based on clan and fraction emerge. The state becomes embedded in society and *vice versa* (cf. Evans 1995). We see here, in other words, a pattern of contact and cooperation between the public and private spheres, but not the sort characteristic of the interactive state. In the predatory model, the two spheres mix and blend, often in a diffuse fashion. There is contact between them, but the contact surface is indistinct. The difference between public and private here is rubbed out; as a result, both spheres lose autonomy. This lack of autonomy entails a mutual handicap. The organizations of civil society are linked together with the state, and they become highly dependent on the resources which can be extracted from that source. The organizations upholding such linkages tend, moreover, to have a pronounced elitist structure. The consequence is a weak civil society, a hierarchically structured and dominated one. But a weak state also results. The rent-seeking that keeps the system going promotes administrative decay. The governing capacity of the state is thus undermined too. If this weakness cannot be compensated for by an ample influx of resources, as a result of external exploitation, access to natural resources, and so on, it becomes increasingly difficult to control the process centrally. The result can be an advancing feudalization of the state. The subalterns appropriate their prebends, as Weber put it. In order to get anything done, the 'prince' must gain the consent of his 'barons'—factional leaders and others—on whom his rule depends. These barons, who constitute the state's links with society, are fed by their connections with the state; at the same time, however, they set limits to its capacity for action. The state which seeks to rule by capturing elite actors in society becomes itself captured by these actors. Many of the great empires of history entered this stage in the course of their decline. But there have also been many examples of this in modern times. The states of the Third World have been marked in a high degree by predatory rule, and many still are today. Many of the states which had formerly been part of the Soviet Union exhibit such a character too. Such countries as Mexico, Nigeria, Indonesia, and Russia may serve as clear examples of the predatory model today[11] (see for example Clapham 1982; Migdal 1988; Bratton and de Walle 1997; Varese 1997).

Such a state can, if the disintegration is not halted, end up losing its governance capacity altogether. Society then breaks free. What remains is the *marginal state*: a state which exhibits certain outward attributes of statehood, but which can penetrate its territory only to a very low degree. Society here is highly autonomous. The state has but a minimal governance capacity. Its task may be primarily symbolic and ritualistic in nature. For a long time the Japanese emperor had such a role. In India, it was often the case that monarchs performed mainly ceremonial functions. Another example may be seen in the famous 'theatre state' in Bali (Geertz 1980). The organization of civil life in such a case can take many different forms. A scenario which has been very common historically, in cases where the state has in a practical sense collapsed, is the appearance of a more or less anarchical warlord system. Such a system developed in Japan as well as in Europe during the early Middle Ages. It can be seen today in some African countries where the state has disintegrated. In another model, religious bodies bring order to civic life. Such was the case to a great extent in Europe after the fall of Rome. Similar patterns have obtained for long periods in India, where the organization of society took place within the framework of the caste system (Hall 1985). A third variant is a form of local self-government, with certain structures connecting the various units, which has been found in frontier societies. Such an order prevailed, for example, in Scandinavia in the early years.

Like the predatory state, the *interactive state* involves a far-reaching collaboration between the state and society. In both cases, the contacts can take place at all levels of the political system. The more numerous the contact points at the local and regional levels, in addition to the central level, the more open and intensive is the link between society and the state. Its difference from the predatory model lies in the nature of these contacts. In the interactive case, it is a question of an institutionalized collaboration. Contacts between the state and society proceed in regulated and ordered forms—forms which help to maintain clear boundaries between the public and the private spheres. In this way, a reciprocal autonomy is established. The state stands free, in its operative functions, from the various particularistic interests in society, and so can

---

[11] It may be of interest to note that these states have in common the possession of large-scale oil resources, and in some cases other natural resources too. As long as the state leadership retains essential control over such resources, the predatory model can remain relatively stable.

maintain rational administrative practices. This enhances the state's governance capacity; in this there is a similarity with the bureaucratic Leviathan state. Society, for its part, is left in peace to a considerable extent; a wide range of social and economic activities is left to the citizens themselves. This stimulates the growth of lively civic networks; in this there is a similarity with the marginal state. But in contrast to the Leviathan state and the marginal state, where in both cases a barrier is upheld, in differing ways, between the state and society, the interactive state is distinct from society and yet cooperates with it. The two sides are in certain respects autonomous from each other, but they are joined in an ongoing linkage. This 'formula', in which autonomy and inclusion are combined, can be favourable to both sides. In as much as society gets the opportunity to exert influence over the state, the state acquires roots in society. This provides the state with information and possibilities of support from the 'territory' it is to govern. That makes governance easier. At the same time, civil society is strengthened.[12]

The interactive model presupposes, first of all, that society is accorded considerable autonomy, in the form of institutionalized freedoms—immunities—and access to resources of its own. The state serves as a guarantee that these conditions will be upheld. Second, the state establishes institutions for the legal regulation of conflicts in society, thus reinforcing the coordination capacity of citizens. Third, the channels and arenas which have been established

---

[12] Cf. Migdal (1988: 35), who assumes that a strong society presupposes a weak state, and *vice versa*. In Migdal's view, society and the state are involved in a zero-sum game: the one side dominates at the expense of the other. This assumption might hold true in the case of power over political norm-setting, but not in the case of power over implementation—in the area, that is, where actual governance capacity is at issue, which is the explicit objective of Migdal's inquiry (1988: 22). The process of implementation is potentially a positive-sum game, to the extent that all parties involved, state as well as society actors, may get a better outcome (Evans 1995: 37; Weiss 1998: 24ff; Edin 2000: 42–3). In his empirical section, Migdal furnishes many highly readable reports of the rise and fall of the Leviathan model. The result has indeed been a weak state stamped by the logic of predatory rule. But the societies described are hardly strong for that, which is what Migdal claims. Rather, the capacity possessed by these societies in their own right is extremely low. They function primarily through the opportunities they provide for exploiting the resources of the state, which become ever more meagre with time. The outcome is negative, in other words, both for the state and for society. The deviant case in Migdal's study—Israel, where the state succeeds in governing—represents a different model: here we encounter the interactive state. See also Wade (1990) and Doner (1992), who claim, with reference to the 'tiger states' of East Asia, that a strong state must be insulated from societal forces. On the theoretical level, cf. also Skocpol (1985).

have a stimulating effect. These institutions furnish, as we know, important incentives to organize at various levels in society. They also provide a space for continuous interaction and mixture between different segments of the population. Society's conciliatory faculty is strengthened thereby. Herein lies its difference from the marginal state. The marginal state leaves considerable room for the growth of a large-scale civil 'mosaic'. But the different elements tend to be sharply divided and separate. In the absence of the incentives and structures supportive of organizing which the state can provide, no intermediate structures are created, whether horizontal or vertical, in society. The passive and socially uninvolved state creates a civil society boasting but a small coordination capacity.[13]

An active state structured in the right manner, institutionally speaking, can strengthen society's collective capacity. The state thus acquires a strong counterpart with which to interact, a counterpart which can hinder the state, but which can also furnish it with valuable support. Herein lies the strength which has contributed to the historical success of the interactive model. Yet herein lies as well the weakness which prevented this model from constituting a practical option over long periods.[14]

The Interactive State: Strengths and Weaknesses

In his comments on the American case, Tocqueville (1969: 244–5, 254–5, 665–6) noted that the European states of which he knew functioned more effectively in certain respects. The absolutist monarchies had often built up a more efficient administrative apparatus. Their bureaucracy displayed greater professionalism, and their methods of decision-making were more suitable for ensuring uniformity and consistency in the actions of the state. The state had one will rather than many. This enabled it to create empires and to

[13] The interactive state is pluralist in character, it operates on the basis of rules, and it exhibits considerable power division. It is active and yet restricted in relation to society. As noted in Part I, such characteristics make for institutionally favourable conditions for the evolution of democratic development.

[14] These state models should be seen, of course, as ideal types. In real life, they may to some extent be combined, so that certain parts of the state function according to one logic, others according to another. At the time of its demise, for example, the Soviet state displayed features both of the Leviathan model and of—increasingly—the predatory model. The German state formed in the late 1800s sought to combine elements of the garrison state with elements of the interactive state. A more common combination is that between interactive and predatory rule. Many young democracies exhibit such a combination.

erect enormous monuments to its rulers. Its strength was most evident in the domain of war, in the ability to target society's resources on military objectives. Government by the people has usually proved inferior in this respect. It has demonstrated a deficient capacity for marshalling forces in times of crisis. Its strength has lain rather at another level: in the social vitality and capacity for collaboration between the state and society which it makes possible. With its population behind it, such a state can achieve many things which a despot cannot. Above all, it has the ability to create social and economic progress, and thus to endow its citizens with wealth. Left in peace for a hundred years, Tocqueville concluded, such a state would 'be richer, more populated, and more prosperous than neighbouring despotic states; but during that century it would often have run the risk of being conquered by them' (1969: 224).

The weakness of the interactive state has to do with the costs arising in connection with decision-making (Wintrobe 1998: 227–8). The Leviathan model exhibits a greater capacity for decision-making. This applies particularly when there is just one decision-maker. A powerful policy for handling crises can thus be upheld more easily. A pluralist form of government, in which power is dispersed, displays a certain inertia, rendering decisive action difficult. Different groups may be gravely at odds over what should be done. This can delay decisions or even produce downright paralysis. Intensively interactive forms of government were long possible only within small and relatively homogeneous units. The city-states are an example here. The interactive forms introduced at the national level in Europe during the Middle Ages were, as a rule, extremely limited in terms of collective potential. The public sector, which was mainly military in character, was extremely small. When new techniques of warfare were introduced at the dawn of the New Era, these interactive units found it hard to survive. It was now necessary to marshall forces in a way that the pluralist systems could not. The advantage now went to actors who ruled over large areas and could gather large-scale resources. Economies of scale were at a premium. Interactive states could not usually compete in this new 'race'. For such societies lacked the coordination capacity which would have made such a competition possible—a problem which got worse as the states expanded geographically. The garrison state, in varying degrees of purity, became the winning concept. Thus were the large cohesive units created which the New Era demanded.

However, in some areas enjoying special conditions for geographical reasons, the interactive form could be kept alive. It was these countries, England and the United States in particular, that were to clear the way for the spread of the interactive and increasingly democratic state. What made this possible? The answer is that the interactive state possesses, as Tocqueville suggested, a superior performance capacity over the long run. Notwithstanding its deficiencies in the area of decision costs, which can be drawbacks in every short-term 'race', it possesses the greater governance potential, and thus enjoys the advantage in the long term.

We return then to the question of the various governance methods at the disposal of states. Governing solely through coercion has its drawbacks, as we know. It necessitates a rule of terror which stifles both society and the institutions of the state. It is simpler, and altogether less costly, when the citizens give their consent in some form and allow themselves to be governed. This can be achieved if, as often is said in the spirit of Weber, the state manages to uphold its legitimacy.[15] There are many ways this subject can be divided up, and many different questions can accordingly be addressed (see for example Connolly 1984; Beetham 1991). In order to illustrate the problem at hand, however, it may suffice to point out that legitimacy can be established primarily in three ways: (1) on the basis of the nature of the decision-making procedure; (2) on the basis of the special qualities displayed by the person or persons making the decisions; and (3) on the basis of the results achieved.

1. As far as the decision-making procedure is concerned, I may give my consent on the grounds that I myself have been able, directly or indirectly, to take part in making the decision in question. Alternatively, and irrespective of the first reason, I may have respect for the rules and underlying norms applied in the process.

2. Where the qualities of the decision-maker(s) are concerned, it may be a matter of competence and professional skill. But it can also be a question of charisma. Our attitudes may further be based on tradition, or on ritualistic and cultural identifications with the person or persons who govern.

3. When it is primarily accomplished results which form the basis for our consent, the critical question is the degree to which public policy accords with our wishes. To what extent does public policy satisfy our various interests, whether of a material or

[15] Deborah Brautigam (1992: 9) summarizes the argument as follows: 'A legitimate system is legal, but more importantly, citizens believe in its appropriateness and adhere to its rules. Legitimacy thus influences the effectiveness of a government: greater efficiency comes from the promotion of voluntary compliance with laws and regulations rather than from reliance on coercion, threats, and personal loyalties.'

normative nature? These interests can also—to make yet another distinction—be of a universal sort applying in principle to all, or of a more particularist kind directed primarily to certain groups.

The strength of interactive state is that it can, in principle, base its rule on all of these different kinds of legitimacy. This is especially true when it is highly inclusive, and based on a broad participation of citizens: when it is democratic, in other words. This gives it a unique basis for gaining the consent of the governed. As a result, a state of this kind can apply a wide register of governance methods. A weakness of the predatory state is that it depends, for its legitimacy, on its ability to deliver particularistic advantages, typically of a material nature, to the groups in society which support it. In order to accomplish this objective, it sets various institutional rules aside. This undermines its administrative capacity, thus endangering its capacity to produce results over the long run. The processes employed contribute, moreover, to a low procedural legitimacy. The marginal state is more limited still. At times it can adduce no more than a traditional or ritualistic legitimacy. The Leviathan state, for its part, can of course be much more potent. It is above all this state which has been, over the last 500 years, the rival of the interactive state for hegemony. For a long time it had the upper hand. Well into the twentieth century, it seemed that the Leviathan model, as personified by Stalin, Hitler, and Mao, might be the model of the future. The strengths of the model are known to us. It leaves a great deal of room for coercion—indeed, almost a boundless expanse. In the long run, however, coercion is a blunt instrument. To function effectively, therefore, a state of this sort needs a group of loyal supporters coopted by privilege. A *nomenklatura* system thus comes into being, which contains the embryo of development in a predatory direction. It is a further advantage if the regime has support, or at any rate acceptance, from the broad mass of the population. Such a regime can, under opportune conditions, point to certain favourable results. Through propaganda and schooling, moreover, it can foster support for the norms which it represents. In the same way, it can pay homage and impart splendour to the person or persons who furnish its outward face. Although denying any real influence to their citizens, such regimes too have sought to maintain a facade of citizen participation in modern times. Citizens have been strongly encouraged to participate in state-controlled elections, as well as in controlled 'mobilizations' of other sorts. What has been the impact of such measures? Education and missionary activity had an appreciable impact in former times. It was in large part Catholic priests who administered the Spanish Empire in South America during its first years (Haring 1975). In modern times, with higher educational levels and richer, and thus harder-to-control, information sources, it would seem that attempts to 'foster' forth legitimacy can have only a limited effect. The risk is that the propaganda and indoctrination will boomerang on the regime itself, as evidently happened in communist eastern Europe. A forced participation in faked elections and other fraudulent displays can have the same effect. The Leviathan model's legitimacy lies above all in its capacity to produce results appreciated by citizens. Above and beyond benefits of a material nature, such results have often had to do with achieving '*gloire*' for the nation. With a rationally functioning bureaucracy, the state becomes more proficient at such tasks. Such an institutional order can also impart legitimacy to the regime due to the professionalism and regularity with which the state apparatus operates. Successful garrison states have been structured in accordance with this pattern. Nevertheless, this model has failed it over the long haul.

In the many trials of strength which have taken place over the last couple of centuries, it is the mainly interactive side which has emerged victorious (Lake 1992). In struggle after struggle, whether with 'hot' weapons or 'cold', the garrison state has been defeated. It has lost, in other words, in the domain where it should have been strongest: the military. How has this been possible? It is two capacities above all which have given the upper hand to the interactive state. We have already touched upon one, namely, its superior politico-administrative potential, which is grounded in its broader legitimacy. A clear indication of this emerged already in the contest between England and France, up to and including the Napoleonic Wars. England was able, due to the greater element of consent on which its regime was founded, to extract far greater resources, proportionally speaking, from its population. On account of their guaranteed immunities and their right to participate in government, the leading social strata were prepared to make great sacrifices for the sake of the nation (North and Weingast 1998). This applied most especially in the area of taxes. By contrast, the autocratic French state, which displayed a mixture of predatory rule and garrison state under the kings, and which acquired more of the latter stamp under Napoleon, possessed no comparable capacity.[16] In war after

---

[16] In his study of France under the monarchy *vis-à-vis* England, Hilton Root (1989: 253) writes that 'because the king claimed full discretion, he had less power'. Otherwise put, in Mann's terminology (1986*b*), a high degree of despotic power contributed to a low degree of infrastructural power. Analyzing the connection between

war, interactive states have displayed a great, and sometimes astonishing, capacity for mobilization. Tocqueville's pessimism about the military capacity of states ruled by the people has proved exaggerated. Through a long-standing application of the interactive model, such states have developed a coordination capacity which enables them more than to hold their own in the contest with states based on the Leviathan model.

A further factor has been important here too. As Paul Kennedy (1987) shows, this factor has, more than any other, decided which side wins out over the long run. States enjoying access to a wealthy economy win out over states with a weaker economic basis. Military discipline and skilful leadership have certainly many times determined the outcome of individual battles; the Swedish king Charles XII was a brilliant example.[17] But in long drawn-out military struggles, Kennedy shows, access to economic resources makes the difference. When the resources run dry, neither the genius of commanders nor the bravery of soldiers can prevent defeat in the end. Germany learned this painful truth in the course of two world wars. Military dominance is determined by economic potential. States which fall behind economically cannot hold their own in military competition over the long term. The Soviet Union is a latter-day example.[18]

The interactive state appears, in other words, not merely to enjoy a politico-administrative superiority, in the form of a greater ability to utilize a given tax base. It also seems to be better at nourishing and developing the source of its revenues. The interactive state provides, in other words, a better environment for economic progress. This was also, we may recall, Tocqueville's judgement of the matter; he did not, however, connect economic progress with military capacity; rather, he saw a conflict between them. What accounts, then, for this economic advantage? The answer is that the patterns and structures which constitute the interactive state also promote economic growth. The interactive state provides considerable space for autonomous civic and economic activity, thus promoting innovation. It is furthermore based on institutions which encourage efficiency

taxation and political organization in France and England, Margaret Levi (1988: 120) makes the following remark: ' . . . the monarchs of France had greater absolute power, but their costs of achieving compliance were much higher than those of their counterparts in England. Without a forum in which to engage in repeated transactions and renegotiations, they were more subject to tax resistance in the form of noncompliance and actual rebellion.'

[17] See Chapter 8, pp. 209–10.

[18] Piquantly enough, Kennedy offered a mistaken forecast of the future strength of the Soviet Union relative to the US.

and promote long-term and productive investment. The critical elements on which the interactive state is founded—the rule of law and predictable administration—are also necessary conditions for economic growth.[19] This relationship is not wholly symmetrical, however. If we distinguish three components in a state based on the rule of law—constitutional law, administrative law, and civil law—the relationship can be illustrated in Fig. 9.1.

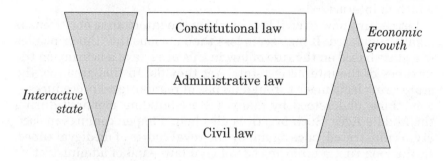

FIGURE 9.1: *Rule of law, interactive state, and economic growth*

Constitutional law bears on the rights of citizens *vis-à-vis* the state, as well as on the distribution of powers within the state. The maintenance of these rights is fundamental to the interactive state. It was on the foundation of constitutionalism, involving the separation of powers and the maintenance of liberties, that the interactive concept was introduced. Less obvious but still important is administrative law, which concerns the exercise of authority by the state apparatus. Administration on the basis of rules facilitates interaction with society, in that it contributes to a high degree of procedural legitimacy. Few phenomena would appear to be so demoralizing, and so detrimental to popular consent, as widespread corruption, nepotism, and public 'kleptomania'. Such practices violate what appears to be a virtually universal conception of fairness.[20] Administration on the basis of rules has another positive

[19] The fact that empirical studies of the link between economic growth and democracy have often demonstrated such weak and irregular connections can be explained against this background. Not all democracies are alike with respect to their institutional foundation. Many contain substantial predatory elements. The relation between democracy and growth is the object of study in Helliwell (1993), Bhalla (1997), Leblang (1997), Przeworski and Limongi (1997).

[20] In a survey done recently in India, respondents described corruption as the greatest evil, much greater than such problems as unemployment, rising prices, and caste conflicts (*India Today* 1997, No. 18; see also Della Porta and Vannucci 1997)

effect as well. It means that state organs observe impartiality in their operations *vis-à-vis* the various special interests in society. Such administrative practices do not, therefore, reinforce conflicts of interest between different population groups. As a neutral regulator of conflict, the state can thus facilitate cooperation between society's various segments. The effect is to reinforce the coordination capacity of civil society, and to strengthen the state's governance capacity in turn—for the state now has a forceful partner with which to interact.

Let us turn now to civil law, in which the intercourse of citizens is legally regulated. It may seem less than obvious that the principles of a state based on the rule of law in this area have a bearing on the fortunes of the interactive state. Yet they do. In this area too, the state gains legitimacy through its use of regular legal procedures—something understood by many a state-building monarch during the Middle Ages. Such practices also help dampen conflicts in society, as illustrated, once again, by the royal courts of medieval times. In the long run, a uniform code of civil law—and of administrative law too, for that matter—may contribute to integration and national cohesion (Poggi 1978). Hence it strengthens both civil society and the state. A people with a common identity is easier to govern through consent, but it is also, due to the collective capacity in its hands, harder to dominate through coercion. Despotic regimes maintain their power through strategies of 'divide and rule' (Weingast 1997). Regimes which based their statecraft on legitimacy work instead to achieve integration. Legal standardization is a tool for realizing this objective.

When we look at the other side of the figure, that bearing on economic growth, it becomes clear that civil law is fundamental. According to institutionalist economic theory, entrepreneurship and productive investments can come about only within a framework of fixed and predictable legislation which serves to uphold contracts and ownership. If economic actors try to arrange this on their own, the risks and transaction costs become so large as to preclude productive economic investment (North 1990). It is only the state which can furnish the legal infrastructure necessary for entrepreneurship.

How then is it with administrative law, which concerns such matters as controls on production, the levying of taxes, and the granting of licences to set up in business? Here too, of course, substantial transaction costs can arise. Unclear rules create uncertainty and impose costs, in terms of time and money, on persons trying to get something done. Such rules—or, more precisely, their absence—feed corruption. Among economists there are, or at any rate have been, a range of views on this phenomenon. One school has argued that corruption should be seen as an administrative lubricant, a method for moving forward through a system characterized by great administrative inertia. One purchases precedence for oneself. Corruption is thus a cost among others. Even so, one may justifiably object, it imposes extra costs. Studies have shown that corruption reduces the will to invest. Unfair conditions of competition are created besides, in which companies obtain contracts, licences, tax breaks, and the like through the offer of bribes rather than on the basis of rational economic and administrative considerations. Such conditions place a general drag on economic life[21] (Ades and Di Tella 1997; Della Porta and Vannucci 1997; World Bank 1997; Rose-Ackerman 1999).

Let us turn, finally, to the constitutional level. Opinions are yet more divided here. According to one long-prevalent conception, a constitutionally unfettered state leadership has a better chance of establishing conditions favourable to economic advancement. It is the 'reform prince' one has in mind here: the strong leader, autonomous from society, who is able to make a clean sweep of corruption and mismanagement and to create institutions providing good incentives for productive entrepreneurship. Such figures have certainly existed; in recent years it has become common to adduce the example of General Pinochet, Chile's brutal dictator. Yet the counter-examples are many.[22] The problem is that the autonomy enjoyed by the reform prince also supplies excellent conditions for efforts in another direction: rent-seeking, or the pursuit of riches through office. If corruption and other forms of public kleptomania furnish poor incentives for economic progress, the situation is worst where this process is orchestrated from the highest level. Such activities then acquire wholly new proportions and become virtually impossible to halt (Myrdal 1968; Theobald 1990; Della Porta and Vannucci 1997; Della Porta 2000). A system in which the state leadership is free of constitutional restrictions, and thus escapes efforts to inspect and control its doings, contains few barriers to political and administrative degeneration. The result can be very costly for society.

[21] The negative effects are in some measure mitigated, many argue, if the money derived from corruption is reinvested domestically, instead of being spent, as so often, on luxury consumption overseas (Theobald 1990).

[22] As illustrated by such names as Batista (Cuba), Somoza (Nicaragua), Mobutu (Zaire), Marcos (the Philippines), Suharto (Indonesia) and Brezhnev (the Soviet Union).

This exposes a general dilemma of third-party enforcement, the logical rationale of the Leviathan model. The problem, as North (1990: 58) has pointed out, is the following: how can we be assured that the third party plays the role presupposed by this model? How can we induce this actor, who is autonomous from society, to function as the neutral, impartial administrator of the common interest? For the 'prince' makes a private calculation of utility too. After all, the third party is a party as well. What then is there to hinder him, if no countervailing powers are present, from furthering his own interest primarily, and becoming a parasitic power in society?

Political power has always implied access to privilege. Unrestricted power opens the floodgates to the unrestrained appropriation of privileges. The Leviathan model does not just provide an opportunity for forcefully promoting the common good, as Hobbes— and Plato before him, and Lenin after—somewhat naively assumed. This mode of government also yields excellent opportunities for promoting the self-interest of the ruling elite. Herein lies a latent weakness: the tendency to develop predatory practices.

The bureaucratic form of the Leviathan state, however, contains an inhibiting factor in this regard, functionally albeit not formally. The bureaucracy in such a system enjoys a professionally grounded autonomy which places limits on the discretionary power of the 'prince'. It is on account of this, and due to the competence and administrative order which can thereby be maintained, that this model has become the most stable form of autocracy. The successful empires of history have been bureaucratic garrison states in the main. In order to get anything done, however, such a state must have roots in society if it is to be able, for example, to recruit officials to its military and administrative apparatus and to gain a group of loyal supporters within the population. Thus does a privileged social stratum, a *nomenklatura*, arise. In a garrison state where the tasks of the public sector are relatively limited, the apparatus can be kept rather small, and the group of supporters required by the state can be kept small as well. Both the apparatus and the privileged stratum can thus be centrally controlled fairly easily: for as long, at any rate, as the centre retains access to the economic resources sustaining both the apparatus and the system of privileges. Conditions change, however, when the social-transformation state takes the stage. The ambitions of the state are substantially greater here, as is its need to penetrate society in order to control the various activities contained therein. A far larger administrative apparatus is now needed, and the state must be rooted in society more widely if it is to realize its goals. This particularly applies when the object is both to push forward economic development and to carry out reforms of a redistributive character, as has often been the case in so-called developmental states. These states have in many cases gone to great lengths to call forth a controlled popular 'participation' in support of their policies. One-party states have tended to undertake such efforts, as have certain 'populist' military regimes. A difficulty arises here, however, in that the growth of the apparatus, and the fragmentation following therefrom, makes the system much harder to control. In the same way, it becomes progressively less feasible to maintain a firm grasp on the system of privileges. These conditions, together with the fact that the space for rent-seeking expands naturally in step with the growth of the state, have in many cases led to an increasing fiscal and administrative disorder. The great and resolute developmental Leviathan state turns into a crumbling hulk torn apart by a multitude of particularistic interests, and it becomes progressively less able to implement any coherent policies. Many 'technocratic' military dictatorships in Latin America have met such a fate, as have a range of 'mobilizing' one-party states in Africa and elsewhere.[23] The result is a spread of predatory practices, which at times can be halted in part through a despotic and tyrannical government. The basic problem is that the Leviathan model, embodying as it does the principle of top-down rule, possesses but a limited governance capacity. When it attempts to exceed its potential, it falls prey to self-destruction, with administrative incapacity, poor macroeconomic performance, and diminishing legitimacy the result.

The strength of the interactive state lies in a developed governance capacity founded on cooperation and consent. The institutions which have made this model possible have at the same time yielded good incentives for economic development, thus endowing the state with a favourable resource base. Taken together, these elements have brought forth a statecraft which the Leviathan model cannot match. It was the introduction of this model at an early stage, and its continuation in certain countries, that contributed to the unique dynamism characterizing the European state system. It was not, in

[23] The example of Brazil may be of interest here. Kurt Weyland (1998: 53) describes the evolution of the development model pursued in that country under military auspices as follows: 'Starting as a powerful Leviathan in the 1940s . . . Brazil's development state ended up as an obese, uncoordinated Gulliver, unable to turn its weight into strength and tied down by innumerable bonds to narrow interest groups and clientelistic networks.' One detail he reports is especially telling: at the end of the 1970s, the Planning Ministry did not even knew the number of public agencies that existed. It was estimated at 1,000, as compared with about 150 in the US at the same time (Weyland 1998: 55).

other words, the state system in itself, with the constant military competition it entailed, that was the critical factor. What made Europe exceptional was the special terms of the competition, namely, the participation within it of a model exhibiting a higher level of performance. This produced an upward pressure on all of the parties involved. What made up for the unique vigour of Europe, accordingly, was the evolution over a long period of time of a unique mode of state.

In its most inclusive form, the interactive state is democratically founded. Its structure, marked as it is by power division, rule-governed governance, and an autonomous civil sphere, has laid the basis for a growing pool of collective capacities in society, thus furthering democratic vitality. With its good economic performance, moreover, this form of government has encouraged the development of resources—political human capital—at the mass level. Hence in both respects, as regards the evolution of democratic citizenship, democracy is able, with the right institutional framework, to reinforce its own preconditions. Herein lies its relative strength.

References

Ades, Alberto and Di Tella, Rafael (1997). 'The New Economics of Corruption: A Survey and Some New Results'. *Political Studies*, 45: 496–515.

Ake, Claud (1997). 'Dangerous Liaisons: The Interface of Globalization and Democracy', in Axel Hadenius (ed.), *Democracy's Victory and Crisis*. Cambridge: Cambridge University Press.

Al-Sayyid, Mustapha, K. (1993). 'A Civil Society in Egypt?' *The Middle East Journal*, 47: 228–42.

Aminzade, Ronald (1995). 'Between Movement and Party: The Transformation of Mid-Nineteenth-Century French Republicanism', in Craig Jenkins and Bert Klanderman (eds), *The Politics of Social Protest*. London: UCL Press.

Anderson, Benedict (1991). *Imagined Communities*. London: Verso.

Anderson, Perry (1978). *Den absoluta statens utveckling*. Lund: Cavefors.

Anners, Erik (1990*a*). *Den europeiska rättens historia 1*. Stockholm: Norstedts.

—— (1990*b*). *Den europeiska rättens historia 2*. Stockholm: Norstedts.

Axelrod, Robert (1984). *The Evolution of Cooperation*. New York: Basic Books.

—— and Keohane, Robert O. (1985). 'Achieving Cooperation under Anarchy: Strategies and Institutions'. *World Politics*, 38: 226–54.

Badie, Bertrand and Birnbaum, Pierre (1983). *The Sociology of the State*. Chicago: University of Chicago Press.

Barkan, Joel D. (1987). 'The Electoral Process and Peasant-State Relations in Kenya', in Fred M. Hayward (ed.), *Elections in Independent Africa*. Boulder, CO: Westview.

—— (1997). 'Can Established Democracies Nurture Democracy Abroad? Lessons from Africa', in Axel Hadenius (ed.), *Democracy's Victory and Crisis*. Cambridge: Cambridge University Press.

Barry, Brian (1970). *Sociologists, Economists and Democracy*. London: Collier-Macmillan.

—— (1975). 'Political Accommodation and Consociational Democracy'. *British Journal of Political Science*, 5: 477–505.

Bates, Robert (1994). 'The Impulse to Reform in Africa', in Jennifer Widner (ed.), *Economic Change and Political Liberalization in Sub-Saharan Africa*. Baltimore: The Johns Hopkins Press.

Beetham, David (1991). *The Legitimation of Power*. London: Macmillan Press.

Bendix, Reinhard (1978). *Kings or People: Power and the Mandate to Rule.* Berkeley: University of California Press.

—— (1986). 'The Special Position of Europe'. *Scandinavian Political Studies*, 9: 301–16.

Bennett, Vivienne (1992). 'The Evolution of Urban Popular Movements in Mexico between (1968 and (1988)', in Arturo Escobar and Sonia Alvarez (eds), *The Making of Social Movements in Latin America.* Boulder, CO: Westview.

Beremo, Nancy (1992). 'Democracy and the Lessons of Dictatorship'. *Comparative Politics*, 24: 273–91.

Berg-Schlosser, Dirk (1985). 'Elements of Consociational Democracy in Kenya'. *European Journal of Political Research*, 13: 95–109.

Berman, Harold J. (1983). *Law and Revolution: The Formation of the Western Legal Tradition.* Cambridge, MA: Harvard University Press.

Berman, Sheri (1997). 'Civil Society and the Collapse of the Weimar Republic'. *World Politics*, 49: 401–29.

Bhagwati, Jagdish (1997). 'Globalization, Sovereignty, and Democracy', in Axel Hadenius (ed.), *Democracy's Victory and Crisis.* Cambridge: Cambridge University Press.

Bhalla, Surjit S. (1997). 'Freedom and Economic Growth: A Virtuous Cycle?', in Axel Hadenius (ed.), *Democracy's Victory and Crisis.* Cambridge: Cambridge University Press.

Bienen, Henry and Herbst, Jeffrey (1996). 'The Relationship between Political and Economic Reform in Africa'. *Comparative Politics*, 29: 23–42.

Birnbaum, Pierre (1988). *States and Collective Action: The European Experience.* Cambridge: Cambridge University Press.

Blomkvist, Hans (1988). *The Soft State: Housing Reform and State Capacity in Urban India.* Uppsala: Department of Government, Uppsala University.

Bollen, Kenneth A. (1979). 'Political Democracy and Timing of Development'. *American Sociological Review*, 44: 572–87.

—— and Paxton, Pamela M. (1997). 'Democracy before Athens', in Manus I. Midlarsky (ed.), *Inequality, Democracy and Economic Development.* Cambridge: Cambridge University Press.

Bonime-Blanc, Andrea (1987). *Spain's Transition to Democracy: The Politics of Constitution-Making.* Boulder, CO: Westview Press.

Booth, John, A. and Richard, Patricia Bayer (1998). 'Civil Society, Political Capital, and Democratization in Central America'. *The Journal of Politics*, 60: 780–800.

Brady, Henry E., Verba, Sidney and Lehman Schlozman, Kay (1995). 'Beyond SES: A Resource Model of Political Participation'. *American Political Science Review*, 89: 271–94.

Brass, Paul R. (1984). *Caste, Faction and Party in Indian Politics: Faction and Party. Vol. 1.* Delhi: Chanakya.

Bratton, Michael (1994). 'Peasant-State Relations in Postcolonial Africa: Patterns of Engagement and Disengagement', in Joel S. Migdal, Atul

Kohli, and Vivienne Shue (eds), *State Power and Social Forces: Domination and Transformation in the Third World*. Cambridge: Cambridge University Press.

—— and van de Walle, Nicolas (1997). *Democratic Experiments in Africa: Regime Transitions in Comparative Perspective*. New York: Cambridge University Press.

Brautigam, Deborah (1992). 'Governance, Economy, and Foreign Aid'. *Studies in Comparative International Development*, 27: 3–25.

Brehm, John and Rahn, Wendy (1997). 'Individual-Level Evidence for the Causes and Consequences of Social Capital'. *American Journal of Political Science*, 41: 999–1023.

Bridenbaugh, Carl (1981). *Early Americans*. Oxford: Oxford University Press.

Brooker, Paul (1995). *Twentieth-century Dictatorships: The Ideological One Party State*. New York: New York University Press.

Brown, Judith M. (1994). *Modern India: The Origins of an Asian Democracy*. Oxford: Oxford University Press.

Bryce, James (1921). *Modern Democracies*. London: Macmillan

Burke, Peter (1986). 'City-States', in John A. Hall (ed.), *States in History*. Oxford: Basil Blackwell.

Burkholder, Mark A. and Johnson, Lyman L. (1994). *Colonial Latin America*. Oxford: Oxford University Press.

Canovan, Margaret (1981). *Populism*. New York: Harcourt.

Carlsson, Sten (1964). *Sveriges Historia II*. Stockholm: Bonniers.

Carr, Raymond (1982). *Spain 1808–1975*. Oxford: Clarendon Press.

Castañeda, Jorge G. (1994). *Utopia Unarmed: The Latin American Left After the Cold War*. New York: Vintage Books.

Chalmers, Douglas A. (1977). 'Parties and Society in Latin America', in Steffen W. Schmidt, James C. Scott, Carl H. Landé, and Laura Guasti (eds), *Friends, Followers and Factions: A Reader in Political Clientelism*. Berkeley: University of California Press.

Chazan, Naomi (1994). 'Engaging the State: Associational Life in Sub-Saharan Africa', in Joel S. Migdal, Atul Kohli, and Vivienne Shue (eds), *State Power and Social Forces: Domination and Transformation in the Third World*. Cambridge: Cambridge University Press.

Chhibbar, Pradeep K. (1999). *Democracy Without Associations: Transformation of the Party System and Political Cleavages in India*. Ann Arbor: University of Michigan Press.

Chirot, Daniel (1985). 'The Rise of the West'. *American Sociological Review*, 50: 181–95.

—— (1994). *Modern Tyrants: The Power and Prevalence of Evil in Our Time*. Princeton: Princeton University Press.

Clapham, Christopher (1982). *Private Patronage and Public Power: Political Clientelism in the Modern State*. London: Frances Pinter.

Coleman, James (1990). *Foundations of Social Theory*. Cambridge, MA: Harvard University Press.

Collier, Ruth Berins and Collier, David (1991). *Shaping the Political Arena: Critical Junctures, the Labor Movement, and Regime Dynamics in Latin America*. Princeton: Princeton University Press.

Connolly, William (1984). 'The Dilemma of Legitimacy', in William Connolly (ed.), *Legitimacy and the State*. Oxford: Basil Blackwell Publisher.

Cooper, Alice H. (1996). 'Public-Good Movements and the Dimensions of Political Process: Postwar German Peace Movements', *Comparative Political Studies*, 29: 267–289.

Coppedge, Michael (1994). *Strong Parties and Lame Ducks: Presidential Partyarchy and Factionalism*. Stanford: Stanford University Press.

Crewe, Ivor (1981). 'Electoral Participation', in David Butler, Howard R. Penniman, and Austin Ranney (eds), *Democracy at the Polls: A Comparative Study of National Elections*. Washington, DC: American Enterprise Institute.

Crook, Richard C. and Manor, James (1998). *Democracy and Decentralization in South Asia and West Africa: Participation, Accountability and Performance*. Cambridge: Cambridge University Press.

Crowley, Stephen (1994). 'Barriers to Collective Action: Steelworkers and Mutual Dependence in the Former Soviet Union', *World Politics*, 46: 589–615.

Dahl, Robert A (1971). *Polyarchy: Participation and Opposition*. New Haven and London: Yale University Press

—— (1982). *Dilemmas of Pluralist Democracy: Autonomy vs. Control*. New Haven: Yale University Press.

—— (1989). *Democracy and its Critics*. New Haven: Yale University Press.

—— and Tufte, Edward R. (1973). *Size and Democracy*. Stanford: Stanford University Press.

Dahrendorf, Ralf (1990). *Reflections on the Revolution in Europe*. London: Chatto and Windus.

D'Anieri, Paul, Ernst, Claire, and Kier, Elisabeth (1990). 'New Social Movements In Historical Perspective'. *Comparative Politics*, 22: 445–58.

Dasgupta, Jyotirindra (1997). 'Federal Design and National Development: Autonomy, Democracy, and Institutional Responsiveness in India'. Paper presented at the conference 'Against the Odds: Fifty Years of Democracy in India', Princeton University.

Davies, Michael, Davies, Henry, and Davies, Kathryn (1992). *Humankind the Gatherer-Hunter: From Earliest Times to Industry*. Kent: Myddle-Brockton Publishers.

Della Porta, Donatella. (2000). 'Social Capital, Beliefs in Government, and Political Corruption', in Susan Pharr and Robert Putnam (eds), *Disaffected Democracies: What's Troubling the Trilateral Countries?* Princeton: Princeton University Press.

—— and Vannucci, Alberto (1997). 'The "Perverse Effects" of Political Corruption'. *Political Studies*, 45: 516–38.

Demker, Marie (1996). *Från Bastiljen till Maastricht*. Arlöv: Almqvist & Wiksell.

Deutsch, Karl W. (1961). 'Social Mobilization and Political Development'. *American Political Science Review*, 55: 403–514.

Diamond, Larry (1992). 'Economic Development and Democracy Reconsidered', in Gary Marks and Larry Diamond (eds), *Reexamining Democracy: Essays in Honor of Seymour Martin Lipset*. Newbury Park: Sage Publications.

—— (1994). 'Introduction: Political Culture and Democracy', in Larry Diamond (ed.), *Political Culture and Democracy in Developing Countries*. Boulder, CO: Lynne Rienner.

—— (1996). 'Is the Third Wave Over?' *Journal of Democracy*, 7: 20–37.

—— (1999). *Developing Democracy: Toward Consolidation*. Baltimore: The Johns Hopkins University Press.

—— and Linz, Juan J. (1989). 'Introduction: Politics, Society, and Democracy in Latin America', in Larry Diamond, Juan J. Linz, and Seymour Martin Lipset (eds), *Democracy in Developing Countries: Latin America*. Boulder, CO: Lynne Rienner.

Di Palma, Guiseppe (1990). *To Craft Democracies*. Berkeley: University of California Press.

Diani, M. (1992). 'The Concept of Social Movements'. *Sociological Review*, 40: 1–25.

Dix, Robert H. (1994). 'History and Democracy Revisited'. *Comparative Politics*, 27: 91–105.

Domingo, Pilar (1999). 'Judicial Independence and Judicial Reform in Latin America', in Andreas Schedler, Larry Diamond, and Marc F. Platter (eds), *The Self-Restraining State: Power and Accountability in New Democracies*. Boulder, CO: Lynne Rienner.

Doner, Richard (1992). 'Limits of State Strength: Toward an Institutionalist View of Economic Development'. *World Politics*, 44: 398–431.

Dorwart, Reinhold A. (1971). *The Prussian Welfare State Before 1740*. Cambridge, MA: Harvard University Press.

Downing, Brian M. (1992). *The Military Revolution and Political Change: Origins of Democracy and Autocracy in Early Modern Europe*. Princeton: Princeton University Press.

Dryzek, John S. (1996). 'Political Inclusion and the Dynamics of Democratization'. *American Political Science Review*, 90: 475–87.

Durkheim, Emile (1958). *Professional Ethics and Civic Morals*. Glencoe: Free Press.

—— (1964). *The Division of Labor in Society*. New York: Free Press.

Duverger, Maurice (1954). *Political Parties: Their Organization and Activity in the Modern State*. London: Methuen.

Dyker, David (1992). *Restructuring the Soviet Economy*. London: Routledge.

Eckstein, Harry (1996). 'Culture as a Foundation Concept for the Social Sciences'. *Journal of Theoretical Politics*, 8: 471–97.

Edin, Maria (2000). *Market Forces and Communist Power: Local Political Institutions and Economic Development in China*. Department of Government, Uppsala University.

Eisenstadt, S. N. and Roninger, L. (1984). *Patrons, Clients and Friends: Interpersonal Relations and the Structure of Trust in Society*. Cambridge: Cambridge University Press.

Ekeh, Peter (1975). 'Colonialism and the two Publics in Africa: A Theoretical Statement'. *Comparative Studies in Society and History*, 17: 91–112.

Elster, Jon (1978). *Logic and Society: Contradictions and Possible Worlds*. Chichester: Wiley.

Eriksen, Erik Oddvar (ed.) (1995). *Deliberativ politikk: Demokrati i teori og praksis*. Oslo: Tano Forlag.

Ertman, Thomas (1997). *Birth of the Leviathan*. Cambridge: Cambridge University Press.

Escobar, Arturo (1992). 'Culture, Economics, and Politics in Latin American Social Movements Theory and Research', in Arturo Escobar and Sonia E. Alvarez (eds), *The Making of Social Movements in Latin America*. Boulder, CO: Westview Press.

Etzioni, Amitai (1968). *The Active Society: A Theory of Societal and Political Processes*. New York: Free Press.

Evans, Geoffrey and Whitefield, Stephen (1995). 'The Politics and Economics of Democratic Commitment: Support for Democracy in Transition Societies'. *British Journal of Political Science*, 25: 485–514.

Evans, Peter (1979). *Dependent Development: The Alliance of Multinational, State, and Local Capital in Brazil*. Princeton: Princeton University Press.

—— (1995). *Embedded Autonomy: States and Industrial Transformation*. Princeton: Princeton University Press

Fairbank, John King (1992). *China: A New History*. Cambridge: The Belknap Press of Harvard University Press.

Finer, S. E. (1988). *The Man on Horseback: The Role of the Military in Politics*. London: Pinter; Boulder, CO: Westview.

—— (1997). *History of Governments from the Earliest Time*, Vols I-III. Oxford: Oxford University Press.

Fish, Steven M. (1996). *Democracy from Scratch: Opposition and Regime in the New Russian Revolution*. Princeton: Princeton University Press.

Foley, Michael W. and Edwards, Bob (1996). 'The Paradox of Civil Society'. *Journal of Democracy*, 7: 38–52.

Fox, Jonathan (1994*a*). 'The Difficult Transition from Clientelism to Citizenship: Lessons from Mexico'. *World Politics*, 46: 151–84.

—— (1994*b*). 'Latin America's Emerging Local Politics'. *Journal of Democracy*, 5: 105–16.

—— (1997). 'How Does Civil Society Thicken? The Political Construction of Social Capital in Rural Mexico', in Peter Evans (ed.), *State-Society Synergy: Government and Social Capital in Development*. Berkeley, CA: Institute of International Affairs.

Frankel, Francine R. (1969). 'Democracy and Political Development: Perspectives from the Indian Experience'. *World Politics*, 21: 448–68.

Friedman, Milton (1962). *Capitalism and Freedom*. Chicago: University of Chicago Press.

Furet, Francois (1996). *The French Revolution 1770–1814*. Oxford: Blackwell.

Gallagher, Michael, Laver, Michael, and Mair, Peter (2001). *Representative Government in Modern Europe*. New York: McGraw-Hill.

Gamble, Clive (1986). 'Hunter-Gatherers and the Origin of States', in John A. Hall (ed.), *States in History*. Oxford: Blackwell.

Gellner, Ernest (1994). *Conditions of Liberty: Civil Society and its Rivals*. London: Hamish Hamilton.

Geertz, Clifford (1980). *Negara: The Theatre State in Nineteenth-Century Bali*. Princeton: Princeton University Press.

Gill, Graeme (1994). *The Collapse of a Single-Party System: The Disintegration of the Communist Party of the Soviet Union*. Cambridge: Cambridge University Press.

Granovetter, Mark S. (1973). 'The Strength of Weak Ties'. *American Journal of Sociology*, 6: 1360–80.

Grant, Michael (1990). *The Fall of the Roman Empire*. London: Weidenfeld and Nicholson.

Grindle, Merilee S. (1996). *Challenging the State: Crisis and Innovation in Latin America and Africa*. Cambridge: Cambridge University Press.

Gutman, Amy (1998). 'Freedom of Association', in Amy Gutman (ed.), *Freedom of Association*. Princeton: Princeton University Press.

Gyimah-Boadi, E. (1996). 'Civil Society in Africa'. *Journal of Democracy*, 7: 118–32.

Hadenius, Axel (1992a). *Democracy and Development*. Cambridge: Cambridge University Press.

—— (1992b). *When the Hour Came: On the Process of Democratization in Zambia* (Uppsala Studies in Democracy, No. 3). Uppsala: Department of Government, Uppsala University.

—— (1994a). 'From One-Party Rule to Multipartism in Africa', in Stuart S. Nagel (ed.), *African Development and Public Policy*. New York: St Martin's Press.

—— (1994b). *Kenya: Preconditions for Democratic Development in an Aid-oriented Perspective* (Uppsala Studies in Democracy, No. 7). Uppsala: Department of Government, Uppsala University.

—— (2001). Power-Sharing and Democracy: Pros and Cons of the Rustow-Lijphart Approach, in Ole Elgström and Göran Hydén (eds). *Development and Democracy: What Have We Learnt and How?* London: Routledge.

—— and Karvonen, Lauri (2001). 'The Paradox of Integration in Intra-State Conflicts'. *Journal of Theoretical Politics*, 13: 35–51.

—— and Uggla, Fredrik (1996). 'Making Civil Society Work, Promoting Democratic Development: What Can States and Donors Do?'. *World Development*, 24: 1621–39.

Hadenius, Stig (1994). *Riksdagen: En svensk historia*. Stockholm: Sveriges Riksdag.

Haggard, Stephan and Kaufman, Robert R. (1995). *The Political Economy of Democratic Transition*. Princeton: Princeton University Press.

Hale, William M. (1994). *Turkish Politics and the Military*. London: Routledge.

Hall, John A. (1985). *Powers and Liberties: The Causes and Consequences of the Rise of the West*. Oxford: Blackwell.

—— (1986). 'States and Economic Development: Reflections on Adam Smith', in John A. Hall (ed.), *States in History*. Oxford: Blackwell.

Hamilton, Alexander, Madison, James, and Jay, John (1961). *The Federalist Papers*. New York: New American Library.

Hardgrave, Robert L., Jr (1993). 'India: The Dilemmas of Diversity'. *Journal of Democracy*, 4: 54–68.

Harik, Iliya (1994). 'Pluralism in the Arab World'. *Journal of Democracy*, 5: 43–56.

Haring, C. H. (1975). *The Spanish Empire in America*. Orlando: Harcourt Brace Jovanovich.

Hayek, F. A. (1944). *The Road to Serfdom*. Chicago: University of Chicago Press.

Helliwell, John (1993). 'Empirical Linkages Between Democracy and Democratic Growth'. *British Journal of Political Science*, 24: 225–48.

Hellman, Judith Adler (1992). 'The Study of New Social Movements in Latin America and the Question of Autonomy', in Arturo Escobar and Sonia E. Alvarez (eds), *The Making of Social Movements in Latin America*. Boulder, CO: Westview Press.

Higley, John and Richard Gunter (eds) (1995). *Elites and Democratic Consolidation in Latin America and Southern Europe*. Cambridge: Cambridge University Press.

Hintze, Otto (1975). *The Historical Essays of Otto Hintze* (ed. Felix Gilbert). New York: Oxford University Press.

Hirschman, Albert (1970). *Exit, Voice, and Loyalty: Responses to Decline in Firms, Organizations, and States*. Cambridge, MA: Harvard University Press.

Hobbes, Thomas (1982). *Leviathan*. Harmondsworth: Penguin Books.

Holmes, Leslie (1993). *The End of Communist Power: Anti- Corruption Campaigns and Legitimation Crisis*. Cambridge: Polity Press.

Horowitz, Donald, L. (1985). *Ethnic Groups in Conflict*. Berkeley: University of California Press.

—— (1991). 'Ethnic Conflict Management for Policymakers', in Joseph V. Montville (ed.), *Conflict and Peacemaking in Multiethnic Societies*. New York: Lexington.

Huntington, Samuel P. (1968). *Political Order in Changing Societies*. New Haven: Yale University Press.

—— (1991). *The Third Wave: Democratization in the Late Twentieth Century*. Norman, Oklahoma: University of Oklahoma Press.

Hydén, Göran (1983). *No Shortcuts to Progress: African Development Management in Perspective*. London: Heinemann.

India Today (1997), No. 18.

Inglehart, Ronald (1990). *Culture Shift in Advanced Industrial Society*. Princeton: Princeton University Press.

Inglehart, Ronald (1997). *Modernization and Postmodernization: Cultural, Economic and Political Change in 43 Societies*. Princeton; Princeton University Press.

Inkeles, Alex (1974). *Becoming Modern: Individual Change in Six Developing Countries*. London: Heinemann.

Israel, Jonathan (1995). *Dutch Republic: Its Rise, Greatness and Fall*. Oxford: Oxford University Press.

Jacob, Margaret and Mijnhardt, Winjnand (eds) (1992). *The Dutch Republic in the Eighteenth Century: Decline, Enlightenment and Revolution*. Ithaca, NY: Cornell University Press.

Jackson, Robert H. and Rosberg, Carl (1982). *Personal Rule in Black Africa*. Berkeley: University of California Press.

—— —— (1986). 'Sovereignty and Underdevelopment: Juridical Statehood in the African Crisis'. *The Journal of Modern African Studies*, 24: 1–31.

Johnson, Allen W. and Earle, Timothy (1987). *The Evolution of Human Societies: From Foraging Group to Agrarian State*. Stanford: Stanford University Press.

Jones, Eric L. (1987). *The European Miracle: Environments, Economies, and Geopolitics in the History of Europe and Asia*. Cambridge: Cambridge University Press.

Joseph, Richard A. (1987). *Democracy and Prebendal Politics in Nigeria: The Rise and Fall of the Second Republic*. Cambridge: Cambridge University Press.

Karatnycky, Adrian (2000). 'A Century of Progress'. *Journal of Democracy*, 11: 187–99.

Kaufman, Chaim (1996). 'Possible and Impossible Solutions to Ethnic Civil Wars'. *International Security*, 20: 136–76.

Keep, John (1995). *The Last of the Empires: A History of the Soviet Union*. Oxford: Oxford University Press.

Kennedy, Paul (1987). *The Rise and Fall of the Great Powers: Economic Change and Military Conflict from 1500 to 2000*. New York: Random House.

Keyder, Caglar (1997). 'The Ottoman Empire', in Karen Barkey and Mark van Hagen (eds), After Empire: Multiethnic Societies and Nation-Building. *Bolder, CO: Westview.*

Khilnani, Sunil (1992). 'India's Democratic Career', in John Dunn (ed.), *Democracy: The Unfinished Journey 508BC to AD1993*. Oxford: Oxford University Press.

Klingemann, Hans-Dieter (1999). 'Mapping Political Support in the 1990s: A Global Analysis', in Pippa Norris (ed.), *Critical Citizens: Global Support for Democratic Governance*. Oxford: Oxford University Press.

Kohli, Atul (1987). *The State and Poverty in India: The Politics of Reform*. Cambridge: Cambridge University Press.

—— (1990). *Democracy and Discontent: India's Growing Crisis of Governability*. Cambridge: Cambridge University Press.

—— (1994). 'Centralization and Powerlessness: India's Democracy in a Comparative Perspective', in Joel S. Migdal, Atul Kohli, and Vivienne

274   References

Shue (eds), *State Power and Social Forces: Domination and Transformation in the Third World*. Cambridge: Cambridge University Press.

Kohli, Atul (1997). 'On Sources of Social and Political Conflicts in Follower Democracies', in Axel Hadenius (ed.), *Democracy's Victory and Crisis*. Cambridge: Cambridge University Press.

Korchak, Alexander (1994). *Contemporary Totalitarianism: A Systems Approach*. New York: Columbia University Press.

Kornhauser, William (1960). *The Politics of Mass Society*. London: Routledge and Kegan Paul.

Kriesi, Hanspeter (1995). 'The Political Opportunity Structure of New Social Movements: Its Impact on Their Mobilization', in Craig Jennings and Bert Klandermans (eds), *The Politics of Social Protest*. London: ULC Press.

Kulke, Hermann and Rothermund, Dietmar (1997). *A History of India*. London: Routledge.

Lagos, Marta (1997). 'Latin Americans' Smiling Mask'. *Journal of Democracy*, 8: 124–38.

Lake, David A. (1992). 'Powerful Pacifists: Democratic States under War'. *American Political Science Review*, 86: 8–23.

Lane, David (1996). *The Rise and Fall of State Socialism: Industrial Society and the Socialist State*. Cambridge: Polity Press.

Lakoff, Sanford (1996). *Democracy: History, Theory, Practice*. Boulder, CO: Westview Press.

Lawrence, Leder H. (1972). *America 1603–1789: Prelude to a Nation*. Minneapolis: Burgess.

Leblang, David A. (1997). 'Political Democracy and Economic Growth: Pooled Cross-Sectional and Time-Series Evidence'. *British Journal of Political Science*, 27: 453–72.

Leftwich, Adrian (1995). 'Model of the Developmental State'. *Journal of development Studies*, 24: 400–27.

Lerner, Daniel (1958). *The Passing of Traditional Society*. Glencoe: Free Press.

Levi, Margaret (1988). *Of Rule and Revenue*. Berkeley: University of California Press.

Lewin, Leif (1970): *Folket och eliterna. En studie i modern demokratisk teori*. Stockholm: Alqvist och Wiksell.

—— (1985). *Ideologi och strategi: Svensk politik under 100 år*. Stockholm: Norstedts.

Lewis, Arthur W. (1965). *Politics in West Africa*. London: Allen and Unwin.

Lijphart, Arend (1977). *Democracy in Plural Societies: A Comparative Exploration*. New Haven: Yale University Press.

—— (1992). 'Introduction', in Arend Lijphart (ed.), *Parliamentary versus Presidential Government*. Oxford: Oxford University Press.

—— (1996). 'The Puzzle of Indian Democracy: A Consociational Interpretation'. *American Political Science Review*, 90: 258–68.

—— (1999). *Patterns of Democracy. Government Forms and Performance in Thirty-Six Countries*. New Haven: Yale University Press.

Lindblom, Charles (1977). *Politics and Markets: The World's Political-Economic Systems*. New York: Basic Books.

Lindegren, Jan (1985). 'The Swedish "Military" State, 1560–1720'. *Scandinavian Journal of History*, 10: 305–36.

Lindström, Ulf (1985). *Fascism in Scandinavia 1920–1940*. Stockholm: Almqvist and Wiksell International.

Lintott, Andrew William (1993). *Imperium Romanum: Politics and Administration*. London: Routledge.

Linz, Juan J. (1975). 'Totalitarian and Authoritarian Regimes', in F. I. Greenstein and Nelson W. Polsby (eds), *The Handbook of Political Science*. Reading, MA: Addison-Wesley.

—— (1978). *The Breakdown of Democratic Regimes: Crisis, Breakdown, and Reequilibration*. Baltimore: Johns Hopkins University Press.

—— (1994). 'Presidential or Parliamentary Democracy: Does it Make a Difference?', in Juan J. Linz and Arturo Valenzuela (eds), *The Failure of Presidential Democracy: Comparative Perspectives*. Baltimore: The John Hopkins University Press.

—— (1997). 'Some Thoughts on the Victory and Future of Democracy', in Axel Hadenius (ed.), *Democracy's Victory and Crisis*. Cambridge: Cambridge University Press.

—— and Stepan, Alfred (1996). *Problems of Democratic Transition and Consolidation: Southern Europe, South America, and Post-Communist Europe*. Baltimore: The Johns Hopkins University Press.

Lipset, Seymour M. (1960). *Political Man: The Social Bases of Politics*. New York: Doubleday.

—— (1983). 'Radicalism or Reformism. The Source of Working-Class Politics'. *American Political Science Review*, 77: 1–18.

—— and Rokkan, Stein (1967). 'Cleavage Structures, Party Systems, and Voter Alignments: An Introduction', in Seymour M. Lipset and Stein Rokkan (eds), *Party Systems and Voter Alignments: Cross-National Perspectives*. New York: The Free Press.

——, Trow, Martin, and Coleman, James (eds) (1956). *Union Democracy: The Internal Politics of the International Typographical Union*. Glencoe, Ill.: Free Press.

Lundahl, Mats (1997). 'Inside the Predatory State: The Rationale, Methods, and Economic Consequences of Kleptocratic Regimes'. *Nordic Journal of Political Economy*, 24: 31–50.

Lynch, John (1986). *The Spanish American Revolutions 1808–1826*. New York: W.W. Norton and Company.

Mainwaring, Scott (1993). 'Presidentialism, Multipartism, and Democracy: The Difficult Combination'. *Comparative Political Studies*, 26: 21–43.

—— and Scully, Timothy R. (1995). 'Party Systems in Latin America', in Scott Mainwaring and Timothy R. Scully (eds), *Building Democratic Institutions: Party Systems in Latin America*. Stanford: Stanford University Press.

Malloy, James M. (1987). 'The Politics of Transition in Latin America', in James M. Malloy and Mitchell A. Seligson (eds), *Authoritarians and*

Democrats: Regime Transition in Latin America. Pittsburgh: University of Pittsburgh Press.

Mann, Michael (1986a). *The Sources of Social Power: A History of Power from the Beginning to* A.D. *1760.* Cambridge: Cambridge University Press.

—— (1986b). 'The Autonomous Power of the State: Its Origins, Mechanisms and Results', in John A. Hall (ed.), *States in History.* Oxford: Basil Blackwell.

—— (1993). *The Sources of Social Power: The Rise of Classes and Nation-states, 1760–1914.* Cambridge: Cambridge University Press.

Manor, James (1997). 'Centre-State Relations'. Paper presented at the conference 'Against the Odds: Fifty Years of Democracy in India', Princeton University.

March, James and Olsen, Johan P. (1989). *Rediscovering Institutions: The Organizational Basis of Politics.* New York: The Free Press.

Mardin, Serif (1997). 'The Ottoman Empire', in Karen Barkey and Mark von Hagen (eds), *After Empire: Multiethnic Societies and National-Building.* Boulder, CO: Westview.

Marongiu, Antonio (1968). *Medieval Parliaments: A Comparative Study.* London: Eyre and Spottiswoode.

Marshall, T. H. (1977). *Class, Citizenship and Social Development.* Chicago: Chicago University Press.

McFarlane, Anthony (1996). 'Political Corruption and Reform in Bourbon Spanish America', in Walter Little and Eduardo Posada-Carbó (eds), *Political Corruption in Europe and Latin America.* London: Macmillan.

McNeill, William H. (1982). *The Pursuit of Power: Technology, Armed Force, and Society since* A.D. *1000.* Chicago: The University of Chicago Press.

Migdal, Joel S. (1988). *Strong Societies and Weak States: State-Society Relations and Capabilities in the Third World.* Princeton: Princeton University Press.

Mill, John Stuart (1991). *Considerations on Representative Government.* Buffalo, NY: Prometheus Books.

Miller, Gary (1992). *Managerial Dilemmas: The Political Economy of Hierarchy.* Cambridge: Cambridge University Press.

Miller, Rory (1996). 'Foreign Capital, the State and Political Corruption in Latin America between Independence and Depression', in Walter Little and Eduardo Posada-Carbó (eds), *Political Corruption in Europe and Latin America.* London: Macmillan.

Mitra, Subrata K. (1997). 'Making Local Government Work: Rural Elites, Panchayati Raj and Legitimacy of India'. Paper presented at the conference 'Against the Odds: Fifty Years of Democracy in India', Princeton University.

Mo, Jongryn (1996). 'Political Learning and Democratic Consolidation: Korean Industrial Relations, 1987–1992'. *Comparative Political Studies,* 29: 290–311.

Moe, Terry M. (1984). 'The New Economics of Organization'. *American Journal of Political Science,* 28: 739–77.

Moore, Barrington Jr (1967). *Social Origins of Dictatorship and Democracy: Lords and Peasants in the Making of the Modern World*. Boston: Beacon Press.

Morone, James A. (1990). *The Democratic Wish: Popular Participation and the Limits of American Government*. New York: Basic Books.

Mouzelis, Nicos P. (1986). *Politics in the Semi-Periphery: Early Parliamentarism and Late Industrialisation in the Balkans and Latin America*. Basingstoke: Macmillan.

Muller, Edward N. (1997). 'Economic Determinants of Democracy', in Manus I. Midlarsky (ed.), *Inequality, Democracy and Economic Development*. Cambridge: Cambridge University Press.

Muslih, Muhammad. (1993). 'Palestinian Civil Society'. *The Middle East Journal*, 47: 258–74.

Myers, A. R. (1975). *Parliaments and Estates in Europe to 1789*. London: Thames and Hudson.

Myers, David A. and O'Connor, Robert E. (1998). 'Support for Coups in a Democratic Political Culture: A Venezuelan Exploration'. *Comparative Politics*, 30: 193–212.

Myrdal, Gunnar (1968). *Asian Drama: An Inquiry into the Poverty of Nations* (3 vols). New York: Twentieth Century Fund.

Nettels, Curtis P. (1963). *Roots of American Civilization: A History of American Colonial Life*. New York: Meredith.

Newton, Kenneth. (1999). 'Social and Political Trust in Established Democracies', in Pippa Norris (ed.), *Critical Citizens: Global Support for Democratic Government*. Oxford: Oxford University Press.

Nilsson, Sven A. (1990). *The Era of the Great Wars: Sweden as a Military State and its Agrarian Society*. Stockholm: Almqvist & Wiksell International.

Nordlund, Per (1996). *Organising the Political Agora: Domination and Democratisation in Zambia and Zimbabwe*. Uppsala: Uppsala University.

North, Douglass C. (1989). 'Institutions and Economic Growth: An Historic Introduction'. *World Development*, 17: 1319–32.

—— (1990). *Institutions, Institutional Change and Economic Performance*. Cambridge: Cambridge University Press.

—— and Weingast, Barry (1998). 'Constitutions and Commitment: The Evolution of Institutions Governing Public Choice in Seventeenth-Century England', in Paul W. Drake and Mathew D. McCubbins (eds), *The Origins of Liberty: Political and Economic Liberalization in the Modern World*. Princeton: Princeton University Press.

Nove, Alec (1989). *An Economic History of the U.S.S.R.* Harmondsworth: Penguin Books.

Nyerere, Julius (1967). *Freedom and Unity*. Dar Es Salaam: Oxford University Press.

Öberg, Per-Ola (1994). *Särintresse och allmänintresse: korporatismens ansikten*. Stockholm: Almqvist & Wiksell International.

O'Donnell, Guillermo (1994). 'Delegative Democracy'. *Journal of Democracy*, 5: 55–69.

Offe, Claus (1990). 'Reflections on the Institutional Self-Transformation of Movement Politics: A Tentative Stage Model', in Russell J. Dalton and Manfred Kuechler (eds), *Challenging the Political Order: New Social Movements in Western Democracies*. Cambridge: Polity Press.

—— (1997). 'Micro-aspects of Democratic Theory: What Makes for the Deliberative Competence of Citizens', in Axel Hadenius (ed.), *Democracy's Victory and Crisis*. Cambridge: Cambridge University Press.

Olson, Mancur (1965). *The Logic of Collective Action: Public Goods and the Theory of Groups*. Cambridge, MA: Harvard University Press.

—— (1982). *The Rise and Decline of Nations: Economic Growth, Stagflation, and Social Rigidities*. New Haven: Yale University Press.

—— (1993). 'Dictatorship, Democracy, and Development'. *American Political Science Review*, 87: 567–76.

O'Neil, Patrick H. (1996). 'Revolution from Within: Institutional Analysis, Transitions from Authoritarianism, and the Case of Hungary'. *World Politics*, 48: 579–603.

Ostrom, Elinor (1990). *Governing the Commons: The Evolution of Institutions for Collective Action*. Cambridge: Cambridge University Press.

Palmer, Robert R. (1959). *The Age of the Democratic Revolution: A Political History of Europe and America, 1760–1800: The Challenge*. Princeton: Princeton University Press.

—— (1964). *The Age of the Democratic Revolution: A Political History of Europe and America, 1760–1800: The Struggle*. Princeton: Princeton University Press.

Pennock, Roland J. (1979). *Democratic Political Theory*. Princeton: Princeton University Press.

Petersson, Olof, Westholm, Anders, and Blomberg, Göran (1989). *Medborgarnas makt*. Stockholm: Carlssons.

Pipes, Richard (1991). *The Russian Revolution*. New York: Vintage.

—— (1995). *Russia under the Old Regime*. London: Penguin Books.

Piven, Frances F. and Cloward, Richard (1979). *Poor People's Movements: Why They Succeed, How They Fail*. New York: Vintage Books.

Poggi, Gianfranco (1978). *The Development of the Modern State: A Sociological Introduction*. Stanford: Stanford University Press.

—— (1990). *The State: Its Nature, Development and Prospects*. Cambridge: Polity Press.

Powell, G. Bingham Jr (1982). *Contemporary Democracies: Participation, Stability, and Violence*. Cambridge, MA: Harvard University Press.

Przeworski, Adam. (1986). *Paper Stones: A History of Electoral Socialism*. Chicago: University of Chicago Press.

—— (1991). *Democracy and the Market: Political and Economic Reforms in Eastern Europe and Latin America*. Cambridge: Cambridge University Press.

—— (1992). 'The Games of Transition', in Scott Mainwaring, Guillermo O'Donnell, and J. Samuel Valenzuela (eds), *Issues in Democratic*

Consolidation: The New South American Democracies in Comparative Perspective. Notre Dame, Indiana: University of Notre Dame Press.

—— and Limongi, Fernando (1997). 'Democracy and Development', in Axel Hadenius (ed.), *Democracy's Victory and Crisis*. Cambridge: Cambridge University Press.

——, Alvarez, Michael, Cheibub, José Antonio, and Limongi, Fernando (1996). 'What Makes Democracy Endure?'. *Journal of Democracy*, 7: 39–55.

Putnam, Robert (1993). *Making Democracy Work: Civic Traditions in Modern Italy*. Princeton: Princeton University Press.

—— (1995). 'Tuning In, Tuning Out: The Strange Disappearance of Social Capital in America'. *PS: Political Science and Politics*, 28: 664–83.

—— (1997). 'Democracy in America at Century's End', in Axel Hadenius (ed.), *Democracy's Victory and Crisis*. Cambridge: Cambridge University Press.

—— (2000). *Bowling Alone: The Collapse and Revival of American Community*. New York: Simon and Schuster.

Pye, Lucian W. (1965). *Political Culture and Political Development*. Princeton: Princeton University Press.

—— (1985). *Asian Power and Politics: The Cultural Dimensions of Authority*. Cambridge, MA: Harvard University Press.

Rae, Douglas W. and Taylor, Michael (1970). *The Analysis of Political Cleavages*. New Haven: Yale University Press.

Reno, William (1998). *Warlord Politics and African States*. Boulder, CO: Lyenne Rienner.

Reynolds, Andrew (1999). *Electoral Systems and Democratization in Southern Africa*. Oxford: Oxford University Press.

Riggs, Fred W. (1992). 'Presidentialism: A Problematic Regime Type', in Arend Lijphart (ed.) *Parliamentary versus Presidential Government*. Oxford: Oxford University Press.

Roberts, Kenneth M. (1997). 'Beyond Romanticism: Social Movements and the Study of Political Change in Latin America'. *Latin American Research Review*, 32: 137–51.

—— and Wibbels, Erik (1999). 'Party System and Electoral Volatility in Latin America: A test of Economic, Institutional, and Structural Explanations'. *American Political Science Review*, 93: 575–90.

Roberts, Michael (1979). *The Swedish Imperial Experience, 1560–1718*. Cambridge: Cambridge University Press.

Rokkan, Stein (1970). *Citizens Elections Parties: Approaches to the Comparative Study of the Processes of Development*. Oslo: Universitetsforlaget.

—— (1975). 'Dimensions of State Formation and Nation-Building: A Possible Paradigm for Research on Variations within Europe', in Charles Tilly (ed.), *The Formation of National States in Western Europe*. Princeton: Princeton University Press.

Roninger, Luis and Günes-Ayata, Ayse (eds) (1994). *Democracy, Clientelism, and Civil Society*. Boulder, CO: Lynne Rienner.

Root, Hilton (1989). 'Tying the King's hands: Credible Commitments and Royal Fiscal Policy during the Old Regime'. *Rationality and Society*, 1: 240–58.

Rose, Richard (1995). 'Russia as an Hour-Glass Society: A Constitution Without Citizens'. *East European Constitutional Review*, 4: 34–42.

Rose-Ackerman, Susan (1999). *Corruption and Government: Causes, Consequences and Reform.* Cambridge: Cambridge University Press.

Rosenberg, Hans (1958). *Bureaucracy, Aristocracy and Autocracy: The Prussian Experience 1660–1815.* Cambridge, MA: Harvard University Press.

Rosenberg, Nathan and Birdzell, L. E. (1986). *How the West Grew Rich: The Economic Transformation of the Industrial World.* New York: Basic Books.

Roth, Guenther (1963). *The Social Democrats in Imperial Germany: A Study in Working-class Isolation and National Integration.* Totowa, NJ: The Bedminster Press.

Rothchild, Donald and Lawson, Letitia (1994). 'The Interactions Between State and Civil Society in Africa: From Deadlock to New Routines', in John W. Harbeson, Donald Rothchild, and Naomi Chazan (eds), *Civil Society and the State in Africa.* Boulder, CO: Lynne Rienner.

Rothstein, Bo (1992). *Den korporativa staten. Den korporativa staten: intresseorganisationer och statsförvaltning i svensk politik.* Stockholm: Norstedts juridik: Allmänna förlaget.

—— (2000). 'Trust, Social Dilemmas and Collective Memories'. *Journal of Theoretical Politics*, 12: 473–97.

Rousseau, Jean Jacques (1919). *Om samhällsfördraget eller statsrättens grunder.* Stockholm: Bonniers.

Rudolph, Lloyd I. and Hoeber Rudolph, Susanne (1987). *In Pursuit of Lakshmi: The Political Economy of the Indian State.* Chicago: The University of Chicago Press.

Ruedy, John (ed.) (1994). *Islamism and Secularism in North Africa.* New York: St. Martin's Press.

Rueschemayer, Dietrich (1998). 'The Self-Organization of Society and Democratic Rule. Specifying the Relationship', in Dietrich Rueschemayer, Marilyn Rueschemayer, and Bjorn Wittrock (eds), *Participation and Democracy East and West: Comparisons and Interpretations.* Armonk: Sharpe.

——, Huber Stephens, Evelyne, and Stephens, John D. (1992). *Capitalist Development and Democracy.* Cambridge: Polity Press.

Rustow, Dankwart A. (1970). 'Transitions to Democracy: Toward a Dynamic Model', *Comparative Politics*, 2: 337–63.

Sadowski, Christine (1994). 'Autonomous Groups as Agents of Democratic Change in Communist and Post-Communist Eastern Europe', in Larry Diamond (ed.), *Political Culture and Democracy in Developing Countries.* Boulder, CO: Lynne Rienner.

Sartori, Giovanni (1976). *Parties and Party Systems: A Framework for Analysis, Vol. 1.* Cambridge: Cambridge University Press.

—— (1987). *The Theory of Democracy Revisited*. Chatham, NJ: Chatham House.

—— (1994). *Comparative Constitutional Engineering: An Inquiry into Structures, Incentives and Outcomes*. London: Macmillan.

Schmitter, Philippe C. (1974). 'Still the Century of Corporatism'. *The Review of Politics*, 36: 85–135.

Schumpeter, Joseph A. (1947). *Capitalism, Socialism, and Democracy*. New York: Harper.

Shefter, Martin (1977). 'Party and Patronage: Germany, England, and Italy'. *Politics and Society*, 7: 403–51.

Shklar, Judith N. (1991). *American Citizenship: The Quest for Inclusion*. Cambridge, MA: Harvard University Press.

Shue, Vivienne (1994). 'State Power and Social Organisation in China', in Joel S. Migdal, Atul Kohli, and Vivienne Shue (eds), *State Power and Social Forces: Domination and Transformation in the Third World*. Cambridge: Cambridge University Press.

Shugart, Matthew, S. (1998). 'The Inverse Relationship Between Party Strength and Executive Strength: A Theory of Politicians' Constitutional Choices'. *British Journal of Political Science*, 28: 1–29.

—— and Carey, John (1992). *Presidents and Assemblies*. Cambridge: Cambridge University Press.

Sides, John (1999). 'It Takes Two: The Reciprocal Relationship Between Social Capital and Democracy'. Paper delivered at the 1999 Annual Meeting of the American Political Science Association.

Siedentop, Larry (1994). *Tocqueville*. Oxford: Oxford University Press.

Sisson, Richard (1994). 'Culture and Democratization in India', in Larry Diamond (ed.), *Political Culture and Democracy in Developing Countries*. Boulder, CO: Lynne Rienner.

Skidmore, Thomas E. and Smith, Peter H. (eds) (1989). *Modern Latin America*. New York: Oxford University Press.

Skinner, Quentin (1992). 'The Italian City-Republics', in John Dunn (ed.), *Democracy: The Unfinished Journey 508BC to AD1993*. Oxford: Oxford University Press.

Skocpol, Theda (1979). *States and Social Revolutions: A Comparative Analysis of France, Russia and China*. Cambridge: Cambridge University Press.

—— (1985). 'Bringing the State Back in', in Peter B. Evans, Dietrich Rueschmeyer, and Theda Skocpol (eds), *Bringing the State Back In*. Cambridge: Cambridge University Press.

Spruyt, Hendrik (1994). *The Sovereign State and Its Competitors*. Princeton: Princeton University Press.

Stepan, Alfred (1985). 'State Power and the Strength of Civil Society in the Southern Cone of Latin America', in Peter B. Evans, Dietrich Rueschmeyer, and Theda Skocpol (eds), *Bringing the State Back In*. Cambridge: Cambridge University Press.

Stern, Fritz (1997). 'The New Democracies in Crisis in Interwar Europe', in Axel Hadenius (ed.), *Democracy's Victory and Crisis*. Cambridge: Cambridge University Press.

Stolle, Dietlind (1998). 'Bowling Together, Bowling Alone: The Development of Generalized Trust in Voluntary Associations'. *Political Psychology*, 19: 497–525.

Stoner-Weiss, Kathryn (2000). 'The Limited Research on Russia's Party System: Under-Institutionalization in Dual Transitions'. ESRC Research Seminar, London School of Economics.

Sulieman, Ezra N. (1994). 'Presidentialism and Political Stability in France', in Juan J. Linz and Arturo Valenzuela (eds), *The Failure of Presidential Democracy: Comparative Perspectives*. Baltimore: The John Hopkins University Press.

Szücs, Stefan (1998). *Democracy in the Head: A Comparative Analysis of Democratic Leadership Orientations Among Local Elites in Three Phases of Democratization*. Göteborg: CEFOS.

Tagapera, Rein and Shugart, Matthew (1989). *Seats and Votes: The Effects and Determinants of Electoral Systems*. New Haven: Yale University Press.

Tangri, Roger (1985). *Politics in Sub-Saharan Africa*. London: Currey/Heinemann.

Tarrow, Sidney (1994). *Power in Movement: Social Movements, Collective Action and Politics*. Cambridge: Cambridge University Press.

—— (1996). 'Making Social Science Work Across Space and Time: A Critical Reflection on Robert Putnam's *Making Democracy Work*'. *American Political Science Review*, 90: 389–97.

Thapar, Romila (1986). 'State Formation in Early India', in Ali Kazancigil (ed.), *The State in Global Perspective*. Aldershot: Gower/Unesco.

Theobald, Robin (1990). *Corruption, Development and Underdevelopment*. London: Macmillan.

Therborn, Göran (1977). 'The Rule of Capital and the Rise of Democracy'. *New Left Review*, 103: 3–41.

Tilly, Charles (ed.) (1975). *The Formation of National States in Western Europe*. Princeton: Princeton University Press.

—— (1985). 'War Making and State Making as Organized Crime', in Peter Evans, Dietrich Rueschemeyer, and Theda Skocpol (eds), *Bringing the State Back In*. Cambridge: Cambridge University Press.

—— (1992). *Coercion, Capital, and European States, AD 900–1992*. Cambridge, MA: Blackwell.

Tingsten, Herbert (1971). *Demokratins problem*. Stockholm: Bonnier.

Tocqueville, Alexis de (1966). *The Ancien Regime and the French Revolution*. Manchester: Fontana.

—— (1969). *Democracy in America*. Garden City: Anchor Press.

Tong, Yanqi (1994). 'State, Society, and Political Change in China and Hungary'. *Comparative Politics*, 26: 333–53.

Torres, Liv (1999). *Amandla! Ngawethu? The Trade Union Movement in South Africa Change*. Department of Political Science, University of Oslo.

Transparency International (1998). *Corruption Perception Index*. Berlin: Transparency International.

Uphoff, Norman Thomas (1992). *Learning from Gal Oya: Possibilities for Participatory Development and Post-Newtonian Social Science*. Ithaca, NY: Cornell University Press.

Usher, Dan (1981). *The Economic Prerequisite to Democracy*. New York: Columbia University Press.

Valenzuela, Samuel (1989). 'Labour Movements in Tradition to Democracy'. *Comparative Politics*, 21: 445–72.

van Caenegem, R. C. (1992). *An Historical Introduction to Private Law*. Cambridge: Cambridge University Press.

van Crevald, Martin (1999). *The Rise and Decline of the State*. Cambridge: Cambridge University Press.

Vanhanen, Tatu (1997). *Prospects of Democracy: A Study of 172 Countries*. London: Routledge.

Varese, Federico (1997). 'The Transition to the Market and Corruption in Post-Socialist Russia'. *Political Studies*, 45: 579–97.

Vedung, Evert (1997). *Public Policy and Program Evaluation*. New Brunswick, NJ: Transaction Publishers.

Veliz, Claudio (1980). *The Centralist Tradition of Latin America*. Princeton: Princeton University Press.

Verba, Sidney, Nie, Norman H., and Kim, Jae-On (1978). *Participation and Political Equality: A Seven Nation Comparison*. Cambridge: Cambridge University Press.

Verba, Sidney, Lehman Schlozman, Kay, and Brady, Henry E. (1995). *Voice and Equality: Civic Voluntarism in American Politics*. Cambridge, MA: Harvard University Press.

Villagrán de Leon, Francisco (1993). 'Thwarting the Guatemalan Coup'. *Journal of Democracy*, 4: 117–24.

Voslensky, Michael (1984). *Nomenklatura: Anatomy of the Soviet Ruling Class*. London: Bodley Head.

Wade, Robert (1990). *Governing the Market: Economic Theory and the Role of Government in East Asian Industrialization*. Princeton: Princeton University Press.

Weber, Max (1987). *Ekonomi och Samhälle: Förståendesociologins grunder*. Lund: Argos.

Weiner, Myron (1989). *The Indian Paradox: Essays in Indian Politics*. New Delhi: Sage Publications.

Weingast, Barry R. (1997). 'The Political Foundations of Democracy and the Rule of Law'. *American Political Science Review*, 91: 245–63.

—— (1998). 'Constructing Trust: The Political and Economic Roots of Ethnic and Regional Conflict', in Karol Soltan, Eric M. Uslander, and Virginia Haufler (eds), *Institutions and Social Order*. Ann Arbor: University of Michigan Press.

Weiss, Linda (1998. *The Myth of the Powerless State*. Ithaca, NY: Cornell University Press.

Weyland, Kurt (1998). 'From Leviathan to Gulliver? The Decline of the Developmental State in Brazil'. *Governance*, 11: 51–75.

Whitehead, Laurence (1986). 'International Aspects of Democratization', in Guillermo O'Donnell, Phillippe C. Schmitter, and Laurence Whitehead (eds), *Transitions from Authoritarian Rule: Prospects for Democracy*. Baltimore: The Johns Hopkins University Press.

Widlund, Ingrid (2000). *Paths to Power and Patterns of Influence: The Dravidian Parties in South Indian Politics*. Uppsala: Acta Universitatis Upsaliensis.

Widmalm, Sten (1997). *Democracy and Violent Separatism in India: Kashmir in a Comparative Perspective*. Uppsala University, Department of Government.

Wildavsky, Aaron (1987). 'Choosing Preferences by Constructing Institutions: A Cultural Theory of Preference Formation'. *American Political Science Review*, 81: 3–21.

Wintrobe, Ronald (1998). *The Political Economy of Dictatorships*. Cambridge: Cambridge University Press.

Wood, Gordon S. (1969). *The Creation of the American Republic, 1776–1787*. New York: Norton.

—— (1991). *The Radicalism of the American Revolution*. New York: Vintage Books.

World Bank (1978). *Development Report*. Washington, DC: World Bank.

—— (1995). *Development Report*. Washington, DC: Oxford University Press.

—— (19970. *World Development Report 1997; The State in a Changing World*. Oxford: Oxford University Press.

Wuthnow, Robert (1986). 'Processes of Early State Development'. *Comparative Studies in Society and History*, 28: 107–13.

Young, M. Crawford (1998). 'The African Colonial State Revisited'. *Governance*, 11: 101–20.

Zakaria, Fareed (1997). 'The Rise of Illiberal Democracy'. *Foreign Affairs*, 76/November-December: 22–43.

Zolberg, Aristide R. (1966). *Creating Political Order: The Party States of West Africa*. Chicago: Rand McNally.

—— (1986). 'Strategic Interactions and the Formation of Modern States: France and England', in Ali Kazancigil (ed.), *The State in Global Perspective*. Aldershot: Gower/Unesco.

Index